Bloom's Classic Critical Views

ALFRED,
LORD TENNYSON

Bloom's Classic Critical Views

Bloom's Classic Critical Views

ALFRED, LORD TENNYSON

Edited and with an Introduction by
Harold Bloom
Sterling Professor of the Humanities
Yale University

BLOOM'S
LITERARY CRITICISM
An imprint of Infobase Publishing

Bloom's Classic Critical Views: Alfred, Lord Tennyson

Copyright © 2010 Infobase Publishing
Introduction © 2010 by Harold Bloom

Bloom's Literary Criticism
An imprint of Infobase Publishing
132 West 31st Street
New York NY 10001

Library of Congress Cataloging-in-Publication Data
Alfred, Lord Tennyson / edited and with an introduction by Harold Bloom.
    p. cm. — (Bloom's classic critical views)
    Includes bibliographical references and index.
    ISBN 978-1-60413-640-1 (alk. paper)
    1. Tennyson, Alfred Tennyson, Baron, 1809–1892—Criticism and interpretation.
    I. Bloom, Harold.
    PR5588.A444 2010
    821"8—dc22
                                      2010005830

Bloom's Literary Criticism books are available at special discounts when purchased in bulk quantities for businesses, associations, institutions, or sales promotions. Please call our Special Sales Department in New York at (212) 967-8800 or (800) 322-8755.

You can find Bloom's Literary Criticism on the World Wide Web at
http://www.chelseahouse.com

Volume editor: Paul Fox
Cover design by Takeshi Takahashi
Composition by IBT Global, Troy NY
Cover printed by IBT Global, Troy NY
Book printed and bound by IBT Global, Troy NY
Date printed: July 2010
Printed in the United States of America
10 9 8 7 6 5 4 3 2 1

This book is printed on acid-free paper.

All links and Web addresses were checked and verified to be correct at the time of publication. Because of the dynamic nature of the Web, some addresses and links may have changed since publication and may no longer be valid.

Contents

Series Introduction

Bloom's Classic Critical Views is a new series presenting a selection of the most important older literary criticism on the greatest authors commonly read in high school and college classes today. Unlike the Bloom's Modern Critical Views series, which for more than 20 years has provided the best contemporary criticism on great authors, Bloom's Classic Critical Views attempts to present the authors in the context of their time and to provide criticism that has proved over the years to be the most valuable to readers and writers. Selections range from contemporary reviews in popular magazines, which demonstrate how a work was received in its own era, to profound essays by some of the strongest critics in the British and American tradition, including Henry James, G.K. Chesterton, Matthew Arnold, and many more.

Some of the critical essays and extracts presented here have appeared previously in other titles edited by Harold Bloom, such as the New Moulton's Library of Literary Criticism. Other selections appear here for the first time in any book by this publisher. All were selected under Harold Bloom's guidance.

In addition, each volume in this series contains a series of essays by a contemporary expert, who comments on the most important critical selections, putting them in context and suggesting how they might be used by a student writer to influence his or her own writing. This series is intended above all for students, to help them think more deeply and write more powerfully about great writers and their works.

Introduction by Harold Bloom

When I began to write I avowed for my principles those of Arthur Hallam in his essay upon Tennyson. Tennyson, who had written but his early poems when Hallam wrote, was an example of the school of Keats and Shelley, and Keats and Shelley, unlike Wordsworth, intermixed into their poetry no elements from the general thought, but wrote out of the impression made by the world upon their delicate senses.

—W. B. Yeats, *Art and Ideas*

So vivid was the delight attending the simple exertions of eye and ear, that it became mingled more and more with trains of active thought, and tended to absorb their whole being into the energy of sense.

—Arthur Henry Hallam on Shelley and Keats, in his review of Tennyson's *Poems, Chiefly Lyrical* (1830)

The laureate of "Despair" and "The Ancient Sage" is of course one of the memorable disasters of poetic tradition, surpassing the Wordsworth of the *Ecclesiastical Sonnets* and even the Arnold of *Merope*. The whole being of Tennyson was at no single time absorbed into the energy of sense, and for this failure of experience the price was paid, alas even overpaid:

And more—think well! Do-well will follow thought,
And in the fatal sequence of this world
An evil thought may soil thy children's blood;

But curb the beast would cast thee in the mire,
And leave the hot swamp of voluptuousness
A cloud between the Nameless and thyself,
And lay thine uphill shoulder to the wheel,
And climb the Mount of Blessing, whence, if thou
Look higher, then—perchance—thou mayest—beyond
A hundred ever-rising mountain lines,
And past the range of Night and Shadow-see
The high-heaven dawn of more than mortal day
Strike on the Mount of Vision!
So, farewell.

There are still Tennyson scholars who can read this, or say they can, but the indefensible badness of it all is plain enough. Sixty years or so before this, as a boy of fourteen, Tennyson possessed the verbal exuberance of an absolute poetic genius and manifested it in the splendid speeches of the Devil in *The Devil and the Lady* and in the remarkable movement of an exercise like the "Ode: O Bosky Brook." The extremes of a poet's values, if they are manifested merely as a chronological continuum, do not much matter. Vision darkens, life triumphs, the poet becomes the man whose pharynx is bad. So went Wordsworth, the founder of modern poetry, and where a Moses was lost, other losses must follow. Yeats and Wallace Stevens appear today to be the first and only poets in the romantic tradition who flowered anew both in middle and in old age, and yet it can be questioned if either will rival Tennyson and Browning after the fogs of fashion have been dispelled.

At the center of Tennyson the problem is not whether or why he hardened and kept hardening in poetic character, or just how his vision darkened perpetually into the abysses of much of the later verse, but why and how the sensibility of a major romantic poet was subverted even in his earlier years. What the most sympathetic reader can still find wanting in the best of Tennyson is a power of imagination shown forth uncompromisingly in *The Fall of Hyperion* and "The Triumph of Life," in "Resolution and Independence" and "The Mental Traveller," and on the largest scale in *The Prelude* and "Jerusalem." Romance, lyric, epic were raised to greatness again in the two generations just before Tennyson. In a lyrical monologue like "Andrea del Sarto," a romance like "Childe Roland to the Dark Tower Came," and in the curious epic of *The Ring and the Book* a poet of Tennyson's own generation comes close to approximating the romantic achievement. Tennyson was as legitimately the heir of Keats as Browning was of Shelley and as much a betrayal of Keats's imaginative honesty and autonomy as Browning was of Shelley's. To make such a point is to reveal in oneself an unreconstructed romantic bias, like that of Swinburne, or Yeats, or Shaw or Hardy, to bring in four Shelleyans who were contemporaries of the older Browning and Tennyson. There are achievements in Tennyson that are not romantic, but they are small enough. The Tennyson who counts for most, seen in the longest and clearest perspective we now can begin to recover, is certainly a romantic poet and not a Victorian antiromantic resembling the Arnold of *Merope* or the straining Hopkins of "The Wreck of the Deutschland." He is a major romantic poet, but not perhaps one of the greatest, though there is an antithetical storm cloud drifting through the center of his work that sometimes shows us what his proper greatness should have been. His affinities in his own time were to no other poet but to Ruskin, a great ruin of a romantic critic, and his value to us now is rather like Ruskin's, since he shows forth as a most crucial instance of the dilemma of postromantic art.

Hallam, who remains Tennyson's best critic, found "five distinctive excellences" in his friend's poetic manner: (1) the control of a luxuriant imagination; (2) accuracy of adjustment in "moods of character," so that narration and feeling naturally corresponded with each other; (3) skill in emotionally fusing a vivid, "picturesque" portrayal of objects ("picturesque" being opposed here to Wordsworthian descriptiveness); (4) modulation of verbal harmony; (5) "mellow soberness of tone," addressed to the understanding heart rather than the mere understanding. Yeats, in his old age, spoke of "the scientific and moral discursiveness of *In Memoriam*," but I cannot recognize the poem from that description. What lives in the elegies for Hallam are precisely the excellences that Hallam picked out in his friend's earlier manner and the various tracts of discursiveness one learns to step over quickly. Discursiveness became a Tennysonian vice, but it did not in itself inhibit the development of Tennyson's poetry. Tennyson, like Browning, but to a still worse extent, never achieved even a pragmatic faith in the autonomy of his own imagination. Such a faith was a ruling passion in Blake, Shelley, and Keats, and such a faith, though held with earnest misgivings, for a while allowed Wordsworth and Coleridge to yield themselves to their greatest achievements. Though the overt Victorian romantics of the Pre-Raphaelite group struggled back to a version of this faith, it was not held again with similar intensity in Tennyson's age except by Pater, who fostered Yeats even as he gave the more disjunctive and ironical Stevens a fresh point of departure in America. To trace the conflict in Tennyson's earlier poetry between a romantic imagination and an emergent societal censor is hardly to conduct a fresh investigation, and I will not attempt it here. Such conflicts, whether

found in a Spenser or even in a D. H. Lawrence, seem recurrent in the history
of poetry and belong more to the study of consciousness than to the study
of poetic tradition. The more rewarding problem for pondering is the young
Tennyson's profounder distrust of his own creative powers. A god spoke in
him, or a demon, and a revulsion accompanied the maturing of this voice. No
really magical poem by Tennyson ever became quite the work he intended it
to be, and this gap between his intention and his actual achievement saved
him as a poet, though it could not save him altogether. Most considerable
poems by Tennyson do not mean what they meant to mean, and while this
is true of all poets whatsoever to some degree, Tennyson is the most extreme
instance I know of the imagination going one way and the will going quite
another. Blake thought that the Milton of *Paradise Lost* had to be rescued
from himself, an opinion that most recent Miltonists find dubious, perhaps
without fully understanding it. But Tennyson's best poems are a much more
radical version of Blake's paradox; they address themselves simultaneously
and overtly to both a conventional and a "diabolic" reading.

Partly this is due to the prevalence in Tennyson's poetic mind of the
"damned vacillating state" of the early *Supposed Confessions*. No lyric by
Tennyson is more central to his sensibility than "Mariana," entirely a poem of
the autonomous imagination running down into isolated and self-destructive
expectation. Wordsworth, in his sublime "The Affliction of Margaret,"
wrote the contrary to Tennyson's poem, for Margaret is destroyed by an
imaginative hope that will not take account of the mundane. The hope is
all too willing to be fed, and the prevalence of the imagination could hardly
be more dangerous. Wordsworth does, here and in *Michael*, what Tennyson
could only approximate in "Dora"; the poet creates a consciousness narrower
and purer than his own and measures his own malady of self-concern by
its distance from that pure intensity. Mariana, unlike Margaret, is a poetess,
and she sings a dejection ode that Tennyson scarcely ventured to write in his
own person. Her disease is romantic self-consciousness, and no bridegroom
can come to heal her. "She could not look on the sweet heaven," for much
the same cause as the singer of Blake's "Mad Song" turns his back to the
east and rejects the comforts of the sun. Willful and unwilling, she is poised
between two states of being, one in which the world has been taken up into
the mind (the mind of a picturesque rather than descriptive poet) and the
other in which the solipsistic mind rejects the world as an unreal intruder;
hence the landscape of her poem, which as a poetic achievement could not
be overpraised. The poplar, seen as a phallic symbol by some recent Tennyson
critics, is rather an indication of the border realm between the two states in
which Mariana lives. She can neither absorb its presence nor utterly reject

it, and it serves therefore to show how precarious her mode of existence is. The poem's strongest impulse is to see the world as phantasmagoria, in which case Mariana's lament would be transvalued and appear as an ironic cry of triumph for the autonomy of her vision. But there are other impulses in the poem, and "He cometh not" remains a lament.

The Shelleyan origins of Tennyson's female solitary, in "Mariana" and other poems, has been demonstrated ably by Lionel Stevenson, who unfortunately reduces this emblematic figure in both Shelley and Tennyson to Jung's archetype of the *anima*. The reduction is unnecessary in any case, since *Epipsychidion* demonstrates how consciously and deliberately Shelley used his epipsyche figure. Tennyson's use of his cynosure-female is presumably not as conscious or as deliberate, though no theory of the two Tennysons, and no prosaic psychoanalytic reduction, need be ventured in consequence. Tennyson's poetry is too many-sided for anyone to suggest plausibly that it was written by uneasy collaboration between a Shelley-Keats and a Victorian Christian humanist, and I intend no such notion in this essay. There is a profound sense of the limitations of poetry in both Keats and Shelley, but each learned how to convert this sense into an overt poetic strength. Tennyson wrote in an age of reform, both voluntary and involuntary, while the younger romantics faced a time of apparent stasis, an exhaustion following an apocalyptic fervor. The temper of poetic imagination is peculiarly and favorably responsive to the thwarting of political hope, and Shelley and Keats and Byron gained immensely by their good fortune of having the era of Metternich and Castlereagh to contend against, little as they would appreciate so cynical a judgment. Like Beddoes and Darley, a half-generation before him, Tennyson found himself with a fiercely autonomous imagination confronting a time that neither challenged nor repelled such an imagination, yet also gave it no proper arena in which to function. Keats was of course not a political poet, indeed was far less one than Tennyson, but there still existed provocations for Keats's humanism and his naturalism to become combative. Browning found provocation enough in the evangelicism of his parents, particularly his mother, but "Pauline" records too clearly how his Shelleyan sensibility failed guiltily before such a stimulus. Tennyson had no combative use to which an assertion of the imagination could be put and no antidote therefore against any aesthetic corrosion that his moral doubts of imagination might bring about. The pride of imagination, and the distrust of it, had nowhere to go but within.

Sexual virginity for any poet, even a Jesuit, as Hopkins shows, is a kind of sickness unto action, a time of fear before the potential disorder of the strange. That Tennyson's Muse was (and always remained) Hallam has given

Robert Graves occasion for innocent merriment but need disturb no one any longer. The death of a beautiful young man strikes our social sense as a less appropriate theme for poetry than Poe's pervasive theme but is, of course, much more traditional than Poe's preference in corpses. The sexual longings of a poet *qua* poet appear to have little relation to mere experience anyway, as for instance in the contrast between the sexually highly active Shelley, with his crucial antithetical theme of the inadequacy of nature to the imagination from *Alastor* on, and the probably virginal Keats of *Endymion*, with his profoundly primary sense of satisfaction in natural experience. Still, there is a line of poetry that goes from the complexly sensual aspirations of Spenser through the bitter sexual frustrations of Milton and Blake (particularly relevant to his *Notebook* poems and *Visions of the Daughters of Albion*), then to the curious argument between Shelley and Keats in *Alastor* and *Endymion*, and on to the astonishingly delayed entries into sexual experience of Tennyson and of Yeats. The analytical sophistication in aesthetic realms that would allow a responsible sexual history of English poetry to be written is not available to us, and yet such a history must and should come. The hidden fulfillment of Wordsworth is the aesthetic puzzle of *The Prelude*, since the 1805 version is marred by the inclusion of the Julia and Vaudracour episode, and the 1850 version suffers from its exclusion. The malaise of Tennyson's early poetry is very like that of *The Wanderings of Oisin*, and the existence of Shelley and Keats as fellow ancestor-poets is insufficient to explain the likeness. The tragedy of sexual intercourse, according to the older Yeats, was the perpetual virginity of the soul. The comedy of sexual intercourse is presumably the initial virginity of the body, but in poetry poised before experience the comedy tends to be negated, or rather displaced into the phantasmagoria of a Mariana, whose poem would be destroyed by the slightest touch of a comic spirit.

I am not, I would hope, alone in my puzzlement as to why Tennyson has not had the prestige of the hieratic in our time, while the more limited but precisely similar Mallarmé has. Tennyson's poems of the "Mariana" kind, centered on a self-embowered consciousness, are not less artful or persuasive than Mallarmé's and are rather more universal in their implications. The English Decadence has, as its true monument, not Swinburne, admirable poet as he certainly was, but the more masterful Tennyson, whose "metaphysics of night" go beyond Mallarmé's in their elaborately indeliberate subtleties. Hallam's is necessarily a theory of pure poetry (as H. M. McLuhan shows), and while Tennyson could not allow himself to share the theory overtly, he inspired it by his early practice and fell back on it implicitly to save his poetry time and time again. In a way that *In Memoriam* does not apprehend, the dead Hallam remained Tennyson's guardian angel.

"Mariana" is too pure a poem to test any argument by, so that an overview of its neighbors in early Tennyson seems likely to be helpful. "Recollections of the Arabian Nights" is a clearly Shelleyan poem, more confident indeed in its Shelleyan faith of imagination than anything else of Tennyson's. It echoes "Kubla Khan" also, but not the third part of that poem in which Coleridge to some degree withdraws from the full implications of his own vision. Like the poet-hero of *Alastor*, Tennyson voyages through nature in search of a center transcending nature, and he finds it in a pleasure dome like that of "Kubla Khan" or "The Palace of Art" or *The Revolt of Islam*:

The fourscore windows' all alight
As with the quintessence of flame,
A million tapers flaring bright
From twisted silvers look'd to shame
The hollow-vaulted dark, and stream'd
Upon the mooned domes aloof
In inmost Bagdat, till there seem'd
Hundreds of crescents on the roof
Of night new-risen . . .

This is the young Tennyson's Byzantium, and perhaps it lingered in the mind of the old Yeats, though more likely both poets were recalling, however involuntarily, visions seen by Coleridge and by Shelley. Reasonable sophisticates will smile at my connecting Tennyson's playful "Recollections" to Yeats's supreme lyric, but there is a great deal legitimately to claim (or reclaim) for "Recollections of the Arabian Nights." It was Hallam's favorite among the 1830 *Poems*, and his choice was a justified one, for the lyric is a complete and perfected miniature of Tennyson's poetic mind and is even an *In Memoriam* in little. A very great, a consummate poet is at work in the full strength of his sensibility and can be felt with especial power from the fifth line of this stanza on:

Far off, and where the lemon grove
In closest coverture upsprung,
The living airs of middle night
Died round the bulbul as he sung;
Not he: but something which possess'd
The darkness of the world, delight,
Life, anguish, death, immortal love,
Ceasing not, mingled, unrepress'd,

Apart from place, withholding time,
But flattering the golden prime
Of good Haroun Alraschid.

This stanza is at the poem's center of vision and properly recalls the song
of Keats's nightingale, also sung to a poet in darkness, and like this chant
an overcoming of the limitations of space and time. The companion poem
to "Recollections" is the impressive "Ode to Memory," and it is palpable
that both lyrics are love poems addressed to Hallam. Palpable to us and not
presumably to Tennyson and Hallam, I suppose I ought to add, but then the
"Ode to Memory" ends:

My friend, with you to live alone,
Were how much better than to own
A crown, a sceptre, and a throne!
O strengthen me, enlighten me!
I faint in this obscurity,
Thou dewy dawn of memory.

The "Recollections" opens with an inspiriting breeze that takes the poet
back to what Hart Crane in "Passage" beautifully called "an improved infancy."
In that unitary joy, Tennyson emulates the poet-hero of *Alastor* and sets forth
on his quest for the good Haroun Alraschid, who is already the supernatural
Hallam of *In Memoriam*, a poet-king dwelling at the center of vision, a type
of god-man still to come. To reach this absolute being, the poet-voyager sails,
with "a majesty of slow motion in every cadence," as Hallam observed, until he
enters "another night in night," an "imbower'd" world of "imprisoning sweets."
The voyage suggests not only the quest of *Alastor* but also the journey to the
Bower of Bliss in book 2 of *The Faerie Queene*. Tennyson, as many critics by
now have noted, is the most discreetly powerful erotic poet in the language,
and this early lyric is a masterpiece of subdued erotic suggestiveness. The
penultimate stanza, with its confectioner's delight of a Persian girl, is merely
an erotic evasion, but the final stanza, directly celebrating Hallam, is sustained
by a lyric rapture remarkable even in the younger Tennyson.

In section 103 of *In Memoriam*, Tennyson finds an after-morn of content
because of another voyage-vision in which Hallam is again at the center, the
Muse presiding over a realized quest. But the playfulness of "Recollections
of the Arabian Nights" is now gone, that poem's greatest admirer being dead.
Perhaps remembering how much Hallam had loved the poem, Tennyson
returns to its design at one of the climaxes in his book of elegies, in which

his grief is assuaged by the compensatory imagination, and Hallam is resurrected as a Titan capable of reviving Tennyson's lesser Muses. In itself, section 103 has rightly been judged to be one of Tennyson's great lyrics, but one can wonder how many of the poet's readers have seen how very little the poem has to do with the supposed faith of *In Memoriam*. Bradley, the definitive commentator on the elegies for Hallam, interpreted the dream of section 103 with his usual good sense but declined to see its clearly Promethean pattern of consolation. In Numbers 13:32–33, the spies of Moses report on the Anakim, "which come of the giants," and the report appalls the murmuring Israelites. Like the Titans, the Anakim testify to a time when there were giants in the earth, when men walked with gods as equals. In the titanic section 103, Tennyson dreams "a vision of the sea" during his last sleep in the house of his childhood, and in the vision he leaves behind him not only childhood but all that precedes a rising Prometheanism as well. The poet's lesser Muses, his Daughters of Beulah as Blake patronizingly would have named them, sing "of what is wise and good / And graceful" to a veiled statue of Hallam, the unknown god who must lead them to a greater music. A dove summons Tennyson to an apocalyptic sea, an outward-flowing tide on which he will be reunited with "him I loved, and love / For ever." The weeping Muses sail with the poet:

> And still as vaster grew the shore
> And rolled the floods in grander space,
> The maidens gather'd strength and grace
> And presence, lordlier than before;
> And I myself, who set apart
> And watch'd them, wax'd in every limb;
> I felt the thews of Anakim,
> The pulses of a Titan's heart.

Watching the ministering spirits of his own creativity, Tennyson suddenly shares their participation in a daemonic possession, an influx of power as the poet rises in the body to be one again with the giants in the earth. With this transformation his Muses sing not of what is but ought to be: the death of war, the great race that is to come, and a new cosmos—the shaping of a star. The New Man, the first of the crowning race, Tennyson's Albion "appearing ere the times were ripe" and so dying an early and unnatural death, is necessarily Hallam, whose epiphany "thrice as large as man" is the saving culmination of section 103 and indeed of all the elegies. The ship of the reunited lovers, both now Titans and accompanied by the nervous Muses, fearful lest their function be gone, sails at last toward a land of crimson cloud, a realm where vapor, sea, and earth come together, a world out of space and time and free of all merely human moralities.

One never ceases to be puzzled that *In Memoriam*, an outrageously personal poem of romantic apotheosis, a poem indeed of vastly eccentric mythmaking, should have been accepted as a work of consolation and moral resolution in the tradition of Christian humanism. *In Memoriam*, viewed as one poem, is rather a welter of confusions, but its main movement is clear enough and establishes the work as having considerably less relation to a Christian elegy than even *Adonais* has. Whatever Tennyson thought he was doing, the daemon of imaginative autonomy got hold of the poem's continuity and made the poem an argument for a personal love about as restrained and societal as Heathcliff's passion or Blake's in *Visions of the Daughters of Albion* or Shelley's in *Epipsychidion*. The vision of Hallam in sections 126 to 130, for instance, is a more extreme version of the transfiguration of Keats in the final stanzas of Adonais and is a victory for everything in Tennyson that could accept neither God nor nature as adequate to the imaginative demands of a permanently bereaved lover who was also a professional poet.

No poet in English seems to me as extreme and fortuitous as Tennyson in his sudden moments of recognition of his own powers, bursts of radiance against a commonplace conceptual background that cannot accommodate such radiance. The deeply imaginative reader learns instinctively to listen to the song and not the singer, for Lawrence's adage is perfectly relevant to Tennyson. More relevant still was the prophetic warning of Hallam, in one sentence of his review that one wishes Tennyson had brooded on daily and so perhaps saved for poetry more fully than he did one of the major romantic sensibilities:

> That delicate sense of fitness which grows with the growth of artist feelings, and strengthens with their strength, until it acquires a celerity and weight of decision hardly inferior to the correspondent judgments of conscience, is weakened by every indulgence of heterogeneous aspirations, however pure they may be, however lofty, however suitable to human nature.

Had Tennyson heeded this, he might have ended like the sinful soul of his own "The Palace of Art," howling aloud, "I am on fire within." One cannot be sure it would not have been the fitting end his imagination required.

BIOGRAPHY

ALFRED, LORD TENNYSON
(1809–1892)

Alfred Tennyson, first baron Tennyson, was born in Somersby, Tennyshire, on August 6, 1809. He attended the Louth Grammar School between 1815 and 1820 and was subsequently educated at home by his father, the Reverend George Clayton Tennyson. In 1827, Alfred and his brother Charles published *Poems by Two Brothers*. Later that same year, Alfred entered Trinity College, Cambridge, where he formed a friendship with Arthur Henry Hallam and became a member of the exclusive intellectual society The Apostles. In 1829, Tennyson was awarded the Chancellor's Gold Medal for his poem "Timbuctoo," and in the following year, he published *Poems, Chiefly Lyrical* (1830), containing "Mariana."

In 1831, following his father's death, Tennyson left school without taking a degree. In December 1832, he published a further volume, *Poems* (dated 1833), which included "The Two Voices," "Oenone," "The Lotos-Eaters," and "A Dream of Fair Women." Tennyson's friend Arthur Henry Hallam died in Vienna in September 1833, and as a tribute to him, Tennyson began to compose *In Memoriam A.H.H.*, which was first published anonymously in 1850. In 1837, Tennyson moved from Somersby to High Beech, Epping, and in the following year, he became engaged to Emily Sellwood; the engagement was, however, broken off in 1840, and they were not married until 1850. They had two children, Hallam and Lionel.

In 1842, Tennyson published another collection of *Poems*. Volume 1 included revised selections from the collections of 1830 and 1832, while volume 2 was made up of of new work, including "Morte d'Arthur," "Locksley Hall," "Ulysses," and "St. Simeon Stylites." In 1845, Tennyson was awarded a civil list pension of £200 a year, which he received for the rest of his life. His narrative poem *The Princess* appeared in 1847, and in 1850, he was chosen to succeed Wordsworth as poet laureate. *Ode on the Death of the Duke of Wellington* appeared in 1852 and was followed, in 1854, by "The Charge of the Light Brigade." Also in 1854, Tennyson settled in Farringford on the Isle of Wight, where he entertained many celebrities and was visited by numerous admirers.

In 1855, Tennyson published *Maud and Other Poems*, followed in 1859 by the first four *Idylls of the King; Enoch Arden* appeared in 1864. In 1868, Tennyson began building a second residence, Aldworth, near Haslemere, Surrey. In 1869, he published *The Holy Grail and Other Poems* (December 1869; dated 1870), and, in 1872, *Gareth* and *Lynette*, intended as part of the *Idylls of the King*. *Queen Mary*, Tennyson's first play, was published in 1875 and followed by other dramas, including *Harold* (1876), *The Cup* (1884), *The Falcon* (1884), and *Becket* (1884). *Ballads and Other Poems*, containing "The Voyage of Maeldune," "Rizpah," and "The Revenge," appeared in 1880. In 1883, Tennyson accepted the baronetcy he had refused in 1865, 1873, and 1874, and, in 1884, he was seated in the House of Lords. *Balin and Balan*, the last of the *Idylls of the King*, although written in 1872–74, was first published in 1885, when *Tiresias and Other Poems* also appeared. In 1886, Tennyson's son Lionel died at sea. After suffering a severe illness during 1888, Tennyson published, in 1889, *Demeter and Other Poems*. His play *The Foresters* appeared early in 1892, and on October 6 of that year, Tennyson died at home in Surrey. *The Death of Oenone, Akbar's Dream, and Other Poems* appeared posthumously in 1892, and in 1897, Tennyson's son Hallam published a two-volume memoir.

PERSONAL

The following section details various personal reminiscences of Tennyson by a number of individuals who were, or were to become, famous in their own rights. The extracts are in prose and in verse, and many respond to Tennyson's seemingly striking appearance, at least in his younger years. Several entries touch on the character of the younger man, while others present a portrait of a mysterious, semireclusive individual. Other writers discuss the family man at home, while additional extracts give a glimpse of the public poet; we are even given a scene of an old man before his monarch. The extracts are written from both sides of the Atlantic and range from Tennyson's earliest years as an artist to the year of his death. They provide a fascinating overview of others' impressions of the poet across his long career.

FRANCES ANNE KEMBLE (1832)

Frances Anne Kemble was a famous British actress. In the following extract, written when she was approximately 20 years old, she describes the young poet, newly published, on the occasion of his dining with her family. The young woman writing in her journal is clearly somewhat attracted to Tennyson, marking those aspects of his appearance that she finds appealing and those she would prefer to be more so. She is also a little in awe of the young man, finding him quiet and gentle, but fearing he may think slightingly of the company in which he finds himself. Kemble is open about the admiration she feels for the poet's early work, and that esteem borders on possessiveness, as she describes Tennyson as "our" poet.

Mrs. Clarke, Miss James, the Messrs. M; and Alfred Tennyson dined with us. I am always a little disappointed with the exterior of our poet when I look at him, in spite of his eyes, which are very fine; but his head and face, striking and dignified as they are, are almost too ponderous and massive for beauty in so young a man; and every now and then there is a slightly sarcastic expression about his mouth that almost frightens me, in spite of his shy manner and habitual silence. But, after all, it is delightful to see and be with any one that one admires and loves for what he has done, as I do him.

—Frances Anne Kemble, *Journal,* March 16, 1832,
Record of a Girlhood, 1878, vol. 3, p. 209

HARTLEY COLERIDGE
"TO ALFRED TENNYSON" (1835)

Hartley Coleridge was an English poet, biographer, and critic and was the son of the major romantic poet Samuel Taylor Coleridge. In the following poem, Coleridge praises both Tennyson and his poetry, stating that he has long enjoyed and found benefit in his fellow writer's work. While much of Coleridge's lines might seem "precious" to the modern reader, his conclusion that his admiration could not be greater for Tennyson's art and for the poet himself, described as a "real earth-treading man," are certainly heartfelt. With the latter statement, it seems that Coleridge has now been able to assess the writer against his writing, to meet Tennyson and compare the man with his poetic thought. Coleridge would also appear to suggest that Tennyson is in touch with the everyday, a common man speaking to common men, not overly sentimental nor obsessed by abstractions. In many ways, Hartley here values those aspects of poetry that his own father's verse and critical philosophy had promoted in the previous generation.

Long have I known thee as thou art in song,
And long enjoy'd the perfume that exhales
From thy pure soul, and odour sweet entails
And permanence, on thoughts that float along
The stream of life, to join the passive throng
Of shades and echoes that are memory's being.
Hearing we hear not, and we see not seeing,
If passion, fancy, faith move not among
The never-present moments of reflection.
Long have I view'd thee in the crystal sphere
Of verse, that, like the beryl, makes appear

Visions of hope, begot of recollection.
Knowing thee now, a real earth-treading man,
Not less I love thee, and no more I can.

—Hartley Coleridge, "To Alfred Tennyson," 1835

JANE WELSH CARLYLE (1843)

Jane Welsh Carlyle was the wife of the well-known Victorian man of letters
Thomas Carlyle and a woman Tennyson had praised for her literary interests and skill as a letter writer. In the following missive, Mrs. Carlyle praises
Tennyson's as yet underappreciated poetry and remarks on the poet's handsome appearance and character. The concluding statement concerning
geniuses being too poor to have wives is a witticism that says more about
the Carlyleses' own marriage than it does about the imagined dangers of
falling in love with a great man like Tennyson. Despite the somewhat roman-
tically subjective statement that he has something of the appearance of a
gypsy, Jane Carlyle is a reliable witness for the poet, a matter-of-fact, down-
to-earth individual, appreciative of Tennyson's mind, art, and skill.

Three of the autographs, which I send you to-day, are first-rate. A Yankee
would almost give a dollar apiece for them. Entire characteristic letters from
Pickwick, Lytton Bulwer, and Alfred Tennyson; the last the greatest genius of
the three, though the vulgar public have not as yet recognised him for such.
Get his poems if you can, and read the 'Ulysses,' 'Dora,' the 'Vision of Sin,'
and you will find that we do not overrate him. Besides he is a very handsome
man, and a noble-hearted one, with something of the gipsy in his appearance,
which, for me, is perfectly charming. Babbie never saw him, unfortunately, or
perhaps I should say fortunately, for she must have fallen in love with him on
the spot, unless she be made absolutely of ice; and then men of genius have
never anything to keep wives upon!

—Jane Welsh Carlyle, letter to Helen Welsh, March
1843, *Letters and Memorials of Jane Welsh Carlyle,*
ed. James Anthony Froude, 1883, vol. 1, pp. 191–92

THOMAS CARLYLE (1844)

Thomas Carlyle was one of the nineteenth century's best-known men of
letters and the husband of Jane, the author of the preceding extract. Carlyle
was an essayist, historian, and satirist and exerted a profound influence on

Victorian thought. In the following letter written by Carlyle to the American writer Ralph Waldo Emerson (who wrote the extract that follows this one), several comments made previously in the volume are repeated: about Tennyson's "massive" head and face; concerning his gypsylike complexion (which Carlyle's wife remarks on in the previous extract); on Tennyson's retiring nature. Carlyle gives us some background to Tennyson's life and habits. Readers might note that Carlyle appears to contrast Tennyson's attitude to nature, being brought up as a gentleman on a farm, to those of the previous generation's romantic writers, who more often concerned themselves with a physical world that was wild, brooding, and dynamic. Tennyson, however, according to Carlyle, is not utterly divorced from a more romantic sense of the natural world: Note how many times the following extract describes the poet as possessing within himself some sense of "chaos." This "chaos" is reflected in his appearance, in that "great shock" of "rough" hair, and in his "free" and "loose" clothing. Tennyson, Carlyle tell us, often neglects to meet with his friends when he is in London, perhaps because of his retiring temperament, but, in contrast to the extract's conclusion, Carlyle also notes how delightful and welcome Tennyson's company is.

Alfred is one of the few British or Foreign Figures (a not increasing Number, I think!) who are and remain beautiful to me;—a true human soul, or some authentic approximation thereto, to whom your own soul can say, Brother!—However, I doubt he will not come; he often skips me, in these brief visits to Town; skips everybody indeed; being a man solitary and sad, as certain men are, dwelling in an element of gloom,—carrying a bit of Chaos about him, in short, which he is manufacturing into Cosmos!

Alfred is the son of a Lincolnshire Gentleman Farmer, I think; indeed you see in his verses that he is a native of "moated granges," and green fat pastures, not of mountains and their torrents and storms. He had his breeding at Cambridge, as if for the Law, or Church; being master of a small annuity on his Father's decease, he preferred clubbing with his Mother and some Sisters, to live unpromoted and write Poems. In this way he lives still, now here now there; the family always within reach of London, never in it; he himself making rare and brief visits, lodging in some old comrade's rooms. I think he must be under forty, not much under it. One of the finest looking men in the world. A great shock of rough dusty-dark hair; bright-laughing hazel eyes; massive aquiline face, most massive yet most delicate, of sallow brown complexion, almost Indian-looking; clothes cynically loose, free-and-easy;—smokes infinite tobacco. His voice is musical metallic,—fit for loud laughter and piercing wail, and all that may lie between; speech and speculation free and plenteous: I do not meet, in these late decades, such company over a pipe!—We shall see what he will grow to. He is often unwell; very chaotic,—his way is thro' Chaos and the Bottomless and Pathless; not handy for making out many miles upon.

—Thomas Carlyle, letter to Ralph Waldo
Emerson, August 5, 1844

RALPH WALDO EMERSON (1848)

Ralph Waldo Emerson was one of the United States' foremost nineteenth-century orators, poets, essayists, and philosophers and one of the founders of the transcendentalist movement. In the following extract, Emerson remarks on aspects of Tennyson's character and appearance: the strength of his personality, his naturalness in company, his straightforward and dignified manner and dress. The latter part of Emerson's journal entry describes what seems to have been a potentially dangerous situation. Tennyson's confrontation of a drunk, threatening Irish youth in an Irish public house—offering him his pocket knife and essentially daring the youngster to stab him—is a remarkable story. The young man appears to attempt to save face without resorting to violence by claiming Tennyson is not really English and thus not the target of his threats. Tennyson refuses to disengage from the confrontation and insists upon his nationality. It is unclear what happens next, but it seems that, since it is the young man's friends who intervene and apologize for their compatriot, the situation may have escalated to the point where the argument was about to turn violent.

I saw Tennyson, first, at the house of Coventry Patmore, where we dined together. His friend Brookfield was also of the party. I was contented with him, at once. He is tall, scholastic-looking, no dandy,—but a great deal of plain strength about him, &, though cultivated, quite unaffected.—Quiet sluggish sense & strength, refined, as all English are,—and good humoured. The print of his head in Home's book is too rounded & handsome. There is in him an air of general superiority, that is very satisfactory. He lives very much with his college set, Spedding, Brookfield, Hallam, Rice, & the rest and has the air of one who is accustomed to be petted and indulged by those he lives with, like George Bradford. Take away Hawthorne's bashfulness, & let him talk easily & fast, & you would have a pretty good Tennyson. He had just come home from Ireland, where he had seen much vapouring of the

Irish youth against England, & described a scene in some tavern, I think, where a hot young man was flourishing a drawn sword, & swearing that he would drive it to the hilt into the flesh & blood of Englishmen. Tennyson was disgusted, &, going up to the young man, took out his penknife, & offered it to him. "I am an Englishman," he said, "and there is my penknife, and, you know, you will not so much as stick that into me." The youth was disconcerted, & said, "he knew he was not an Englishman." "Yes, but I am." Hereupon the companions of the youth interfered, & apologized for him, he had been in drink, & was excited, &c.

—Ralph Waldo Emerson, *Journal,* 1848

Walter Savage Landor (1853)

Walter Savage Landor was an English writer and poet, not as well respected in his day as he might have been, and certainly not as he himself believed he deserved to be. He had a witty but volatile temperament, and his some-times acerbic tone landed him in trouble more than once. He was still, by all accounts, a respected gentleman and poet among his fellow writers and had many friends in the Victorian world of letters. The following piece of doggerel speaks to the good company Tennyson affords and the nature of his friendship.

I entreat you, Alfred Tennyson,
Come and share my haunch of venison.
I have too a bin of claret,
Good, but better when you share it.
Tho 'tis only a small bin,
There's a stock of it within,
And as sure as I'm a rhymer,
Half a butt of Rudesheimer.
Come; among the sons of men is one
Welcomer than Alfred Tennyson?

—Walter Savage Landor, untitled poem, 1853

Lewis Carroll (1857)

Lewis Carroll was the pen name of Charles Lutwidge Dodgson, best known today as the author of *Alice's Adventures in Wonderland* and *Through the Looking Glass.* Carroll was an Anglican deacon, a mathematician and logician, a fellow of Christ Church College at Oxford University, and an early amateur photographer. It is in this latter capacity that Carroll tells us, in the following diary entry, he has gone to meet Mr. and Mrs. Tennyson, hoping that the poet will agree to sit for a portrait. Tennyson's wild hair, mentioned in previous extracts, is now matched by an equally wild beard. As others have stated in this volume, the poet's face is striking and his character unaffected and friendly. Carroll reveals the humorous sides to Tennyson's temper, noting the jokes that the man makes while looking through the album of photographs that Carroll brought with him. The remarks on Tennyson's feelings toward John Ruskin, the English poet and critic and one of the most influential minds of his generation, is telling. Tennyson is polite to the other writer, but we are given details of an unexplained impertinence on Ruskin's part. Tennyson, rather than confronting him by return post, chooses to ignore the rudeness and all letters from the man thereafter. Carroll is clearly extremely enthusiastic, almost in awe, after his "miraculous day" with the famous man and finds that he might well have overstayed his welcome in the Tennysons' home, leaving after eleven o'clock at night, had the poet and his wife not been such generous and gregarious hosts.

Left Ambleside by the 9.15 coach for Coniston, where I arrived a little before 12. Put up at the hotel and walked over to call at Tent Lodge, to ask leave to take the children's pictures. I asked for Mrs. Tennyson, as I had seen her before, and was shown into the drawing room. After I had waited some little time the door opened, and a strange shaggy-looking man entered: his hair, moustache and beard looked wild and neglected: these very much hid the character of the face. He was dressed in a loosely fitting morning coat, common grey flannel waist-coat and trousers, and a carelessly tied black silk neckerchief. His hair is black: I think the eyes too; they are keen and restless—nose acquiline—forehead high and broad—both face and head are fine and manly. His manner was kind and friendly from the first: there is a dry lurking humour in his style of talking.

I was disappointed to find that they were going away tomorrow morning; however they will be back by Friday night, so I think I may yet manage the photographs. They will not return to Tent Lodge, but to the Marshalls. Mr. Tennyson took me over there to ask leave to take the pictures on their premises, which was readily granted by Mrs. Marshall, Mr. Marshall being from home. We stayed luncheon there and met a son of Mrs. Marshall's, about sixteen years old; a daughter, Julia, about eleven, and the son's tutor. The little girl has a very striking, animated face, not unlike Katie Murdoch. . . .

After luncheon Mr. Tennyson returned to the lodge, and I took a walk through Coniston, having first brought my books of photographs to Mrs. Marshall to be looked at.

At six I went by invitation to dine at Tent Lodge, and spent a most delightful evening. I saw the little boys for a short time; I had met them in a donkey cart near Coniston during my walk. Mrs. Marshall sent over the books in the course of the evening, and Mr. and Mrs. Tennyson admired some of them so much that I have strong hopes of ultimately getting a sitting from the poet, though I have not yet ventured to ask for it.

Some of the photographs called out a good deal of fun on Mr. Tennyson's part. The picture of Skeffington in a fishing costume, he said, had the expression, (stroking down his beard as he spoke) 'Well! I've come down here to catch trout, and if I don't catch a trout this season, the great business of my life will be gone'; and his half-length portrait 'By Jupiter! all my labour gone for nothing, and not one single trout!' The first portrait of Mr. Webster was interpreted 'Now, sir, I am ready to argue the question with you on any point—What is the particular subject you would like to discuss, predestination or what?' And the second 'Well, it may be so, or it may not: there are differences of opinion'.

He remarked on the similarity of the monkey's skull to the human, that a young monkey's skull is quite human in shape and gradually alters—the analogy being borne out by the human skull being at first more like the statues of the gods, and gradually degenerating into human—and then, turning to Mrs. Tennyson, 'There, that's the second original remark I've made this evening!'

We talked a good deal of Ruskin, whom he seemed to have a profound contempt for as a critic, though he allowed him to be a most eloquent writer. He said that Ruskin had written to him, asking to make his acquaintance, that he had answered it in a friendly spirit, and that Ruskin had then sent him an impertinent letter, of which he had taken no notice, nor of any letter received from him since.

He threw out several hints of his wish to learn photography, but seems to be deterred by a dread of the amount of patience required. I left at what I believed to be a little after nine, but which to my horror I found to be after eleven, having had a most interesting and delightful evening. The hotel was shut up for the night, and I had to wait and ring a long while at the door.

Dies mirabilis!

—Lewis Carroll, *Diary,* September 22, 1857

Nathaniel Hawthorne (1857)

Nathaniel Hawthorne was one of the best-known American short story writers and novelists of the nineteenth century. In this extract, Hawthorne begins by describing Tennyson, a wildish, somewhat poetic figure, as sensitive, not entirely careful about his appearance, sporting a poet's floppy hat, and seemingly uninterested in, if not unaware of, those around him. Having spotted the poet in an exhibition of paintings, he hurries off to find his wife, who he knows would be excited to see the Englishman. On their return, Hawthorne finds that Tennyson has met some acquaintances, is perfectly comfortable in their company, but appears to be uninterested in, perhaps even disinclined toward, the companionship of others. His voice is described as "ragged around the edges" but "pleasant" by Hawthorne, very much the same as how the American describes Tennyson's physical appearance.

The anecdote related at the conclusion of the extract is an amusing misunderstanding suffered between Tennyson and some French waiters whilst the poet was visiting Paris. He had presumably meant to say to the Frenchmen, upon the departure from the hotel of his friend for a walk, that he himself did not want to go out; but what the poet actually said was "Do not allow me to go out." The waiters were happy to oblige, and it seems a rather frenzied struggle ensued, only to be broken up upon the return of Tennyson's friend from his walk.

Tennyson is the most picturesque figure, without affectation, that I ever saw; of middle size, rather slouching, dressed entirely in black, and with nothing white about him except the collar of his shirt, which, methought, might have been whiter the day before. He had on a black wide-awake hat, with round crown and wide, irregular brim, beneath which came down his long black hair, looking terribly tangled; he had a long pointed beard, too, a little browner than the hair, and not so abundant as to encumber any of the expression of his face. His frock coat was buttoned up across the breast, though the afternoon was warm. His face was very dark, and not exactly a smooth face, but worn, and expressing great sensitiveness, though not at that moment the pain and sorrow that is seen in his bust. His eyes were black; but I know little of them, as they did not rest on me, nor on anything but the pictures. He seemed as if he did not see the crowd, nor think of them, but as if he defended himself from them by ignoring them altogether; nor did anybody but myself cast a glance at him. . . .

Knowing how much my wife would delight to see him, I went in search of her, and found her and the rest of us under the music gallery; and we all,

Fanny and Rosebud included, went back to the saloon of the Old Masters. So rapid was his glance at the pictures, that in the little interval Tennyson had got half-way along the other side of the saloon, and, as it happened, an acquaintance had met him—an elderly gentleman and lady—and he was talking to them as we approached. I heard his voice,—a bass voice, but not of a resounding depth,—a voice rather broken, as it were, and ragged about the edges, but pleasant to the ear. His manner, while conversing with these people, was not in the least that of an awkward man, unaccustomed to society; but he shook hands and parted with them, evidently, as soon as he conveniently could, and shuffled away quicker than before. He betrayed his shy and secluded habits more in this than in anything else that I observed; though, indeed, in his whole presence I was indescribably sensible of a morbid painfulness in him,—a something not to be meddled with. Very soon he left the saloon, shuffling along the floor with short, irregular steps,—a very queer gait, as if he were walking in slippers too loose for him. I had observed that he seemed to turn his feet slightly inward, after the fashion of Indians.

I should be glad to smoke a cigar with him. Mr. Ireland says that, having heard he was to be at the Exhibition, and not finding him there, he conjectured that he must have gone into the Botanical Garden to smoke; and, sure enough, he found him there. He told me an anecdote about Tennyson while on a visit to Paris. He had a friend with him who could not speak very good French, any more than the poet himself. They were sitting at the fireside in the parlor of the hotel; and the friend proposed a walk about the city, and finally departed, leaving Tennyson at the fireside, and telling the waiter 'ne souffrez pas le faire sortir.' By and by Tennyson also rose to go out; but the waiter opposed him with might and main, and called another waiter to his assistance; and when Tennyson's friend returned, he found him really almost fit for a straitjacket. He might well enough pass for a madman at any time, there being a wildness in his aspect which doubtless might readily pass from quietude to frenzy. He is exceedingly nervous.

—Nathaniel Hawthorne, 1857, cited in Julian
Hawthorne, *Nathaniel Hawthorne and His Wife*,
1884, vol. 2, pp. 143–46

QUEEN VICTORIA (1883)

Victoria, queen of the United Kingdom of Great Britain and Ireland and empress of India, reigned longer than any previous or, until today, succeeding British monarch. She has, of course, given her name to, and become emblematic of, a period in history. She was, as the following extract shows, a devoted fan of Tennyson's poetry and an admirer of the man himself. The queen is no great literary critic, but the comfort that Tennyson's work has afforded her is not open to question. Tennyson, despite being now infirm, offers Victoria any service she requires of him, saying he will be happy to attend her anytime she requests his company. The poet's mood appears to be somber, gloomy about the state of the world and of modern thought, specifically its attitudes to the afterlife, faith, and the immortality of the soul. He contemplates those friends who have already died, and, in his old age when he believes himself to be only a year or two from death, this conversation with the elderly queen could easily be conceived of as being morbid were it not for the comfort that both derived from art: Victoria from Tennyson's, Tennyson from the great German poet Goethe's.

After luncheon saw the great Poet *Tennyson* in dearest Albert's room for nearly an hour;—and most interesting it was. He is grown very old—his eyesight much impaired *and he is very shaky on his legs.* But he was very kind. Asked him to sit down. He talked of the many friends he had lost and what it would be if he did not feel and know that there was another World, where there would be no partings; and then he spoke with horror of the unbelievers and philosophers who would make you believe there was no other world, no Immortality—who tried to explain *all* away in a miserable manner. We agreed that were such a thing possible, God, who is Love, would be far more cruel than any human being. He quoted some well-known lines from Goethe whom he so much admires. Spoke of the poor Lily of Hanover so kindly—asked after my grandchildren. He spoke of Ireland with abhorrence and the wickedness in ill using poor Animals. 'I am afraid I think the world is darkened, I daresay it will brighten again.'

I told him what a comfort *In Memoriam* had again been to me which pleased him; but he said I could not believe the number of shameful letters of abuse he had received about it. Incredible! When I took leave of him, I thanked him for his kindness and said I needed it, for I had gone through so much—and he said you are so alone on the 'terrible height, it is Terrible. I've only a year or two to live but I'll be happy to do anything for you I can. Send for me whenever you like.' I thanked him warmly.

—Queen Victoria, *Journal*, August 7, 1883

RICHARD LE GALLIENNE
"'TENNYSON' AT THE FARM" (1892)

Richard Le Gallienne was an English writer, critic, and poet who was particularly associated with the 1890s and the decadent period in British literature. This short poem written in the year of Tennyson's death describes the influence that the poet has had on a new generation of English writers, Le Gallienne describing a youth neglecting his duties on his father's farm and instead reading from a poetry collection. Le Gallienne, like the youth on the farm, prefers to follow the great poet's lead and move from the countryside or provinces to the "far-off town." Tennyson's craft is eulogized as "[t]he fairest art, / The sweetest English song" and as an ideal to be emulated and pursued by young men in the manner of disciples following a master.

O you that dwell 'mid farm and fold,
   Yet keep so quick undulled a heart,
   I send you here that book of gold,
       So loved so long;
        The fairest art,
     The sweetest English song.
       And often in the far-off town,
   When summer sits with open door,
     I'll dream I see you set it down
   Beside the churn,
      Whose round shall slacken more and more,
   Till you forget to turn.
      And I shall smile that you forget,
  And Dad will scold—but never mind!
     Butter is good, but better yet,
   Think such as we,
     To leave the farm and fold behind,
And follow such as he.

        —Richard Le Gallienne, "Tennyson' at the Farm,"
                   English Poems, 1892, p. 102

GENERAL

The following section deals with a variety of subjects, several extracts considering Tennyson's entire career as a writer and attempting to develop a sense of aesthetic continuum unifying three-quarters of a century of work. There are reviews of individual poems and collections of poetry (both as they were published and retrospectively) and examinations of Tennyson's style, lyric voice, philosophy (indeed, whether the poet could be said to actually have a consistent philosophical stance), and later dramas. Other extracts detail Tennyson's cultural and spiritual attitudes, his political views, and his relationship to the Victorian age and its several crises. Suggestions to readers for cross-referencing the many contrasting opinions voiced in this section are provided in several of the excerpts' introductions. The passages provided offer the reader the opportunity to not only appreciate the huge variance in attitude to Tennyson's work at different periods in his career but also to note how shifts in culture and taste influenced critical opinions over the course of the Victorian period.

W. J. Fox "Tennyson's Poems" (1831)

W. J. Fox was a newspaper and literary critic. The following extract for the *Westminster Review*, one of London's leading journals, highly praises Tennyson's first published collection. Fox remarks on the natural, sincere, honest, and thoughtful qualities presented by the poet in his verse, his originality and poetic harmonies. Critics would still be praising Tennyson's lyric grace at the end of his poetic career at the end of the nineteenth century, along with the poet's capacity to move his readership through the philosophical insight contained in his works. Fox is correct in stating at the conclusion of this extract that the finer qualities exemplified by the young writer would be felt for a long period of time.

These poems *(Poems, Chiefly Lyrical)* are anything but heavy; anything but stiff and pedantic, except in one particular, which shall be noticed before we conclude; anything but cold and logical. They are graceful, very graceful; they are animated, touching, and impassioned. And they are so, precisely because they are philosophical; because they are not made up of metrical cant and conventional phraseology; because there is sincerity where the author writes from experience, and accuracy whether he writes from experience or observation; and he only writes from experience or observation, because he has felt and thought, and learned to analyze thought and feeling; because his own mind is rich in poetical associations, and he has wisely been content with its riches; and because, in his composition, he has not sought to construct an elaborate and artificial harmony, but only to pour forth his thoughts in those expressive and simple melodies whose meaning, truth, and power, are the soonest recognized and the longest felt.

—W. J. Fox, "Tennyson's Poems," *Westminster Review*, January 1831, p. 214

Arthur Henry Hallam "Extract from a Review of Tennyson's Poems" (1831)

Arthur Henry Hallam was an English poet and Tennyson's closest friend. The two young men had met while at Cambridge University, and Hallam became engaged to marry Tennyson's sister. He died suddenly in Vienna of a brain hemorrhage while traveling with his father at the age of 22. His death had a profound effect on Tennyson, to the extent that some critics and biographers have questioned the nature of the two men's relationship (by far the majority agree that it was platonic, if unusually close). Tennyson dedicated what would perhaps be his most famous poem, *In Memoriam A. H. H.*, to his deceased friend, the initials in the poem's title being, of course, those of the dead Hallam.

Hallam is here writing a review of his friend Tennyson's first publication, and his unbiased critical credentials should therefore be called into question. The extract from the review is, nevertheless, detailed if eulogistic. Readers should note how Hallam positions Tennyson within the English romantic tradition, alongside poets such as John Keats, Percy Bysshe Shelley, and Lord Byron, while simultaneously marking him out as an original author among them. Hallam praises his friend's imagination, passion, love of beauty, appreciation of nature, and his lyric voice, all traits commonly remarked on and valued by the romantic era's critics and artists. The review, as a consequence, is of as much benefit to the reader as a critical analysis of Tennyson's early verse. It is also a marker of the values of a generation that, by the end of the century and Tennyson's life, would be long deceased.

The five "distinctive excellencies" identified by Hallam at the conclusion to the extract are also of note. The first three—the poet's imagination, his portrayal of characters' moods, and his accuracy in depicting objects in vivid detail—would be poetic traits associated in later years, and to Tennyson's detriment, with his great rival Robert Browning. The fourth and fifth qualities, the poet's lyrical modulation and his "elevated habits of thought" would become, for some critics later in the century, problematic with Tennyson's poetry rather than aspects that were praiseworthy. The changing critical and public tastes during the long reign of Queen Victoria should be kept in mind when examining Hallam's review.

Mr. Tennyson belongs decidedly to the class we have already described as Poets of Sensation. He sees all the forms of nature with the "eruditus oculus," and his ear has a fairy fineness. There is a strange earnestness in his worship of beauty which throws a charm over his impassioned song, more easily felt than described, and not to be escaped by those who have once felt it. We think he has more definitiveness and roundness of general conception than the late Mr. Keats, and is much more free from blemishes of diction and hasty capriccios of fancy. He has also this advantage over that poet and his friend Shelley, that he comes before the public unconnected with any political party or peculiar system of opinions. Nevertheless, true to the theory we have stated, we believe his participation in their characteristic excellencies is sufficient to secure him a share of their unpopularity. The volume of *Poems, Chiefly Lyrical*, does not contain above 154 pages; but it shows us much more of the character of its parent mind, than many books we have known of much larger compass, and more boastful pretensions. The features of original genius are clearly and strongly marked. The author imitates nobody; we recognise the spirit of his age, but not the individual form of this or that writer. His thoughts bear no more resemblance to Byron or Scott, Shelley or Coleridge, than to Homer or Calderon, Firdusi or Calidasa. We have remarked five distinctive excellencies of his own manner. First his luxuriance of imagination, and at the same time, his control over it. Secondly, his power of embodying himself in ideal characters, or rather moods of character, with such extreme accuracy of adjustment, that the circumstances of the narration seem to have a natural correspondence with the predominant feeling, and, as it were, to be evolved from it by assimilative force. Thirdly, his vivid, picturesque delineation of objects, and the peculiar skill with which he holds all of them *fused,* to borrow a metaphor from science, in a medium of strong emotion. Fourthly, the variety of his lyrical measures, and exquisite modulation of harmonious words and cadences to the swell and fall of the feelings expressed. Fifthly, the elevated habits of thought, implied in these compositions, and imparting a mellow soberness of tone, more impressive to our minds, than if the author had drawn up a set of opinions in verse, and sought to instruct the understanding rather than to communicate the love of beauty to the heart.

—Arthur Henry Hallam, "Extract from a Review
of Tennyson's Poems," 1831, *Remains in Verse and
Prose,* 1863, pp. 304–05

John Wilson "Tennyson's Poems" (1832)

In the following extract, John Wilson reviews Tennyson's earliest publications for the esteemed Edinburgh-based literary journal *Blackwood's Magazine.* The review is a humorous, but vitriolic, attack on the Scottish journal's great rival, the *Westminster Review.* Wilson attacks the London publication's critic for several extravagant statements made concerning Tennyson's capacity to transfer his own ideas and thought into the characters inhabiting his verse. Tennyson does not fare well in the review by association, but he rarely surfaces above the scathing wit of Wilson's attack on his rival journalist. The reader should, however, note that, on Tennyson's initially being published, not every critic or journal was as full of praise as the others.

⸺⸺⸺

Mr. Tennyson's admirers say he excels wondrously in personating mermen and mermaids, fairies, *et id genus omne,* inhabiting sea-caves and forest glades, "in still or stormy weather," the "gay creatures of the element," be that element air, earth, fire, or water, so that the denizens thereof be but of "imagination all compact." We beg of you to hear, for a few sentences, the quack in the Westminster. "Our author has the secret of the transmigration of the soul. He can cast his own spirit into any living thing, real or imaginary. Scarcely Vishnu himself becomes incarnate more easily, frequently, or perfectly. And there is singular refinement, as well as solid truth, in his impersonations, whether they be of inferior creatures, or of such elemental beings as sirens, as mermen, and mermaidens. He does not merely assume their external shapes, and exhibit his own mind masquerading. He takes their senses, feelings, nerves, and brain, along with their names and local habitations; still it is himself in them, modified but not absorbed by their peculiar constitution and mode of being. In the 'Merman,' one seems to feel the principle of thought injected by a strong volition into the cranium of the finny worthy, and coming under all the influences, as thinking principles do, of the physical organization to which it is for the time allied: for a moment the identification is complete; and then a consciousness of contrast springs up between the reports of external objects brought to the mind by the senses, and those which it has been accustomed to receive, and this consciousness gives to the description a most poetical colouring." We could quote another couple of critics—but as the force of nature could no farther go, and as to make one fool she joined the other two, we keep to the Westminster. It is a perfect specimen of the super-hyperbolical ultra-extravagance of outrageous Cockney eulogistic foolishness, with which not even a quantity of common sense less than nothing has been suffered, for an indivisible moment of time, to mingle; the purest mere matter of moonshine ever mouthed by an idiot-lunatic, slavering in the palsied dotage of the extremest superannuation ever inflicted on a being, long ago, perhaps, in some slight respects and low degrees human, but now sensibly and audibly reduced below the level of the Pongos. "Coming under all the influences, as thinking principles do, of the physical organization to which it is for the time allied!" There is a bit of Cockney materialism for you! "The principle of thought injected by a strong volition into the cranium of the finny worthy!" Written like the Son of a Syringe. O the speculative sumph! 'Tis thus that dishonest Cockneys would fain pass off in their own vile slang, and for their own viler meaning, murdered and dismembered, the divine Homeric philosophy of the Isle of Circe. Was not Jupiter still Jove—aye, every inch the thunderous king of heaven, whose throne was Olympus—while to languishing Leda the godhead seemed a Swan? In the eyes of a grazier, who saw but Smithfield, he would have been but a bull in the Rape of Europa. Why, were the Cockney critic's principle of thought injected by a strong volition into the skull of a donkey—has he vanity to imagine, for a moment, that he would be a more consummate ass than he now brays? Or if into that of the Great Glasgow Gander, that his quackery would be more matchless still? O no, no, no! He would merely be "assuming their external shapes;" but his asinine and anserine natural endowments would all remain unchanged—a greater goose than he now is, depend upon it, he could not be, were he for a tedious lifetime to keep waddling his way through this weary world on web-feet, and with uplifted wings and outstretched neck, hissing the long-red-round-cloaked beggar off the common; a superior ass he might in no ways prove, though untethered in the lane where gipsy gang had encraal'd, he were left free to roam round the canvass walls, eminent among all the "animals that chew the thistle."

—John Wilson, "Tennyson's Poems," *Blackwood's Edinburgh Magazine*, May 1832, pp. 728–29

SAMUEL TAYLOR COLERIDGE (1833)

Samuel Taylor Coleridge was an English poet, philosopher, and critic and, along with his friend and fellow poet William Wordsworth, was a leading figure in the English romantic movement. This extract comes from a volume written the year before the by-then-old poet's death. In it, Coleridge laments what he perceives to be the lack of rhythm and meter in Tennyson's verse, while simultaneously praising the "good deal of beauty" also contained therein. There is something of the curmudgeon in evidence in this extract, certainly in the final line, where Coleridge seems almost to throw up his hands in exasperation on attempting to scan Tennyson's verse. It is interesting to contrast the older poet's opinions with other reviewers of Tennyson's early work; most critics had praised the young poet's sense of lyrical harmony and the "music" contained in his poetic lines.

I have not read through all Mr. Tennyson's poems, which have been sent to me; but I think there are some things of a good deal of beauty in what I have seen. The misfortune is, that he has begun to write verses without very well understanding what metre is. Even if you write in a known and approved metre, the odds are, if you are not a metrist yourself, that you will not write harmonious verses; but to deal in new metres without considering what metre means and requires, is preposterous. What I would, with many wishes for success, prescribe to Tennyson,—indeed without it he can never be a poet in act,—is to write for the next two or three years in none but one or two well-known and strictly defined metres, such as the heroic couplet, the octave stanza, or the octosyllabic measure of the "Allegro" and "Penseroso." He would, probably, thus get imbued with a sensation, if not a sense, of metre without knowing it, just as Eton boys get to write such good Latin verses by conning Ovid and Tibullus. As it is, I can scarcely scan his verses.

—Samuel Taylor Coleridge, *Table Talk*, April 24, 1833

MARGARET FULLER (1842)

Margaret Fuller was an American women's rights advocate, critic, and journalist. In the following extract, Tennyson is described by Fuller as having
moved away from the passionate expressions of his earliest poetry and as
having arrived at an earnest and noble expression of "the problems of life."
She states, however, that Tennyson's work, nevertheless, retains its music,
its sense of profound feeling, and its thoughtful appreciation of human
existence. The extract provides a valuable and sensitive assessment of the
strengths of some of Tennyson's most enduring verse. Readers might also
note that Fuller, like so many of her contemporaries in both Great Britain
and the United States, felt that she "found herself" in Tennyson's poetic
characters and in his poetry's portrayal of life.

I have just been reading the new poems of Tennyson. Much has he thought,
much suffered, since the first ecstasy of so fine an organization clothed all the
world with rosy light. He has not suffered himself to become a mere intellectual
voluptuary, nor the songster of fancy and passion, but has earnestly revolved
the problems of life, and his conclusions are calmly noble. In these later
verses is a still, deep sweetness; how different from the intoxicating, sensuous
melody of his earlier cadence! I have loved him much this time, and taken
him to heart as a brother. One of his themes has long been my favorite,—the
last expedition of Ulysses,—and his, like mine, is the Ulysses of the *Odyssey*,
with his deep romance of wisdom, and not the worldling of the *Iliad*. How
finely marked his slight description of himself and of Telemachus. In "Dora,"
"Locksley Hall," the "Two Voices," "Morte D'Arthur," I find my own life, much
of it, written truly out.

—Margaret Fuller, *Journal*, August
1842, *Memoirs*, 1852, vol. 2, p. 66

RALPH WALDO EMERSON (1843)

The following extract was written for the U.S. journal *The Dial*, which, at
the time, was the major publication of the transcendentalist movement.
Margaret Fuller, the author of the preceding extract, initially accepted the
journal's editorship. Ralph Waldo Emerson was one of the leading figures
and proponents of the movement.

In this extract, Emerson praises the musicality of Tennyson's verse, its
harmonies, and its qualities as "song." The review points out that the English

poet's work avoids, at one extreme, the overly sentimental passion of some writers of the time, and at the other a didactic philosophizing, each of which would destroy the power of Tennyson's writing. Emerson sensitively draws a distinction between the poetic representation of objects and their reproduction in verse. Tennyson is not slavishly faithful to reality in his poetry, reproducing what exists in the external world, but reproduces it in the manner of a master painter, with a style and a simple grace all his own. It is a distinction that readers might find in contrasting Tennyson's work with those lesser poets of the same period who produced their verse in a realistic manner and not in the mode which Emerson here suggests is the true poetic one.

Tennyson is more simply the songster than any poet of our time. With him the delight of musical expression is first, the thought second. It was well observed by one of our companions, that he has described just what we should suppose to be his method of composition in this verse from "The Miller's Daughter."

A love-song I had somewhere read,
      An echo from a measured strain,
Beat time to nothing in my head
      From some odd corner of the brain.
It haunted me, the morning long,
      With weary sameness in the rhymes,
      The phantom of a silent song,
      That went and came a thousand times.

So large a proportion of even the good poetry of our time is either over-ethical or over-passionate, and the stock poetry is so deeply tainted with a sentimental egotism, that this, whose chief merits lay in its melody and picturesque power, was most refreshing. What a relief, after sermonizing and wailing had dulled the sense with such a weight of cold abstraction, to be soothed by this ivory lute!

Not that he wanted nobleness and individuality in his thoughts, or a due sense of the poet's vocation; but he won us to truths, not forced them upon us; as we listened, the cope

      Of the self-attained futurity
Was cloven with the million stars which tremble
      O'er the deep mind of dauntless infamy.

And he seemed worthy thus to address his friend,

> Weak truth a-leaning on her crutch,
> Wan, wasted truth in her utmost need,
> Thy kingly intellect shall feed,
> Until she be an athlete bold.

Unless thus sustained, the luxurious sweetness of his verse must have wearied. Yet it was not of aim or meaning we thought most, but of his exquisite sense for sounds and melodies, as marked by himself in the description of Cleopatra.

> Her warbling voice, a lyre of widest range,
> Touched by all passion, did fall down and glance
> From tone to tone, and glided through all change
> Of liveliest utterance.

Or in the fine passage in the "Vision of Sin," where

> Then the music touched the gates and died;
> Rose again from where it seemed to fail,
> Stormed in orbs of song, a growing gale; &c.

Or where the Talking Oak composes its serenade for the pretty Alice;—but indeed his descriptions of melody are almost as abundant as his melodies, though the central music of the poet's mind is, he says, as that of the

>   fountain
> Like sheet lightning,
>   Ever brightening
> With a low melodious thunder;
> All day and all night it is ever drawn
> From the brain of the purple mountain
> Which stands in the distance yonder:
> It springs on a level of bowery lawn,
> And the mountain draws it from heaven above,
> And it sings a song of undying love.

Next to his music, his delicate, various, gorgeous music, stands his power of picturesque representation. And his, unlike those of most poets, are eye-pictures, not mind-pictures. And yet there is no hard or tame fidelity, but a simplicity and ease at representation (which is quite another thing from reproduction) rarely to be paralleled. How, in the "Palace of Art," for instance, they are unrolled slowly and gracefully, as if painted one after another on the same canvass. The touch is calm and masterly, though the result is looked at with a sweet, self-pleasing eye. Who can forget such as this, and of such there are many, painted with as few strokes and with as complete a success?

> A still salt pool, locked in with bars of sand;
>   Left on the shore; that hears all night
>   The plunging seas draw backward from the land
> Their moon-led waters white.

Tennyson delights in a garden. Its groups, and walks, and mingled bloom intoxicate him, and us through him. So high is his organization, and so powerfully stimulated by color and perfume, that it heightens all our senses too, and the rose is glorious, not from detecting its ideal beauty, but from a perfection of hue and scent, we never felt before. All the earlier poems are flower-like, and this tendency is so strong in him, that a friend observed, he could not keep up the character of the tree in his Oak of Summer Chase, but made it talk like an "enormous flower." The song,

> A spirit haunts the year's last hours,

is not to be surpassed for its picture of the autumnal garden.

> —Ralph Waldo Emerson, *The Dial*, April 1843

Edwin P. Whipple "English Poets of the Nineteenth Century" (1845)

Edwin P. Whipple was a literary critic who, in the following extract, reviews Tennyson's place within the nineteenth-century English poetic tradition. Whipple states that Tennyson is the poetic successor to Percy Bysshe Shelley, in terms of his ability to see clearly and insightfully and to eschew passion for intellectual intensity. The extract examines the manner in which each of Tennyson's poems is a unity, with no baroque ornamentation, no unnecessary details or decoration, every idea, image and word an integral part of the whole. No detail could be removed from Tennyson's verse without operating to the detriment of the poem. Both the poet's eye and ear for detail, his lyrics' images and tone, are praised. Those critics who attack Tennyson for being simply a "rhapsodist," or a passionate singer alone, are called to account for their own inability to see the profound meaning in the poet's art.

Whipple's review is certainly full of the highest praise, but it should be of interest to those readers in search of critical disagreement over poetics generally, and Tennyson's verse specifically, in the middle years of the nineteenth century. The shift away from the "passion" and "intensity" cherished by romanticism is not total, but the importance of the philosophical aspect of poetry and the fear of sentimentalism for critics is made obvious from this extract. Tennyson's contemporary, Robert Browning, would find these cultural-critical shifts in perspective to be generally to his benefit. Nonetheless, both poets would continue to be attacked throughout the remainder of the century: Tennyson for being intellectually lightweight, more concerned with the music of his verse than the vague ideas contained therein, and Browning for his philosophizing in verse, for the lack of structure and harmony in his writing. Depending on one's critical camp, one of the two poets would be held aloft as the ideal of the poet for the remainder of Queen Victoria's reign.

⸻ ꝏ/ꝏ/ꝏ ⸻   ⸻ ꝏ/ꝏ/ꝏ ⸻   ⸻ ꝏ/ꝏ/ꝏ ⸻

Of all the successors of Shelley, he possesses the most sureness of insight. He has a subtle mind, of keen, passionless vision. His poetry is characterized by intellectual intensity as distinguished from the intensity of feeling. He watches his consciousness with a cautious and minute attention, to fix, and condense, and shape into form, the vague and mystical shadows of thought and feeling which glide and flit across it. He listens to catch the lowest whisperings of the soul. His imagination broods over the spiritual and mystical elements of his being with the most concentrated power. His eye rests firmly on an object until it changes from film into form. Some of his poems are forced into artistical shape by the most patient and painful intellectual processes. His utmost strength is employed on those mysterious facts of consciousness which form the staple of the dreams and reveries of others. His mind winds through the mystical labyrinths of thought and feeling, with every power awake, in action, and wrought up to the highest pitch of intensity. The most acute analysis is followed, step by step, by a suggestive imagination, which converts refined abstractions into pictures, or makes them audible to the soul through the most cunning combinations of sound. Everything that is done is the result of labor. There is hardly a stanza in his writings but was introduced to serve some particular purpose, and could not be omitted without injury to the general effect. Everything has meaning. Every idea was won in a fair conflict with darkness, or dissonance, or gloom. The simplicity, the barrenness of ornament, in some of his lines, are as much the result of contrivance as his most splendid images. With what labor, for instance, with what attentive watching of consciousness, must the following stanza have been wrought into shape:—

All those sharp fancies, by down-lapsing thought
Streamed onward, lost their edges, and did creep,
Rolled on each other, rounded, smoothed and
brought
Into the gulfs of sleep.

This intense intellectual action is displayed in his delineations of nature and individual character, as well as in his subjective gropings into the refinements of his consciousness. In describing scenery, his microscopic eye and marvellously delicate ear are exercised to the utmost in detecting the minutest relations and most evanescent melodies of the objects before him, in order that his representation shall include everything which is important to their full perception. His pictures of English rural scenery, among the finest in the language, give the inner spirit as well as the outward form of the objects, and represent them, also, in their relation to the mind which is gazing on them. But nothing is spontaneous; the whole is wrought out elaborately by patient skill. The picture in his mind is spread out before his detecting and dissecting intellect, to be transferred to words only when it can be done with the most refined exactness, both as regards color, and form, and melody. He takes into calculation the nature of his subject, and decides whether it shall be definitely expressed in images, or indefinitely through tone, or whether both modes shall be combined. His object is expression, in its true sense; to reproduce in other minds the imagination or feeling which lies in his own; and he adopts the method which seems best calculated to effect it. He never will trust himself to the impulses of passion, even in describing passion. All emotion, whether turbulent or evanescent, is passed through his intellect, and curiously scanned. To write furiously would to him appear as ridiculous, and as certainly productive of confusion, as to paint furiously, or carve furiously. We only appreciate his art when we consider that many of his finest conceptions and most sculptural images originally appeared in his consciousness as formless and mysterious emotions, having seemingly no symbols in nature or thought.

If our position is correct, then most certainly nothing can be more incorrect than to call any poem of Tennyson's unmeaning. Such a charge simply implies a lack in the critic's mind, not in the poet's. The latter always *means* something in everything he writes; and the form in which it is embodied is chosen with the most careful deliberation. It seems to us that the purely intellectual element in Tennyson's poetry has been overlooked, owing perhaps to the fragility of some of his figures, and the dreaminess of outline apparent in others. Many think him to be a mere rhapsodist, fertile in nothing but a kind of melodious empiricism. No opinion is more contradicted by the fact. There are few authors who will bear the probe of analysis better.

The poetry of Tennyson is, moreover, replete with magnificent pictures, flushed with the finest hues of language, and speaking to the eye and the mind with the vividness of reality. We not only see the object, but feel the associations connected with it. His language is penetrated with imagination; and the felicity of his epithets, especially, leaves nothing to desire. "Godiva" combines simplicity of feeling with a subtle intensity of imagination, which remind us half of Chaucer and half of Shelley. Like the generality of Tennyson's poems, though short, it contains elements of interest capable of being expanded into a much larger space. But the poem which probably displays to the best advantage his variety of power is "The Gardener's Daughter." It is flushed throughout with the most ethereal imagination, though the incidents and emotions come home to the common heart, and there is little appearance of elaboration in the style. It is bathed in beauty—perfect as a whole, and finished in the nicest details with consummate art. There is a seeming copiousness of expression with a real condensation; and the most minute threads of thought and feeling,—so refined as to be overlooked in a careless perusal, yet all having relation to the general effect,—are woven into the texture of the style with the most admirable felicity. "Locksley Hall," "Œnone," "The May Queen," "Ulysses," "The Lotos-Eaters," "The Lady of Shalott," "Mariana," "Dora," "The Two Voices," "The Dream of Fair Women," "The Palace of Art," all different, all representing a peculiar phase of nature or character, are still all characterized by the cunning workmanship of a master of expression, giving the most complete form to the objects which his keen vision perceives. The melody of verse, which distinguishes all, ranging from the deepest organ tones to that

Music which gentlier on the spirit lies
Than tired eyelids upon tired eyes,

is also of remarkable beauty, and wins and winds its way to the very fountains of thought and feeling.

—Edwin P. Whipple, "English Poets of the Nineteenth Century," 1845, *Essays and Reviews,* 1850, vol. 1, pp. 339–42

GEORGE GILFILLAN "ALFRED TENNYSON" (1847)

George Gilfillan was a Scottish poet and critic, one of the so-called spasmodic poets of the 1840s and 1850s. In the following extract, he examines a number of Tennyson's poems and finds in them evidence of poetic talent, but no, as yet, great achievement. The suggestion is that Tennyson is a curious mixture of artistic qualities: on one hand bold, impulsive, and intellectual, on the other morbid, retiring, and delicate. Gilfillan describes how Tennyson's verse can move easily and swiftly between the passions and fervor of the romantic poets and the sedateness of the Victorian drawing room, finding in this movement the "paradox" of Tennyson as a writer: He is equally in love with a grand and haunting beauty and the elegant artifice of Victorian England.

Gilfillan's reading of Tennyson's poetry is a representative example of the mid-nineteenth-century values of the literary critic. The extract references the previous generation's romantic poets several times as points of comparison, usually to Tennyson's detriment (unless he has imitated certain qualities of those earlier writers). His shorter lyrics are praised as original but only for their extreme simplicity and for their capacity to engage the reader's sentiment. Gilfillan states that Tennyson gives his audience wonderful moments of poetic power and beauty but has never been capable of sustaining them. The critic doubts if Tennyson's temperament can ever allow him to maintain the effort required to create a single, unified poetic work of great power. In a wonderful image, Gilfillan says that Tennyson is like a man who is fascinated by hot iron, touching it quickly and then hurrying away; as a poet he touches on great themes but swiftly turns from them. He is not a poet of action or passion but a solitary watcher, a pensive observer of what he witnesses before him. The critic sees this shortcoming as being bound in the character of the poet himself: The extract concludes with a brief biography of Tennyson, describing his retiring nature and distaste for appearing in London. The final words give a brief and, one must say, overly critical, almost begrudging, summary of Tennyson's publications. The "small cohort" of the poet's admirers is quite clearly a critical miscount. By the middle years of the nineteenth century, Tennyson was already a famous and popular artist. Gilfillan, in labeling this small group of loyalists as "zealous," attempts to portray the poet's popularity as a product of noise rather than numbers.

The subject of the following sketch seems a signal example of the intimate relation which sometimes exists between original genius, and a shrinking, sensitive, and morbid nature. We see in all his writings the struggle of a strong intellect to "turn and wind the fiery Pegasus" of a most capricious, volatile, and dream-driven imagination. Tennyson is a curious combination of impulse, strength, and delicacy approaching to weakness. Could we conceive, not an Eolian harp, but a grand piano, played on by the swift fingers of the blast, it would give us some image of the sweet, subtle, tender, powerful, and changeful movements of his verse, in which are wedded artificial elegance, artistic skill, and wild, impetuous impulse. It is the voice and lute of Ariel; but heard not in a solitary and enchanted island, but in a modern drawing-room, with beautiful women bending round, and moss-roses breathing, in their faint fragrance, through the half-opened windows. Here, indeed, lies the paradox of our author's genius. He is haunted, on the one hand, by images of ideal and colossal grandeur, coming upon him from the isle of the Syrens, the caves of the Kraken, the heights of Ida, the solemn cycles of Cathay, the riches of the Arabian heaven; but, on the other hand, his fancy loves, better than is manly or beseeming, the tricksy elegancies of artificial life—the "white sofas" of his study—the trim walks of his garden—the luxuries of female dress—and all the tiny comforts and beauties which nestle round an English parlour. From the sublime to the snug, and *vice versa,* is with him but a single step. This moment toying on the carpet with his cat, he is the next soaring with a roc over the valley of diamonds. We may liken him to the sea-shell which, sitting complacently and undistinguished amid the commonplace ornaments of the mantelpiece, has only to be lifted to give forth from its smooth ear the far-rugged boom of the ocean breakers. In this union of feminine feebleness and imaginative strength, he much resembles John Keats, who at one time could hew out the vast figure of the dethroned Saturn, "quiet as a stone," with the force of a Michael Angelo, and, again, with all the gusto of a milliner, describe the undressing of his heroine in the *Eve of St. Agnes.* Indeed, although we have ascribed, and we think justly, original genius to Tennyson, there is much in his mind, too, of the imitative and the composite. He adds the occasional langour, the luxury of descriptive beauty, the feminine tone, the tender melancholy, the grand aspirations, perpetually checked and chilled by the access of morbid weakness, and the mannerisms of style which distinguish Keats, to much of the simplicity and the philosophic tone of Wordsworth, the peculiar rhythm and obscurity of Coleridge, and a portion of the quaintness and allegorising tendency which were common with the Donnes, Withers, and Quarleses, of the seventeenth century. What is peculiar to himself is a certain carol, light in air and tone, but profound in burden. Hence his little lyrics—such as "Oriana," "Mariana at the Moated Grange," the "Talking Oak," the "May Queen"—are among his most original and striking productions. They tell tales of deep tragedy, or they convey lessons of wide significance, or they paint vivid and complete pictures, in a few lively touches, and by a few airy words, as if caught in dropping from the sky. By sobs of sound, by half-hints of meaning, by light, hurrying strokes on the ruddy chords of the heart, by a ringing of changes on certain words and phrases, he sways us as if with the united powers of music and poetry. Our readers will, in illustration of this, remember his nameless little song, beginning

Break, break, break,
On thy cold grey crags, O sea!

which is a mood of his own mind, faithfully rendered into sweet and simple verse. It is in composition no more complicated or elaborate than a house built by a child, but melts you, as that house would, were you to see it after the dear infant's death. But than this he has higher moods, and nobler, though still imperfect aspirations. In his "Two Voices," he approaches the question of all ages—Whence evil? And if he, no more than other speculators, unties, he casts a soft and mellow light around this Gordian knot. This poem is no fancy piece, but manifestly a transcript from his own personal experience. He has sunk into one of those melancholy moods incident to his order of mind, and has become "aweary of the sun," and of all the sun shines upon—especially of his own miserable idiosyncrasy. There slides in at that dark hour a still small voice: how different from that which thrilled on Elijah's ear in the caves of Horeb! It is the voice of that awful lady whom De Quincey calls *Mater tenebrarum,* our lady of darkness. It hints at suicide as the only remedy for human woes.

Thou are so full of misery,
Were it not better not to be?

And then there follows an eager and uneasy interlocution between the "dark and barren voice," and the soul of the writer, half spurning and half holding parley with its suggestions. Seldom, truly, since the speech by which Despair in Spenser enforces the same sad argument, did misanthropy breathe a more withering blight over humanity and human hopes; seldom did unfortunate by a shorter and readier road reach the conclusion, "there is one remedy for all," than in the utterance of this voice. Death in it looks lovely; nay, the one lovely thing in the universe. Again and again the poet is ready to yield to the desire of his own heart, thus seconded by the mystic voice, and, in the words of one who often listened to the same accents, to "lie down like a tired child, and weep away this life of care." But again and again the better element of his nature resists the temptation, and beats back the melancholy voice. At length, raising himself from his lethargy, he rises, looks forth—it is the Sabbath morn, and, as he sees the peaceful multitudes moving on to the house of God, and as, like the Anciente Mariner, he "blesses them unaware," straightway the spell is broken, the "dull and bitter voice is gone," and, hark!

A second voice is at his ear,
A little whisper, silver-clear,

and it gives him a hidden and humble hope, which spreads a quiet heaven within his soul. Now he can go forth into the fields, and

Wonder at the bounteous hours,
The slow result of winter showers,
You scarce can see the grass for flowers.

All nature calls upon him to rejoice, and to the eye of his heart, at least, the riddle is read. Nay, we put it to every heart if this do not, more than many elaborate argumentations, touch the core of the difficulty. "Look up," said Leigh Hunt to Carlyle, when he had been taking the darker side of the question, and they had both come out under the brilliance of a starry night—"look up, and find your answer there!" And although the reply failed to convince the party addressed, who, looking aloft at the sparkling azure, after a deep pause, rejoined, with a sigh, and in tones we can well imagine, so melancholy and far withdrawn, "Oh! it's a sad sight;" yet, apart from the divine discoveries, it was the true and only answer. The beauty, whether of Tennyson's fields—where we "scarce can see the grass for flowers"—or of Leigh Hunt's skies, "whose unwithered countenance is young as on creation's day," and where we find an infinite answer to our petty cavils—is enough to soothe, if not to satisfy, to teach us the perfect patience of expectancy, if not the full assurance of faith.

Tennyson, in some of his poems as well as this, reveals in himself a current of thought tending towards very deep and dark subjects. This springs partly from the metaphysical bias of his intellect, and partly from the morbid emotions of his heart. And yet he seems generally to toy and trifle with such tremendous themes—to touch them lightly and hurriedly, as one might hot iron—at once eager and reluctant to intermeddle with them. Nevertheless, there is a perilous stuff about his heart, and upon his verse lies a "melancholy compounded of many simples." He is not the poet of hope, or of action, or of passion, but of sentiment, of pensive and prying curiosity, or of simple stationary wonder, in view of the great sights and mysteries of Nature and man. He has never thrown himself amid the heats and hubbub of society, but remained alone, musing with a quiet but observant eye upon the tempestuous pageant which is sweeping past him, and concerning himself little with the political or religious controversies of his age. There are, too, in some of his writings, mild and subdued vestiges of a wounded spirit, of a heart that has been disappointed, of an ambition that has been repressed, of an intellect that has wrestled with doubt, difficulty, and disease.

In "Locksley Hall," for instance, he tells a tale of unfortunate passion with a gusto and depth of feeling, which (unless we misconstrue the mark of the branding-iron) betray more than a fictitious interest in the theme. It is a poem breathing the spirit of, and not much inferior to, Byron's "Dream," in all but that clear concentration of misery which bends over it like a bare and burning heaven over a bare and burning desert. "Locksley Hall," again, is turbid and obscure in language, wild and distracted in feeling. The wind is down, but the sea still runs high. You see in it the passion pawing like a lion who has newly missed his prey, not fixed as yet in a marble form of still and hopeless disappointment. The lover, after a season of absence, returns to the scene of his early education and hapless love, where of old he

Wander'd, nourishing a youth sublime
With the fairy tales of science, and the long result of
time.

A feeling, cognate with, and yet more imperious than those of his high aspirations, springs up in his mind. It arises in spring like the crest of a singing-bird. It is the feeling of love for Amy his cousin, sole daughter of her father's house and heart. The feeling is mutual, and the current of their true love flows smoothly on, till interrupted by the interference of relatives. Thus far he remembers calmly; but here recollection strikes the fierce chord of disappointment, and he bursts impetuously forth—

O, my cousin, shallow-hearted. O, my Amy, mine
    no more.
    O, the dreary, dreary moorland. O, the barren,
barren shore.

Darting then one hasty and almost vindictive glance down her future history, he predicts that she shall lower to the level of the clown she has wedded, and that he will use his victim a little better than his dog or his horse. Nay, she will become

Old and formal, suited to her petty part;
With her little hoard of maxims, preaching down a
    daughter's heart.

But himself, alas! what is to become of him? Live he must—suicide is too base an outlet from existence for his brave spirit. But what to do with this bitter boon of being? There follow some wild and half-insane stanzas expressive of the ambitions and uncertainties of his soul. It is the Cyclops mad with blindness, and groping at the sides of his cave. He will hate and despise all women, or, at least, all British maidens. He will return to the orient land, whose "larger constellations" saw a father die. He will, in his despair, take some savage woman who shall rear his dusky race. But no—the despair is momentary—he may not mate with a squalid savage; he will rather revive old intellectual ambitions, and renew old aspirations, for he feels within him that the "crescent promise of his spirit has not set." It is resolved—but, ere he goes, let every ray of remaining love and misery go forth in one last accusing, avenging look at the scene of his disappointment and the centre of his woe.

Howsoever these things be, a long farewell to
    Locksley Hall.
Now, for me, the woods may wither; now, for me,
  the roof-tree fall,
      Comes a vapour from the margin, blackening over
      heath and holt;
      Cramming all the blast before it, in its breast a
      thunderbolt.
Let it fall on Locksley Hall, with rain, or hail, or fire,
    or snow,
For a mighty wind arises, roaring seaward, and I go.

And thus the ballad closes, leaving, however, with us the inevitable impression that the unfortunate lover is not done with Locksley Hall nor its bitter memories—that Doubting Castle is not down, nor giant Despair dead—that the calls of the curlews around it will still resound in his ears, and the pale face of its Amy, still unutterably beloved, will come back upon his dreams—that the iron has entered into his soul—and that his life and his misery are henceforth commensurate and the same.

Among the more remarkable of Tennyson's poems, besides those already mentioned, are "The Poet," "Dora," "Recollections of the Arabian Nights," "Œnone," "The Lotos Eaters," "Ulysses," "Godiva," and "The Vision of Sin." "The Poet" was written when the author was young, and when the high ideal of his heart was just dawning upon his mind. It is needless to say that his view of the powers and influences of poetry is different with what prevails with many in our era. Poetry is, with him, no glittering foil to be wielded gaily on gala days. It is, or ought to be, a sharp two-edged sword. It is not a baton in the hand of coarse authority—it is a magic rod. It is not a morning flush in the sky of youth, that shall fade in the sun of science—it is a consuming and imperishable fire. It is not a mere amusement for young love-sick men and women—it is as serious as death, and longer than life. It is tuned philosophy—winged science—fact on fire—"truth springing from earth"—high thought voluntarily moving harmonious numbers. His "Poet" is "dowered with the hate of hate, the scorn of scorn, the love of love," and his words "shake the world."

The author, when he wrote "The Poet," was fresh from school, and from Shelley, his early idol. Ere writing "Dora" he had become conversant with the severer charms of Wordsworth; and that poem contains in it not one figure or flower—is bare, literal, and pathetic as the book of Ruth. Its poetry is that which lies in all natural life, which, like a deep quiet pool, has only to be disturbed in the slightest degree to send up in dance those bells and bubbles which give it instantly ideal beauty and interest, and suddenly the pool becomes a poem!

His "Recollections of the Arabian Nights" is a poem of that species which connects itself perpetually, in feeling and memory, with the original work, whose quintessence it collects. It speaks out the sentiments of millions of thankful hearts. We feel in it what a noble thing was the Arabian mind—like the Arabian soil, "all the Sun's"—like the Arabian climate, fervid, golden—like the Arabian horse, light, elegant, ethereal, swift as the wind. "O, for the golden prime of good Haroun Alras-chid!" O, for one look—though it were the last—of that Persian maid, whom the poet has painted in words vivid as colours, palpable almost as sense. Talk of enchantment! The *Thousand-and-One Nights* is one enchantment—more powerful than the lamp of Aladdin, or the "Open Sesame" of Ali Baba. The author, were he *one*—not many—is a magician—a geni—greater than Scott, than Cervantes, equal to Shakspere himself. What poetry, passion, pathos, beauty of sentiment, elegance of costume, ingenuity of contrivance, wit, humour, farce, interest, variety, tact in transition, sunniness of spirit, dream-like wealth of imagination, incidental but precious light cast upon customs, manners, history, religion—everything, in short, that can amuse or amaze, instruct or delight, the human spirit! Like the *Pilgrim's Progress*—devoured by boys, it is a devout study for bearded men.

Tennyson has expressed, especially, the moonlight voluptuousness of tone and spirit which breathes around those delicious productions, as well as the lavish magnificence of dress and decoration, of furniture and architecture, which were worthy of the witch element, the sunny climate, and the early enchanted era, where and when they were written. But we doubt if he mates adequately with that more potent and terrible magic which haunts their higher regions, as in the sublime picture of the Prince's daughter fighting with the Enchanter in mid air, or in the mysterious grandeur which follows all the adventures of Aboulfaouris. With this, too, indeed, he must have sympathy; for it is evident that he abundantly fulfils Coleridge's test of a genuine lover of the *Arabian Nights*. 'Do you admire,' said the author of *Kubla Khan* to Hazlitt, "the *Thousand-and-One Nights?*" "No," was the answer. "That's because you *don't dream*." But surely, since the "noticeable man, with large grey eyes" awoke in death from his long life-dream, no poet has arisen of whom the word were more true than of Tennyson, whether in reproach or commendation, asleep or awake—"Behold this dreamer cometh."

In "Oenone," we find him up on the heights of Ida, with the large foot-prints of gods and goddesses still upon its sward, and the citadel and town of Troy, as yet unfallen, as yet unassailed, visible from its summit. Here the poet sees a vision of his own—a vision which, recorded in verse, forms a high third with Wordsworth's "Laodamia" and Keats's *Hyperion,* in the classical style. Less austere and magnificent than the poem of Keats, which seems not so much a torso of earthly art as a splinter fallen from some other exploded world—less chaste, polished, and spiritual, than "Laodamia," that Elgin marble set in Elysian light, it surpasses both in picturesque distinctness and pathetic power. The story is essentially that of "Locksley Hall," but the scene is not the flat and sandy moorland of Lincolnshire, but the green gorges and lawns of Ida. The deceived lover is Œnone, daughter of a river god. She has been deceived by Paris, and her plaint is the poem. Melancholy her song, as that of a disappointed woman—melodious, as that of an aggrieved goddess. It is to Ida, her mother mountain, that she breathes her sorrow. She tells her

of her lover's matchless beauty—of her yielding up her heart to him—of
the deities descending to receive the golden apple from his hands—of his
deciding it to Venus, upon the promise of the "fairest and most loving wife
in Greece"—of his abandonment of Œnone, and of her despair. Again and
again, in her agony, she cries for Death; but the grim shadow, too busy in
hewing down the happy, will not turn aside at her miserable bidding. Her
despair at last becomes fury; her tears begin to burn; she will arise; she will
leave her dreadful solitude—

> I will rise, and go
> Down into Troy, and, ere the stars come forth,
> Talk with the wild Cassandra; for she says
> A fire dances before her, and a sound
> Rings ever in her ears of armed men.
> What this may be I know not; but I know
> That, wheresoe'er I am, by night and day
> All earth and air seems only burning fire.

And fancy follows Oenone to Ilium, and sees the two beautiful broken-
hearted maidens meeting, like two melancholy flames, upon one funeral
pile, mingling their hot tears, exchanging their sad stories, and joining, in
desperate exultation, at the prospect of the ruin which is already darkening,
like a tempest, round the towers and temples of Troy. It is pleasant to find
from such productions that, after all, the poetry of Greece is not dead—that
the oaks of Delphos and Dodona have not shed all their oracular leaves—that
the lightnings in Jove's hand are still warm—and the snows of Olympus are
yet clear and bright, shining over the waste of years—that Mercury's feet are
winged still—and still is Apollo's hair unshorn—that the mythology of Homer,
long dead to belief, is still alive to the airy purposes of poetry—that, though
the "dreadful infant's hand" hath smitten down the gods upon the capital, it
has left them the freedom of the Parnassian Hill; and that a Wordsworth, or a
Tennyson, may even now, by inclining the ear of imagination, hear the river
god plunging in Scamander—Œnone wailing upon Ida—Old Triton blowing
his wreathed horn; for never was a truth more certain than that "a thing of
beauty is a joy for ever."

We had intended to say something of his "Lotos-Eaters," but are afraid
to break in upon its charmed rest—to disturb its sleepy spell—to venture on
that land "in which it seemed always afternoon"—or to stir its melancholy,
mildeyed inhabitants. We will pass it by, treading so softly that the "blind

mole may not hear a footfall." We must beware of slumbering, and we could hardly but be dull on the enchanted ground.

While the "Lotos-Eaters" breathes the very spirit of luxurious repose, and seems, to apply his own words, a perfect poem in "perfect rest," "Ulysses" is the incarnation of restlessness and insatiable activity. Sick of Ithaca, Argus, Telemachus, and (sub rosa) of Penelope too, the old, much-enduring Mariner King, is again panting for untried dangers and undiscovered lands.

> My purpose holds,
> To sail beyond the sunset, and the baths
> Of all the western stars, until I die.

Tennyson, with his fine artistic instinct, saw that the idea of Ulysses at rest was an incongruous thought, and has chosen rather to picture him journeying ever onwards toward infinity or death—

> It may be that the gulphs will wash us down—
> It may be, we shall reach the happy isles,
> And see the great Achilles, whom we knew.

And with breathless interest, and a feeling approaching the sublime, we watch the grey-headed monarch stepping, with his few aged followers, into the bark, which is to be their home till death, and stretching away toward eternity; and every heart and imagination cry out after him—"Go, and return no more."

"Godiva" is an old story newly told—a delicate business delicately handled—the final and illuminated version of an ancient and world-famous tradition. Its beauty is, that, like its heroine, it is "clothed on with chastity." It represses the imagination as gently and effectually as her naked virtue did the eye. We hold our breath, and shut every window of our fancy, till the great ride be over. And in this trial and triumph of female resolution and virtue, the poet would have us believe that Nature herself sympathised—that the light was bashful, and the sun ashamed, and the wind hushed, till the sublime pilgrimage was past—and that, when it ended, a sigh of satisfaction, wide as the circle of earth and heaven, proclaimed Godiva's victory.

The "Vision of Sin" strikes, we think, upon a stronger, though darker, chord than any of his other poems. There are in it impenetrable obscurities, but, like jet black ornaments, some may think them dearer for their darkness. You cannot, says Hazlitt, make "an allegory go on all fours." A vision must be hazy—a ghost should surely be a shadow. Enough, if there be a meaning in the mystery, an oracle speaking through the gloom. The dream is that of a youth, who is seen riding to the gate of a palace, from which

> Came a child of sin,
> And took him by the curls and led him in.

He is lost straightway in mad and wicked revel, tempestuously yet musically described. Meanwhile, unheeded by the revellers, a "vapour, *(the mist of darkness!)* heavy, hueless, formless, cold," is floating slowly on toward the palace. At length it touches the gate, and the dream changes, and such a change!

> I saw
> A grey and gap-toothed man, as lean as Death,
> Who slowly rode across a wither'd heath,
> And lighted at a ruined inn.

And, lighted there, he utters his bitter and blasted feelings in lines, reminding us, from their fierce irony, their misanthropy, their thrice-drugged despair, of Swift's "Legion Club;" and—as in that wicked, wondrous poem—a light sparkle of contemptuous levity glimmers with a ghastly sheen over the putrid pool of malice and misery below, and cannot all disguise the workings of that remorse which is not repentance. At length this sad evil utterance dies away in the throat of the expiring sinner, and behind his consummated ruin there arises a "mystic mountain range," along which voices are heard lamenting, or seeking to explain the causes of his ruin. One says—

> Behold, it was a crime
> Of sense, avenged by sense, that wove with time.

Another—

> The crime of sense became
> The crime of malice, and is equal blame.

A third—

> He had not wholly quenched his power—
> A little grain of conscience made him sour.

And thus at length, in a darkness visible of mystery and grandeur, the "Vision of Sin" closes:—

At last I heard a voice upon the slope
Cry to the summit, Is there any hope?
To which an answer peal'd from that high land,
But in a tongue no man could understand;
And on the glimmering limit, far withdrawn,
God made himself an *awful rose of dawn.*

A reply there is; but whether in the affirmative or negative we do not know. A revelation there is; but whether it be an interference in behalf of the sinner, or a display, in ruddy light, of God's righteousness in his punishment, is left in deep uncertainty. Tennyson, like Addison in his "Vision of Mirza," ventures not to withdraw the veil from the left side of the eternal ocean. He leaves the curtain to be the painting. He permits the imagination of the reader to figure, if it dare, shapes of beauty, or forms of fiery wrath, upon the "awful rose of dawn," as upon a vast back-ground. It is his only to start the thrilling suggestion.

After all, we have considerable misgivings about placing Tennyson—for what he has hitherto done—among our great poets. We cheerfully accord him great powers; but he is, as yet, guiltless of great achievements. His genius is bold, but is waylaid at almost every step by the timidity and weakness of his temperament. His utterance is not proportionate to his vision. He sometimes reminds us of a dumb man with important tidings within, but only able to express them by gestures, starts, sobs, and tears. His works are loopholes, not windows, through which intense glimpses come and go, but no broad, clear, and rounded prospect is commanded. As a thinker, he often seems like one who should perversely pause a hundred feet from the summit of a lofty hill, and refuse to ascend higher. "Up! the breezes call thee—the clouds marshal thy way—the glorious prospect waits thee, as a bride for her husband—angels or gods may meet thee on the top—it may be thy Mountain of Transfiguration." But, no; the pensive or wilful poet chooses to remain below.

Nevertheless, the eye of genius is flashing in Tennyson's head, and his ear is unstopped, whether to the harmonies of nature, or to the still sad music of humanity. We care not much in which of the tracks he has already cut out he may choose to walk; but we would prefer if he were persuaded more frequently to see visions and dream dreams—like his "Vision of Sin"—imbued with high purpose, and forming the Modern Metamorphoses of truth. We have no hope that he will ever be, in the low sense, a popular poet, or that to him the task is allotted of extracting music from the railway train, or of setting in song the "fairy tales of science"—the great astronomical or geological discoveries of the age. Nor is he likely ever to write anything which, like the poems of Burns, or Campbell, can go directly to the heart of the entire nation. For no "Song of the Shirt" even, need we look from him. But the imaginativeness of his nature, the deep vein of his moral sentiment, the bias given to his mind by his early reading, the airy charm of his versification, and the seclusion in which he lives, like a flower in its own peculiar jar, all seem to prepare him for becoming a great spiritual dreamer, who might write not only "Recollections of the Arabian Nights," but Arabian Nights themselves, equally graceful in costume, but impressed with a deeper sentiment, chastened into severer taste, and warmed with a holier flame. Success to such pregnant slumbers! soft be the pillow as that of his own "Sleeping Beauty;" may every syrup of strength and sweetness drop upon his eyelids, and may his dreams be such as to banish sleep from many an eye, and to people the hearts of millions with beauty!

On the whole, perhaps Tennyson is less a prophet than an artist. And this alone would serve better to reconcile us to his silence, should it turn out that his poetic career is over. The loss of even the finest artist may be supplied— that of a prophet, who has been cut off in the midst of his mission, or whose words some envious influence or circumstance has snatched from his lips, is irreparable. In the one case, it is but a painter's pencil that is broken; in the other it is a magic rod shivered. Still, even as an artist, Tennyson has not yet done himself full justice, nor built up any structure so shapely, complete, and living, as may perpetuate his name.[1]

Alfred Tennyson is the son of an English clergyman in Lincolnshire. He is of a retiring disposition, and seldom, though sometimes, emerges from his retirement into the literary coteries of London. And yet welcome is he ever among them—with his eager physiognomy, his dark hair and eyes, and his small, black tobacco pipe. Some years ago, we met a brother of his in Dumfries, who bore, we were told, a marked, though miniature resemblance to him, a beautiful painter and an expert versifier, after the style of Alfred.

The particulars of his literary career are familiar to most. His first production was a small volume of poems, published in 1831. Praised in the *Westminster* elaborately, and extravagantly eulogised in the *Englishman's Magazine* (a periodical conducted by William Kennedy, but long since defunct, and which, according to some malicious persons, died of this same article)—it was sadly mangled by less generous critics. *Blackwood's Magazine* doled it out some severely-sifted praise; and the author, in his next volume, rhymed back his ingratitude in the well-known lines to "Rusty, musty, fusty, crusty Christopher," whose blame he forgave, but whose praise he could not. Meanwhile, he was quietly forming a small but zealous cohort of admirers; and some of his poems, such as "Mariana," &c, were universally read and appreciated. His second production was less successful, and deserved to be less successful, than the first. It was stuffed with wilful impertinencies and affectations. His critics told him he wrote ill, and he answered them by writing worse. His third exhibited a very different spirit. It consisted of a selection from his two former volumes, and a number of additional pieces— the principal of which we have already analysed. In his selection, he winnows his former works with a very salutary severity; but what has he done with that delectable strain of the "Syrens?" We think he has acted well in stabling and shutting up his "Krakens" in their dim, ocean mangers; but we are not so willing to part with that beautiful sisterhood, and hope to see them again at no distant day, standing in their lovely isle, and singing—

> Come hither, come hither, and be our lords,
> For merry brides are we.
> We will kiss sweet kisses and speak sweet words.
> Ye will not find so happy a shore,
> Weary mariners all the world o'er.
> Oh fly, oh fly no more.

Notes

1. His "Princess," published since the above, is a medley of success, failure, and half-success—not even an attempt towards a whole.

—George Gilfillan, "Alfred Tennyson," 1847,
A Second Gallery of Literary Portraits, 1850, pp. 214–31

THOMAS POWELL "ALFRED TENNYSON" (1849)

Thomas Powell was a literary critic who in the following extract comments upon the relationship between Tennyson's poetry and the literary and social culture of the middle years of the nineteenth century. Powell suggests that critics have focused on a particular aspect of Tennyson's work as both its strength and weakness: Its power resides in its intensity, and this is precisely what appealed to Tennyson's audience. The poet's capacity to elicit feelings of brief, concentrated delight in his readers is claimed in the extract, however, to be not a drawback, as some contemporary critics and "friends" of the poet believed, but rather an aesthetic (and commercial) triumph. Powell maintains that his age is not one for the long, drawn-out epic, nor for lyrics that calm, but that it requires sensation, power, and the brief, intense shock. It is exactly this quality that he presents as being perfectly exemplified in Tennyson's verse.

We do not expect that he will ever produce any great work; his mind is unequal to a long flight; he is master of one or two instruments, and his power over them is perfect; his orchestra is not, however, full enough to bring out that mighty volume of sound which sleeps in the Epic and the Drama. His last production, *The Princess, a Medley,* has been a great disappointment to his friends, as it convinces them he is unequal to a sustained undertaking. We do not see why they should be surprised or grieved at the failure; this is not an age for long narratives, it is essentially the "age of emphasis," every production now must be intensed. Men will not sit to be lectured or read asleep; they want to be aroused, excited and kept awake. They do not look for instruction, they demand power and sensation!—delight is their object, not quiescence or tranquillity. Soothing syrups are past: electrical flashes are in vogue.

—Thomas Powell, "Alfred Tennyson," *The Living Authors of England*, 1849, p. 48

Edgar Allan Poe "The Poetic Principle" (1850)

Edgar Allan Poe is one of the best-known American writers of the nineteenth century. Having already published a work titled "The Philosophy of Composition" in 1846, Poe would presumably have the authority to critically assess Tennyson's verse. The following extract is taken from one of Poe's further explorations of poetic theory, "The Poetic Principle." In the part of the essay presented here, Poe claims for Tennyson the title of the most noble poet who had ever lived. The rationale given by Poe for such an extraordinary statement is that the sensations produced by Tennyson's poetry are the most pure and ennobling at all times. They are not the most intense (and readers might wish to contrast Poe's assessment with Thomas Powell's view on intensity in Tennyson's verse in the previous extract), nor are they the most profound (readers can compare Edwin P. Whipple's opinion of the intellectual worth of Tennyson's poetry previously included in this section). The sensations Tennyson evokes are the most "ethereal" or spiritual, according to Poe.

. . . in perfect sincerity I regard him as the noblest poet that ever lived . . . I call him, and *think* him the noblest of poets—*not* because the impressions he produces are, at *all* times, the most profound—*not* because the poetical excitement which he induces is, at *all* times, the most intense—but because it *is*, at all times, the most ethereal—in other words, the most elevating and the most pure.

—Edgar Allan Poe, "The Poetic Principle," 1850,
Essays and Reviews, ed. G. R. Thompson, 1984, p. 92

CHARLES KINGSLEY "TENNYSON" (1850)

Charles Kingsley was a historian, the Regius Professor of Modern History at Cambridge University, and a novelist. In the following extract, Kingsley, who would resign his professorship to become a canon in the Anglican Church, praises *In Memoriam* as the greatest Christian poem written in England in the past 200 years (the prior poem being, presumably, John Milton's *Paradise Lost*). Tennyson's poem is seen by Kingsley as being the product of a natural progression, from the noble ideas contained in the poet's earlier verse, to "everlasting facts," an intellectual and emotional journey that he hopes the young men at his university will follow themselves (it is for this reason that Kingsley reveals Tennyson to be the author of the anonymous poem: his students already strongly admire the poet's earlier verse).

Kingsley begins by examining Tennyson's previous work and finding the poet's skill in portraying "reverent awe" for "the divineness of Nature" superior to that of the romantic poets John Keats and William Wordsworth (readers might contrast Kingsley's views on Tennyson and nature with those of G. K. Chesterton contained elsewhere in this volume). By 1842, Kingsley believes that Tennyson has developed his poetic gifts sufficiently to embody the doubts and questions of his age: in "Locksley Hall," Tennyson is said to have portrayed man's "faith in the progress of science and civilisation" and "hope in the final triumph of good." But the poet's ultimate statement of faith, Kingsley believes, is that articulated in *In Memoriam*, where Tennyson expresses the overcoming of doubt, the power of love, and the ultimate hope in things divine.

Readers should, of course, be fully aware of Kingsley's own personal background: the son of a religious official becoming one himself. This is not to gainsay Kingsley's spiritual interpretation of Tennyson's verse. But an equally religious man, G. K. Chesterton, provides a different reading of the poet's work, one written more than 50 years after this extract. The times have changed; the perspective on the questioning and doubt of the Victorian era is different: Kingsley wrote this extract nine years

before Darwin published *On the Origin of Species*, and it is that text that
Chesterton will claim radically altered the age, along with Tennyson's
vocation as a poet.

Critics cannot in general be too punctilious in their respect for an incognito.
If an author intended us to know his name, he would put it on his title-
page. If he does not choose to do that, we have no more right to pry into
his secret than we have to discuss his family affairs or open his letters. But
every rule has its exceptional cases; and the book which stands first upon our
list *(In Memoriam)* is surely such. All the world, somehow or other, knows
the author. His name has been mentioned unhesitatingly by several reviews
already, whether from private information, or from the certainty which every
well-read person must feel that there is but one man in England possessed at
once of poetic talent and artistic experience sufficient for so noble a creation.
We hope, therefore, that we shall not be considered impertinent if we ignore
an incognito which all England has ignored before us, and attribute *In
Memoriam* to the pen of the author of *The Princess.*

Such a course will probably be the more useful one to our readers; for this
last work of our only living great poet seems to us at once the culmination of
all his efforts and the key to many difficulties in his former writings. Heaven
forbid that we should say that it completes the circle of his powers. On the
contrary, it gives us hope of broader effort in new fields of thought and forms
of art. But it brings the development of his Muse and of his Creed to a positive
and definite point. It enables us to claim one who has been hitherto regarded
as belonging to a merely speculative and peirastic school as the willing and
deliberate champion of vital Christianity, and of an orthodoxy the more sincere
because it has worked upward through the abyss of doubt; the more mighty for
good because it justifies and consecrates the aesthetics and the philosophy of
the present age. We are sure, moreover, that the author, whatever right reasons
he may have had for concealing his own name, would have no quarrel against
us for alluding to it, were he aware of the idolatry with which every utterance
of his is regarded by the cultivated young men of our day, especially at the
universities, and of the infinite service of which this *In Memoriam* may be
to them, if they are taught by it that their superiors are not ashamed of faith,
and that they will rise instead of falling, fulfil instead of denying the cravings
of their hearts and intellects, if they will pass upwards with their teacher
from the vague though noble expectations of "Locksley Hall," to the assured
and everlasting facts of the proem to *In Memoriam*—in our eyes the noblest
Christian poem which England has produced for two centuries.

To explain our meaning, it will be necessary, perhaps, to go back to Mr. Tennyson's earlier writings, of which he is said to be somewhat ashamed now—a fastidiousness with which we will not quarrel; for it should be the rule of the poet, forgetting those things which are behind, to press on to those things which are before, and "to count not himself to have apprehended but"— no, we will not finish the quotation; let the readers of *In Memoriam* finish it for themselves, and see how, after all, the poet, if he would reach perfection, must be found by Him who found St. Paul of old. In the meantime, as a true poet must necessarily be in advance of his age, Mr. Tennyson's earlier poems, rather than these latter ones, coincide with the tastes and speculations of the young men of this day. And in proportion, we believe, as they thoroughly appreciate the distinctive peculiarities of those poems, will they be able to follow the author of them on his upward path.

Some of our readers, we would fain hope, remember as an era in their lives the first day on which they read those earlier poems; how, fifteen years ago, Mariana in the Moated Grange, "The Dying Swan," "The Lady of Shalott," came to them as revelations. They seemed to themselves to have found at last a poet who promised not only to combine the cunning melody of Moore, the rich fulness of Keats, and the simplicity of Wordsworth, but one who was introducing a method of observing nature different from that of all the three and yet succeeding in everything which they had attempted, often in vain. Both Keats and Moore had an eye for the beauty which lay in trivial and daily objects. But in both of them there was a want of deep religious reverence, which kept Moore playing gracefully upon the surface of phenomena without ever daring to dive into their laws or inner meaning; and made poor Keats fancy that he was rather to render nature poetical by bespangling her with florid ornament, than simply to confess that she was already, by the grace of God, far beyond the need of his paint and gilding. Even Wordsworth himself had not full faith in the great dicta which he laid down in his famous Introductory Essay. Deep as was his conviction that nature bore upon her simplest forms the finger-mark of God, he did not always dare simply to describe her as she was, and leave her to reveal her own mystery. We do not say this in depreciation of one who stands now far above human praise or blame. The wonder is, not that Wordsworth rose no higher, but that, considering the level on which his taste was formed, he had power to rise to the height above his age which he did attain. He did a mighty work. He has left the marks of his teaching upon every poet who has written verses worth reading for the last twenty years. The idea by which he conquered was, as Coleridge well sets forth, the very one which, in its practical results on his own poetry, procured him loud and deserved ridicule. This, which will be the root idea of the whole poetry of this generation, was the dignity of nature in all her manifestations, and not merely in those which may happen to suit the fastidiousness or Manichasism of any particular age. He may have been at times fanatical on his idea, and have misused it, till it became self-contradictory, because he could not see the correlative truths which should have limited it. But it is by fanatics, by men of one great thought, that great works are done; and it is good for the time that a man arose in it of fearless honesty enough to write *Peter Bell* and the "Idiot Boy," to shake all the old methods of nature-painting to their roots, and set every man seriously to ask himself what he meant, or whether he meant anything real, reverent, or honest, when he talked about "poetic diction," or "the beauties of nature." And after all, like all fanatics, Wordsworth was better than his own creed. As Coleridge thoroughly shows in the second volume of the *Biographia Literaria,* and as may be seen nowhere more strikingly than in his grand posthumous work, his noblest poems and noblest stanzas are those in which his true poetic genius, unconsciously to himself, sets at naught his own pseudo-naturalist dogmas.

Now Mr. Tennyson, while fully adopting Wordsworth's principle from the very first, seemed by instinctive taste to have escaped the snares which had proved too subtle both for Keats and Wordsworth. Doubtless there are slight *niaiseries,* after the manner of both those poets, in the first editions of his earlier poems. He seems, like most other great artists, to have first tried imitations of various styles which already existed, before he learnt the art of incorporating them into his own, and learning from all his predecessors, without losing his own individual peculiarities. But there are descriptive passages in them also which neither Keats nor Wordsworth could have written, combining the honest sensuous observation which is common to them both, with a self-restrained simplicity which Keats did not live long enough to attain, and a stately and accurate melody, an earnest songfulness (to coin a word) which Wordsworth seldom attained, and from his inaccurate and uncertain ear, still seldomer preserved without the occurrence of a jar or a rattle, a false quantity, a false rapture, or a bathos. And above all, or rather beneath all—for we suspect that this has been throughout the very secret of Mr. Tennyson's power—there was a hush and a reverent awe, a sense of the mystery, the infinitude, the awfulness, as well as of the mere beauty of wayside things, which invested these poems as wholes with a peculiar richness, depth, and majesty of tone, beside which both Keats's and Wordsworth's methods of handling pastoral subjects looked like the colouring of Julio Romano or Watteau by the side of Correggio or Titian.

This deep simple faith in the divineness of Nature as she appears, which, in our eyes, is Mr. Tennyson's differentia, is really the natural accompaniment of a quality at first sight its very opposite, and for which he is often blamed by a prosaic world; namely, his subjective and transcendental mysticism. It is the mystic, after all, who will describe Nature most simply, because he sees most in her; because he is most ready to believe that she will reveal to others the same message which she has revealed to him. Men like Behmen, Novalis, and Fourier, who can soar into the inner cloud-world of man's spirit, even though they lose their way there, dazzled by excess of wonder—men who, like Wordsworth, can give utterance to such subtle anthropologic wisdom as the "Ode on the Intimations of Immortality," will for that very reason most humbly and patiently "consider the lilies of the field, how they grow." And even so it is just because Mr. Tennyson is, far more than Wordsworth, mystical, and what an ignorant and money-getting generation, idolatrous of mere sensuous activity, calls "dreamy," that he has become the greatest naturalistic poet which England has seen for several centuries. The same faculty which enabled him to draw such subtle subjective pictures of womanhood as Adeline, Isabel, and Eleanor, enabled him to see, and therefore simply to describe, in one of the most distinctive and successful of his earlier poems, how

> The creeping mosses and clambering weeds,
> And the willow branches hoar and dank,
>> And the wavy swell of the soughing reeds,
>> And the wave-worn horns of the echoing bank,
>> And the silvery marish flowers that throng
>> The desolate creeks and pools among,
>> Were flooded over with eddying song.

No doubt there are in the earlier poems exceptions to this style—attempts to adorn nature, and dazzle with a barbaric splendour akin to that of Keats—as, for instance, in the "Recollections of the Arabian Nights." But how cold and gaudy, in spite of individual beauties, is that poem by the side of either of the Marianas, and especially of the one in which the scenery is drawn, simply and faithfully, from those counties which the world considers the quintessence of the prosaic—the English fens.

> Upon the middle of the night
>> Waking she heard the night-fowl crow;
> The cock sang out an hour ere light:
>> From the dark fen the oxen's low
> Came to her: without hope of change,
>> In sleep she seemed to walk forlorn,
> Till cold winds woke the gray-eyed morn
>> About the lonely moated grange.

. . .
About a stone-cast from the wall
   A sluice with blackened waters slept,
And o'er it many, round and small,
   The cluster'd marish-mosses crept.
Hard by a poplar shook alway,
   All silver-green with gnarled bark,
For leagues no other tree did mark
   The level waste, the rounding gray,

Throughout all these exquisite lines occurs but one instance of what the vulgar call "poetic diction." All is simple description, in short and Saxon words, and yet who can deny the effect to be perfect—superior to any similar passage in Wordsworth? And why? Because the passage quoted, and indeed the whole poem, is perfect in what artists call tone—tone in the metre and in the sound of the words, as well as in the images and the feelings expressed. The weariness, the dreariness, the dark mysterious waste, exist alike within and without, in the slow monotonous pace of the metre and the words, as well as in the boundless fen, and the heart of her who, "without hope of change, in sleep did seem to walk forlorn."

The same faith in Nature, the same instinctive correctness in melody, springing from that correct insight into Nature, ran through the poems inspired by medieval legends. The very spirit of the old ballad writers, with their combinations of mysticism and objectivity, their freedom from any self-conscious attempt at reflective epithets or figures, runs through them all. We are never jarred in them, as we are in all the attempts at ballad-writing and ballad-restoring before Mr. Tennyson's time, by discordant touches of the reflective in thought, the picturesque in Nature, or the theatric in action. To illustrate our meaning, readers may remember the ballad of "Fair Emmeline," in Bishop Percy's *Reliques*. The bishop confesses, if we mistake not, to have patched one end of the ballad. He need not have informed us of that fact, while such lines as these following meet our eyes:

The Baron turned aside,
And wiped away the rising tears
He proudly strove to hide.

No old ballad writer would have used such a complicated concetto. Another, and even a worse instance is to be found in the difference between the old and new versions of the grand ballad of "Glasgerion." In the original, we hear how the elfin harper could

> Harp fish out of the water,
>   And water out of a stone,
>   And milk out of a maiden's breast
> That bairn had never none.

For which some benighted "restorer" substitutes—

> Oh, there was magic in his touch,
> And sorcery in his string!

No doubt there was. But while the new poetaster informs you of the abstract notion, the ancient poet gives you the concrete fact; as Mr. Tennyson has done with wonderful art in his exquisite "St. Agnes," where the saint's subjective mysticism appears only as embodied in objective pictures:

> Break up the heavens, oh Lord! and far
> Through all yon starlight keen
> Draw me, thy bride, a glittering star,
> In raiment white and clean.

Sir Walter Scott's ballads fail just on the same point. Even Campbell cannot avoid an occasional false note of sentiment. In Mr. Tennyson alone, as we think, the spirit of the Middle Age is perfectly reflected; its delight, not in the "sublime and picturesque," but in the green leaves and spring flowers for their own sake—the spirit of Chaucer and of the "Robin Hood Garland"—the naturalism which revels as much in the hedgerow and garden as in Alps, and cataracts, and Italian skies, and the other strong stimulants to the faculty of admiration which the palled taste of an unhealthy age, from Keats and Byron down to Browning, has rushed abroad to seek. It is enough for Mr. Tennyson's truly English spirit to see how

> On either side the river lie
> Long fields of barley and of rye,
> That clothe the wold and meet the sky;
> And through the field the road runs by
> To many-tower'd Camelot.

Or how

> In the stormy east wind straining,
> The pale yellow woods were waning,
> The broad stream in his banks complaining,
> Heavily the low sky raining
> Over tower'd Camelot.

Give him but such scenery as that which he can see in every parish in England, and he will find it a fit scene for an ideal myth, subtler than a casuist's questionings, deep as the deepest heart of woman.

But in this earlier volume the poet has not yet arrived at the art of combining his new speculations on man with his new mode of viewing Nature. His objective pieces are too exclusively objective, his subjective too exclusively subjective; and where he deals with natural imagery in these latter, he is too apt, as in "Eleanore," to fall back upon the old and received method of poetic diction, though he never indulges in a commonplace or a stock epithet. But in the interval between 1830 and 1842 the needful interfusion of the two elements has taken place. And in "Locksley Hall" and the "Two Voices" we find the new doubts and questions of the time embodied naturally and organically, in his own method of simple natural expression. For instance, from the Search for Truth in the "Two Voices"—

> Cry, faint not, climb: the summits lope
> Beyond the furthest flights of hope,
> Wrapt in dense cloud from base to cope.
> Sometimes a little corner shines
> As over rainy mist inclines
> A gleaming crag with belts of pines.
> "I will go forward," sayest thou;
> "I shall not fail to find her now.
> Look up, the fold is on her brow."

Or again, in "Locksley Hall," the poem which, as we think deservedly, has had most influence on the minds of the young men of our day:

> Eager-hearted as a boy when first he leaves his father's field,
> And at night along the dusky highway near and nearer drawn,
> Sees in heaven the light of London flaring like a dreary dawn;
> And his spirit leaps within him to be gone before him then,

Underneath the light he looks at, in among the throngs of men;
Men, my brothers, men the workers, ever reaping something new;
That which they have done but earnest of the things which they shall do:

and all the grand prophetic passage following, which is said, we know not
how truly, to have won for the poet the respect of that great statesman whose
loss all good men deplore.

In saying that "Locksley Hall" has deservedly had so great an influence
over the minds of the young, we shall, we are afraid, have offended some who
are accustomed to consider that poem as Werterian and unhealthy. But, in
reality, the spirit of the poem is simply anti-Werterian. It is man rising out
of sickness into health—not conquered by Werterism, but conquering his
selfish sorrow, and the moral and intellectual paralysis which it produces, by
faith and hope—faith in the progress of science and civilisation, hope in the
final triumph of good. Doubtless, that is not the highest deliverance—not
a permanent deliverance at all. Faith in God and hope in Christ alone can
deliver a man once and for all from Werterism, or any other moral disease;
that truth was reserved for "In Memoriam:" but as far as "Locksley Hall" goes,
it is a step forward—a whole moral aeon beyond Byron and Shelley; and a
step, too, in the right direction, just because it is a step forward—because
the path of deliverance is, as "Locksley Hall" sets forth, not backwards
towards a fancied paradise of childhood—not backward to grope after an
unconsciousness which is now impossible, an implicit faith which would
be unworthy of the man, but forward on the road on which God has been
leading him, carrying upward with him the aspirations of childhood, and
the bitter experience of youth, to help the organised and trustful labour of
manhood. There are, in fact, only two deliverances from Werterism possible
in the nineteenth century; one is into Popery, and the other is—

Forward, forward, let us range;
Let the peoples spin for ever down the ringing grooves of change;
Through the shadow of the world we sweep into the younger day:
Better fifty years of Europe than a cycle of Cathay.

But such a combination of powers as Mr. Tennyson's naturally develop
themselves into a high idyllic faculty; for it is the very essence of the idyl
to set forth the poetry which lies in the simpler manifestations of Man and
Nature; yet not explicitly, by a reflective moralising on them, as almost all
our idyllists—Cowper, Gray, Crabbe, and Wordsworth—have been in the
habit of doing, but implicitly, by investing them all with a rich and delightful

tone of colouring, perfect grace of manner, perfect melody of rhythm, which, like a gorgeous summer atmosphere, shall glorify without altering the most trivial and homely sights. And it is this very power, as exhibited in the "Lord of Burleigh," "Audley Court," and the "Gardener's Daughter," which has made Mr. Tennyson, not merely the only English rival of Theocritus and Bion, but, in our opinion, as much their superior as modern England is superior to ancient Greece.

Yet in *The Princess*, perhaps, Mr. Tennyson rises higher still. The idyllic manner alternates with the satiric, the pathetic, even the sublime, by such imperceptible gradations, and continual delicate variations of key, that the harmonious medley of his style becomes the fit outward expression of the bizarre and yet harmonious fairyland in which his fancy ranges. In this work, too, Mr. Tennyson shows himself more than ever the poet of the day. In it more than ever the old is interpenetrated with the new—the domestic and scientific with the ideal and sentimental. He dares, in every page, to make use of modern words and notions, from which the mingled clumsiness and archaism of his compeers shrinks, as unpoetical. Though, as we just said, his stage is an ideal fairyland, yet he has reached the ideal by the only true method—by bringing the Middle Age forward to the Present one, and not by ignoring the Present to fall back on a cold and galvanised Medievalism; and thus he makes his "Medley" a mirror of the nineteenth century, possessed of its own new art and science, its own new temptations and aspirations, and yet grounded on, and continually striving to reproduce, the forms and experiences of all past time. The idea, too, of *The Princess* is an essentially modern one. In every age women have been tempted, by the possession of superior beauty, intellect, or strength of will, to deny their own womanhood, and attempt to stand alone as men, whether on the ground of political intrigue, ascetic saintship, or philosophic pride. Cleopatra and St. Hedwiga, Madame de Stael and the Princess, are merely different manifestations of the same self-willed and proud longing of woman to unsex herself, and realise, single and self-sustained, some distorted and partial notion of her own as to what the "angelic life" should be. Cleopatra acted out the pagan ideal of an angel; St. Hedwiga, the medieval one; Madame de Stael hers, with the peculiar notions of her time as to what "spirituel" might mean; and in *The Princess* Mr. Tennyson has embodied the ideal of that nobler, wider, purer, yet equally fallacious, because equally unnatural, analogue, which we may meet too often up and down England now. He shows us the woman, when she takes her stand on the false masculine ground of intellect, working out her own moral punishment, by destroying in herself the tender heart of flesh: not even her vast purposes of philanthropy can preserve her, for they are built up, not on the womanhood which God has given her, but on her own self-will; they change, they fall, they become inconsistent, even as she does herself, till, at last, she loses all feminine sensibility; scornfully and stupidly she rejects and misunderstands the heart of man; and then falling from pride to sternness, from sternness to sheer inhumanity, she punishes sisterly love as a crime, robs the mother of her child, and becomes all but a vengeful fury, with all the peculiar faults of woman, and none of the peculiar excellences of man.

The poem being, as its title imports, a medley of jest and earnest, allows a metrical licence, of which we are often tempted to wish that its author had not availed himself; yet the most unmetrical and apparently careless passages flow with a grace, a lightness, a colloquial ease and frolic, which perhaps only heighten the effect of the serious parts, and serve as a foil to set off the unrivalled finish and melody of these latter. In these come out all Mr. Tennyson's instinctive choice of tone, his mastery of language, which always fits the right word to the right thing, and that word always the simplest one, and the perfect ear for melody which makes it superfluous to set to music poetry which, read by the veriest schoolboy, makes music of itself. The poem, we are glad to say, is so well known that it seems unnecessary to quote from it; yet there are here and there gems of sound and expression of which, however well our readers may know them, we cannot forbear reminding them again. For instance, the end of the idyl in book vii. beginning "Come down, O maid" (the whole of which is perhaps one of the most perfect fruits of the poet's genius):

Myriads of rivulets hurrying through the lawn,
The moan of doves in immemorial elms,
And murmuring of innumerable bees.

Who, after three such lines, will talk of English as a harsh and clumsy language, and seek in the effeminate and monotonous Italian for expressive melody of sound? Who cannot hear in them the rapid rippling of the water, the stately calmness of the wood-dove's note, and, in the repetition of short syllables and soft liquids in the last line, the

Murmuring of innumerable bees?

Or again, what combination of richness with simplicity in such a passage as this:

Breathe upon my brows;
In that fine air I tremble, all the past

Melts mist-like into this bright hour, and this
I scarce believe, and all the rich to come
Reels, as the golden Autumn woodland reels
Athwart the smoke of burning leaves.

How Mr. Tennyson can have attained the prodigal fulness of thought and imagery which distinguishes this poem, and especially the last canto, without his style ever becoming overloaded, seldom even confused, is perhaps one of the greatest marvels of the whole production. The songs themselves, which have been inserted between the cantos in the last edition of the book, seem, perfect as they are, wasted and smothered among the surrounding fertilty; till we discover that they stand there, not merely for the sake of their intrinsic beauty, but serve to call back the reader's mind, at every pause in the tale of the Princess's folly, to that very healthy ideal of womanhood which she has spurned.

At the end of the first canto, fresh from the description of the female college, with its professoresses, and hostleresses, and other Utopian monsters, we turn the page, and—

As through the land at eve we went,
  And pluck'd the ripen'd ears.
We fell out, my wife and I,
  And kissed again with tears:
And blessings on the falling-out
  That all the more endears,
When we fall out with those we love,
  And kiss again with tears!
For when we came where lies the child
  We lost in other years,
There above the little grave,
  We kissed again with tears.

Between the next two cantos intervenes the well-known cradle-song, perhaps the best of all; and at the next interval is the equally well-known bugle-song, the idea of which is that of twin-labour and twin-fame, in a pair of lovers:

Our echoes roll from soul to soul,
And grow for ever and for ever.

In the next, the memory of wife and child inspirits the soldier in the field; in the next, the sight of the fallen hero's child opens the sluices of his widow's tears; and in the last, and perhaps the most beautiful of all, the poet has succeeded, in the new edition, in superadding a new form of emotion to a canto in which he seemed to have exhausted every resource of pathos which his subject allowed; and prepares us for the triumph of that art by which he makes us, after all, love the heroine whom he at first taught us to hate and despise, till we see that the naughtiness is after all one that must be kissed and not whipped out of her, and look on smiling while she repents, with Prince Harry of old, "not in sackcloth and ashes, but in new silk and old sack:"

> Ask me no more: the moon may draw the sea;
> The cloud may stoop from Heaven and take the shape,
> With fold to fold, of mountain or of cape;
> But, O too fond, when have I answered thee?
> Ask me no more.
> Ask me no more: what answer should I give?
> I love not hollow cheek or faded eye:
> Yet, O my friend, I will not have thee die!
> Ask me no more, lest I should bid thee live;
> Ask me no more.
> Ask me no more: thy fate and mine are seal'd:
> I strove against the stream and all in vain:
> Let the great river take me to the main:
> No more, dear love, for at a touch I yield;
> Ask me no more.

We now come to *In Memoriam;* a collection of poems on a vast variety of subjects, but all united, as their name implies, to the memory of a departed friend. We know not whether to envy more—the poet the object of his admiration, or that object the monument which has been consecrated to his nobleness. For in this latest and highest volume, written at various intervals during a long series of years, all the poet's peculiar excellences, with all that he has acquired from others, seem to have been fused down into a perfect unity, and brought to bear on his subject with that care and finish which only a labour of love can inspire. We only now know the whole man, all his art, all his insight, all his faculty of discerning the *piu nell'uno,* and the *uno nell' piu.* As he says himself:

> My love has talked with rocks and trees,
> He finds on misty mountain-ground,
> His own vast shadow glory-crowned;
> He sees himself in all he sees.

Everything reminds him of the dead. Every joy or sorrow of man, every aspect of nature, from

> The forest crack'd, the waters curl'd,
> The cattle huddled on the lea.
> The thousand waves of wheat
> That ripple round the lonely grange.

In every place where in old days they had met and conversed; in every dark wrestling of the spirit with the doubts and fears of manhood, throughout the whole outward universe of Nature, and the whole inward universe of spirit, the soul of his dead friend broods—at first a memory shrouded in blank despair, then a living presence, a ministering spirit, answering doubts, calming fears, stirring up noble aspirations, utter humility, leading the poet upward, step by step, to faith, and peace, and hope. Not that there runs throughout the book a conscious or organic method. The poems seem often merely to be united by the identity of their metre, so exquisitely chosen, that while the major rhyme in the second and third lines of each stanza gives the solidity and self-restraint required by such deep themes, the mournful minor rhyme of each first and fourth line always leads the ear to expect something beyond, and enables the poet's thoughts to wander sadly on, from stanza to stanza and poem to poem, in an endless chain of

> Linkèd sweetness long drawn out.

There are records of risings and fallings again, of alternate cloud and sunshine, throughout the book; earnest and passionate, yet never bitter; humble, yet never abject; with a depth and vehemence of affection "passing the love of woman," yet without a taint of sentimentality; self-restrained and dignified, without ever narrowing into artificial coldness; altogether rivalling the sonnets of Shakespeare; and all knit together into one spiritual unity by the proem at the opening of the volume—in our eyes, the noblest English Christian poem which several centuries have seen.

　　We shall not quote the very poems which we should most wish to sink into men's hearts. Let each man find for himself those which suit him best, and meditate on them in silence. They are fit only to be read solemnly in our purest and most thoughtful moods, in the solitude of our chamber, or by the side of those we love, with thanks to the great heart who has taken courage to bestow on us the record of his own friendship, doubt, and triumph.

It has been often asked why Mr. Tennyson's great and varied powers had never been concentrated on one immortal work. The epic, the lyric, the idyllic faculties, perhaps the dramatic also, seemed to be all there, and yet all sundered, scattered about in small fragmentary poems. "In Memoriam," as we think, explains the paradox. Mr. Tennyson had been employed on higher, more truly divine, and yet more truly human work than either epos or drama. Within the unseen and alone truly Real world which underlies and explains this mere time-shadow, which men miscall the Real, he had been going down into the depths, and ascending into the heights, led, like Dante of old, by the guiding of a mighty spirit. And in this volume, the record of seventeen years, we have the result of those spiritual experiences in a form calculated, as we believe, to be a priceless benefit to many an earnest seeker in this generation, and perhaps to stir up some who are priding themselves on a cold dilettantism and barren epicurism, into something like a living faith and hope. Blessed and delightful it is to find, that even in these new ages the creeds which so many fancy to be at their last gasp, are still the final and highest succour, not merely of the peasant and the outcast, but of the subtle artist and the daring speculator. Blessed it is to find the most cunning poet of our day able to combine the complicated rhythm and melody of modern times with the old truths which gave heart to martyrs at the stake; and to see in the science and the history of the nineteenth century new and living fulfilments of the words which we learnt at our mother's knee. Blessed, thrice blessed, to find that hero-worship is not yet passed away; that the heart of man still beats young and fresh; that the old tales of David and Jonathan, Damon and Pythias, Socrates and Alcibiades, Shakespeare and his nameless friend, of "love passing the love of woman," ennobled by its own humility, deeper than death, and mightier than the grave, can still blossom out, if it be but in one heart here and there, to show men still how, sooner or later, "he that loveth knoweth God, for God is love."

—Charles Kingsley, "Tennyson," 1850, *Literary
and General Essays*, 1880, pp. 103–24

JOHN RUSKIN (1860)

John Ruskin was nineteenth-century England's foremost art critic, an author, journalist, social commentator, and artist. In this extract, Ruskin writes to Tennyson praising the poet's talent and power but bemoaning the application of these gifts to historical subjects in his poetry. Ruskin, a social reformer, claims that Tennyson should allow readers of all backgrounds to "feel" what poetry was. The average person, he contends, meanders through life incapable of appreciating what beauty there is in the common and the everyday. Ruskin here suggests to Tennyson that this ignorance could be remedied if the poet wrote on contemporary subjects for all people, awakening in them a sense of communion with those who go through grief and pain. These difficulties and the subsequent transcending or dispelling of them is, to Ruskin, the subject for the modern poet; his task must be to allow those ignorant of others' anguish access to it.

In Memoriam, Maud, "The Miller's Daughter," and such like will always be my own pet rhymes, yet I am quite prepared to admit this to be as good as any, for its own peculiar audience. Treasures of wisdom there are in it, and word-painting such as never was yet for concentration, nevertheless it seems to me that so great power ought not to be spent on visions of things past but on the living present. For one hearer capable of feeling the depth of this poem I believe ten would feel a depth quite as great if the stream flowed through things nearer the hearer. And merely in the facts of modern life, not drawing-room formal life, but the far away and quite unknown growth of souls in and through any form of misery or servitude, there is an infinity of what men should be told, and what none but a poet can tell. I cannot but think that the intense masterful and unerring transcript of an actuality, and the relation of a story of any real human life as a poet would watch and analyze it, would make all men feel more or less what poetry was, as they felt what Life and Fate were in their instant workings.

This seems to me the true task of the modern poet. And I think I have seen faces, and heard voices by road and street side, which claimed or conferred as much as ever the loveliest or saddest of Camelot. As I watch them, the feeling continually weighs upon me, day by day, more and more, that not the grief of the world but the loss of it is the wonder of it. I see creatures so full of all power and beauty, with none to understand or teach or save them. The making in them of miracles and all cast away, for ever lost as far as we can trace. And no "in memoriam."

—John Ruskin, letter to Alfred, Lord Tennyson,
1860, cited in Hallam Tennyson, *Alfred Lord
Tennyson: A Memoir*, 1897, vol. 1, pp. 453–54

MATTHEW ARNOLD (1862)

Matthew Arnold was a poet, cultural critic, and essayist and one of Great Britain's most influential nineteenth-century writers. He is generally considered to be, along with Thomas Carlyle and John Ruskin, one of the "Victorian sages," the greatest thinkers and critics of an age replete with remarkable individuals. In the following extract, Arnold describes Tennyson as a type of anti-Homer, the ancient Greek author of the epic poems *The Iliad* and *The Odyssey*. Where the Greek writer is renowned for the natural power of both his thought and expression, Tennyson's verse exemplifies, for Arnold, the most subtle and elaborate ideas and their equally subtle and elaborate presentation. There is no indication by Arnold that he values one poetic manner over the other; he sees in Tennyson the continuation of a tradition going back at least to the Elizabethan poets; he suggests there are even traits suggestive of Shakespeare. Arnold claims that the essential characteristics of Tennyson's verse are his curious expressions of curious thoughts, citing poetic examples as evidence in support of his opinion.

Tennyson is a most distinguished and charming poet; but the very essential characteristic of his poetry is, it seems to me, an extreme subtlety and curious elaborateness of thought, an extreme subtlety and curious elaborateness of expression. In the best and most characteristic productions of his genius, these characteristics are most prominent. They are marked characteristics, as we have seen, of the Elizabethan poets; they are marked, though not the essential, characteristics of Shakspeare himself. Under the influences of the nineteenth century, under wholly new conditions of thought and culture, they manifest themselves in Mr. Tennyson's poetry in a wholly new way. But they are still there. The essential bent of his poetry is towards such expressions as—

> Now lies the Earth all Danae to the stars;
> O'er the sun's bright eye
> Drew the vast eyelid of an inky cloud;
> When the cairned mountain was a shadow, sunned
> The world to peace again;
> The fresh young captains flashed their glittering teeth,
> The huge bush-bearded barons heaved and blew;
> He bared the knotted column of his throat,

The massive square of his heroic breast,
And arms on which the standing muscle sloped
As slopes a wild brook o'er a little stone,
Running too vehemently to break upon it.

And this way of speaking is the least *plain*, the most *un-Homeric*, which can possibly be conceived. Homer presents his thought to you just as it wells from the source of his mind: Mr. Tennyson carefully distils his thought before he will part with it. Hence comes, in the expression of the thought, a heightened and elaborate air. In Homer's poetry it is all natural thoughts in natural words; in Mr. Tennyson's poetry it is all distilled thoughts in distilled words. Exactly this heightening and elaboration may be observed in Mr. Spedding's

While the steeds *mouthed their corn aloof,*

(an expression which might have been Mr. Tennyson's) on which I have already commented; and to one who is penetrated with a sense of the real simplicity of Homer, this subtle sophistication of the thought is, I think, very perceptible even in such lines as these,—

And drunk delight of battle with my peers,
Far on the ringing plains of windy Troy,—

which I have seen quoted as perfectly Homeric. Perfect simplicity can be obtained only by a genius of which perfect simplicity is an essential characteristic.

—Matthew Arnold, *On Translating
Homer: Last Words,* 1862

EDWARD DOWDEN "MR. TENNYSON AND MR. BROWNING" (1867)

Edward Dowden was an Irish poet and literary critic. In the following extract, he begins by suggesting that the foundation of all Tennyson's thought was a faith in "law," the order inherent in the physical and moral worlds. As a consequence, Tennyson would envision God as the embodiment of law, as underpinning the material and moral planes, rather than as a being entering into a personal relationship with humankind. Tennyson's conservative belief in the slow, ordered progress of science, society, and civilization toward some distant futurity is read equally by Dowden as the fulfillment or unfolding of law. The ideals of emotional, intellectual, and moral self-restraint are, for Dowden, the basis not only of Tennyson's portrayal of society and the individual but also of his poetic style. Grief and passion are uncontrolled, outside the law, and are therefore the worst of evils for the poet; these outbursts are not in evidence in his poetic style or expression, a fact pointed out often by critics such as Sara Coleridge and Charlotte Brontë (whose commentary is also included in this volume), who doubt the poet's depiction of his feelings and grief as they are evidenced in *In Memoriam*.

Dowden's reading of Tennyson's "faith" stands in contrast to other critics, such as G. K. Chesterton or Charles Kingsley, included in this section. Many other extracts detail varying views on the emotional aspects of Tennyson's poetry and on his conservative politics (see Walt Whitman's views on the poet's reactionary attitudes). Cross-referencing those discussions with Dowden's should provide students of Tennyson's work several contrasting opinions against which they might consider their own opinions of the poet and his works.

Let us start in our study,—a partial study made from a single point of view,— with what may be an assumption for the present, but an assumption which will lead to its own verification. Let us start by saying that Mr Tennyson has a strong sense of the dignity and efficiency of *law*,—of *law* understood in its widest meaning. Energy nobly controlled, an ordered activity delight his imagination. Violence, extravagance, immoderate force, the swerving from appointed ends, revolt,—these are with Mr Tennyson the supreme manifestations of evil.

Under what aspect is the relation of the world and man to God represented in the poems of Mr Tennyson? Surely,—it will be said,—one who feels so strongly the presence of law in the physical world, and who recognises so fully the struggle in the moral nature of man between impulse and duty, assigning to conscience a paramount authority, has the materials from which arises naturally a vivid feeling of what is called the personal relation of God to his creatures. A little reflection will show that this is not so. It is quite possible to admit in one's thoughts and feelings the existence of a physical order of the material world, and a moral order of the spiritual world, and yet to enter slightly into those intimate relations of the affections with a Divine Being which present him in the tenderest way as a Father,—as a highest Friend. Fichte, the sublime idealist, was withheld from seeing God by no obtruding veil of a material universe. Fichte, if any man ever did, recognised the moral order of the world. But Fichte—living indeed the blessed life in God,—yet annihilated for thought his own personality and that of God, in the infinity of this moral order. No: it is not law but will that reveals will; it is not our strength but our weakness that cries out for the invisible Helper and Divine Comrade; it is not our obedience but our aspiration, our joy, our anguish; it is the passion of self-surrender, the grief that makes desolate, the solitary rapture which demands a partaker of its excess, the high delight which must save itself from as deep dejection by a passing over into gratitude.

Accordingly, although we find the idea of God entering largely into the poems of Mr Tennyson, there is little recognition of special contact of the soul with the Divine Being in any supernatural ways of quiet or of ecstasy. There is, on the contrary, a disposition to rest in the orderly manifestation of God, as the supreme Law-giver, and even to identify him with his presentation of himself, in the physical and moral order of the universe. And if this precludes all spiritual rapture, that "glorious folly, that heavenly madness, wherein true wisdom is acquired,"[1] it preserves the mind from despair or any deep dejection; unless, indeed, the faith in this order itself give way, when in the universal chaos, no will capable of bringing restoration being present, a confusion of mind, a moral obscurity greater than any other, must arise.

Wordsworth in some of his solitary trances of thought really entered into the frame of mind which the mystic knows as union or as ecstacy, when thought expires in enjoyment, when the mind is blessedness and love, when "the waters of grace have risen up to the neck of the soul, so that it can neither advance nor retreat." With Mr Tennyson the mystic is always the visionary, who suffers from an over-excitable fancy. The nobler aspects of the mystical religious spirit, are unrepresented in his poetry. St Simeon upon his pillar is chiefly of interest, as affording an opportunity for studying the phenomena of morbid theopathetic emotion. We find nowhere among the persons of his imagination a Teresa, uniting as she did in so eminent a degree an administrative genius, a genius for action with the genius of exalted piety. The feeble Confessor beholds visions; but Harold strikes ringing blows upon the helms of his country's enemies. Harold is no virgin, no confessor, no seer, no saint, but a loyal, plain, strong-thewed, truth-loving son of England, who can cherish a woman, and rule a people, and mightily wield a battle-axe. In the Idylls when the Grail passes before the assembled knights, where is the king? He is absent, actively resisting evil, harrying the bandits' den; and as he returns, it is with alarm that he perceives the ominous tokens left by the sacred thing:—

> Lo there! the roofs
> Of our great hall are rolled in thunder smoke!
> Pray heaven, they be not smitten by the bolt.

The Grail is a sign to maim the great order which Arthur has reared. The mystical glories which the knights pursue are "wandering fires." If Galahad beheld the vision, it was because Galahad was already unmeet for earth, worthy to be a king, not in this sad yet noble city of men, but in some far-off spiritual city.

> And spake I not too truly, O my knights?
> Was I too dark a prophet when I said
> To those who went upon the Holy Quest,
> That most of them would follow wandering fires,
> Lost in the quagmire?—lost to me and gone,
> And left me gazing at a barren board,
> And a lean Order—scarce return'd a tithe—
> And out of those to whom the vision came
> My greatest hardly will believe he saw;
> Another hath beheld it afar off,
> And leaving human wrongs to right themselves,
> Cares but to pass into the silent life.
> And one hath had the vision face to face,
> And now his chair desires him here in vain,
> However they may crown him otherwhere.

The Round Table is dissolved, the work of Arthur is brought to an end, because two passions have overthrown the order of the realm, which it has been the task of the loyal, steadfast and wise king to create,—first, the sensual passion of Lancelot and Guinevere; secondly, the spiritual passion hardly less fatal, which leaped forth when the disastrous quest was avowed. Only that above all order of human institution, a higher order abides, we might well suppose that chaos must come again; but it is not so:—

> The old order changeth giving place to new,
> And God fulfils himself in many ways.

Thus, as has been already remarked, Mr Tennyson's sense of a beneficent unfolding in our life of a divine purpose, lifts him through and over the common dejections of men. With his own friend, it is as with his ideal king; he will not mourn for any overmuch. The fame which he predicted to his friend is quenched by an early death; but he will not despair:—

> The fame is quench'd that I foresaw,
>   The head hath missed an earthly wreath;
>   I curse not nature, no, nor death;
> For nothing is that errs from law.

Even the thought of the foul corruption of the grave becomes supportable, when it is conceived as a part of the change which permits the spirit to have its portion in the self-evolving process of the higher life:—

> Eternal process moving on,
> From state to state the spirit walks;
> And these are but the shatter'd stalks,
> Or ruin'd chrysalis of one.

It is only when the doubt of a beneficent order of the world cannot be put away—it is only when nature (as discovered by the investigations of geology), seems ruthless alike to the individual and the species, "red in tooth and claw with ravine," it is only then that the voice of the mourner grows wild, and it appears to him that his grief has lost its sanctity and wrongs the quiet of the dead.

Mr Tennyson finds law present throughout all nature, but there is no part of nature in which he dwells with so much satisfaction upon its presence as in human society. No one so largely as Mr Tennyson, has represented in art the new thoughts and feelings, which form the impassioned side of the modern conception of progress. His imagination is for ever haunted by "the vision of the world, and all the wonder that would be." But the hopes and aspirations of Mr Tennyson are not those of the radical or movement character. He is in all his poems conservative as well as liberal. It may be worth while to illustrate the feeling of Shelley, in contrast with that of Mr Tennyson, with reference to this idea of progress. In the year 1819 Shelley believed that England had touched almost the lowest point of social and political degradation:

> An old, mad, blind, despised, and dying king,—
> Princes, the dregs of their dull race, who flow
> Through public scorn, mud from a muddy spring,—
> Rulers, who neither see, nor feel, nor know,

But leech-like to their fainting country cling,
Till they drop, blind in blood, without a blow,—
A people starv'd and stabb'd in the untilled field,—
An army which liberticide and prey
Make as a two-edged sword to all who wield,—
Golden and sanguine laws which tempt and slay,—
Religion Christless, Godless,—a book sealed,
A Senate—time's worst statute unrepealed.—

Such laws, such rulers, such a people Shelley found in his England of half a century since. Did he therefore despair, or if he hoped was the object of his hope some better life of man in some distant future? No: all these things

Are graves, from which a glorious Phantom may
Burst, to illumine our tempestuous day.

The regeneration of society, as conceived by Shelley, was to appear suddenly, splendidly shining with the freshness and glory of a dream; as the result of some bright, brief national struggle; as the consequence of the apparition of some pure being, at once a poet and a prophet, before whose voice huge tyrannies and cruel hypocrisies must needs go down, as piled-up clouds go down ruined and rent before a swift, pure wind; in some way or another which involves a catastrophe, rather than according to the constantly operating processes of nature.

Now Mr Tennyson's conception of progress, which he has drawn from his moral and intellectual environment, and which accords with his own moral temper, is widely different. No idea perhaps occupies a place in his poems so central as that of the progress of the race. This it is which lifts out of his idle dejection and selfish dreaming the speaker in "Locksley Hall;"

Not in vain the distance beacons. Forward, forward
  let us range,
    Let the great world spin for ever down the ringing
      grooves of change.

This it is which suggests an apology for the fantasies of "The Day-Dream." This it is which arms the tempted with a weapon of defence, and the tempter with a deadlier weapon of attack in "The Two Voices." This it is of which Leonard writes, and at which old James girds in "The Golden Year." This it is which gives a broad basis of meditative thought to the Idyll that tells of the passing of Arthur, and renders it something more than a glorious fable. This it is which is the sweetness of "The Poet's Song," making the wild swan pause, and the lark drop from heaven to earth. This it is which forms the closing prophecy of *The Princess*, the full confession of the poet's faith. This it is which is heard in the final chords of the *In Memoriam*, changing the music from a minor to a major key. And the same doctrine is taught from the opposite side in "The Vision of Sin," in which the most grievous disaster which comes upon the base and sensual heart is represented as hopelessness with reference to the purpose and the progress of the life of man:

> Fill the can and fill the cup,
> All the windy ways of men
> Are but dust that rises up
> And is lightly laid again.[2]

But in all these poems throughout which the idea of progress is so variously expressed, and brought into relation with moods of mind so diverse, the progress of mankind is uniformly represented as the evolution and self-realisation of a law; it is represented as taking place gradually and slowly, and its consummation is placed in a remote future. We "hear the roll of the ages;" the "increasing purpose" runs through centuries; it is "with the process of the suns" that the thoughts of men are widened. It is when our sleep should have been prolonged through many decades and quinquenniads that we might wake to reap the flower and quintessence of change:

> For we are Ancients of the earth,
> And in the morning of the times.

It is because millenniums will not bring the advance of knowledge near its term that the tempted soul in "The Two Voices" feels how wretched a thing it must be to watch the increase of intellectual light during the poor thirty or forty years of a life-time. It is "in long years" that the sexes shall attain to the fulness of their mighty growth, until at last, man and Woman

> Upon the skirts of Time
> Sit side by side, full-summ'd in all their powers,
> Dispensing harvest, sowing the To-be,
> . . .
> Then comes the statelier Eden back to man:

Then reign the world's great bridals, chaste and calm;
Then springs the crowning race of humankind.
May these things be!

And the highest augury telling of this "crowning race" is drawn from those who already having moved upward through the lower phases of being become precursors and pledges of the gracious children of the future:

For all we thought and loved and did,
   And hoped, and suffer'd, is but seed
Of what in them is flower and fruit;
Whereof the man, that with me trod
   This planet, was a noble type
   Appearing ere the times were ripe,
That friend of mine who lives in God,
That God, which ever lives and loves,
   One God, one law, one element,
   And one far-off divine event,
To which the whole creation moves.

The great hall which Merlin built for Arthur, is girded by four zones of symbolic sculpture; in the lowest zone, beasts are slaying men; in the second, men are slaying beasts;

And on the third are warriors, perfect men,
And on the fourth are men with growing wings.

To work out the beast is the effort of long ages; to attain to be "a perfect man" is for those who shall follow us afar off; to soar with wings is for the crowning race of the remotest future.

Apart from the growth of the individual that golden age to which the poet looks forward, the coming of which he sees shine in the distance, is characterized, as he imagines it, chiefly by a great development of knowledge, especially of scientific knowledge; this first; and, secondly, by the universal presence of political order and freedom, national and international, secured by a vast and glorious federation. It is quite of a piece with Mr Tennyson's feeling for law, that his imagination should be much impressed by the successes of science, and that its promises should correspond with his hopes. The crowning race will be a company

Of those that, eye to eye, shall look
On knowledge; under whose command
Is Earth and Earth's, and in their hand
Is Nature like an open book.

Were we to sleep the hundred years, our joy would be to wake

On science grown to more,
On secrets of the brain, the stars.

It is the promises and achievements of science which restore sanity to the distraught lover of "Locksley Hall." In *The Princess* the sport half-science of galvanic batteries, model steam-engines, clock-work steamers and fire-balloons, suggest the thought of a future of adult knowledge:

This fine old world of ours is but a child
Yet in the go-cart. Patience! Give it time
To learn its limbs: there is a hand that guides.

But Mr Tennyson's dream of the future is not more haunted by visionary discoveries and revelations of science than by the phantoms of great political organizations. That will be a time

When the war-drum throbs no longer, and the battle flags are furl'd
In the Parliament of men, the Federation of the world.

A time in which

Phantoms of other forms of rule,
New Majesties of mighty states

will appear, made real at length; a time in which the years will bring to being

The vast Republics that may grow,
The Federations and the Powers;
Titanic forces taking birth.

These days and works of the crowning race are, however, far beyond our grasp; and the knowledge of this, with the faith that the progress of mankind is the expression of a slowly, self-revealing law, puts a check upon certain of our hopes and strivings. He who is possessed by this faith will look for no speedy regeneration of men in the social or political sphere, and can but imperfectly sympathise with those enthusiastic hearts whose expectations, nourished by their ardours and desires, are eager and would forestall futurity. Mr Tennyson's justness of mind in a measure forsakes him, when he has to speak of political movements into which passion in its uncalculating form has entered as a main motive power. Yet passion of this type is the right and appropriate power for the uses of certain times and seasons. It is by ventures of faith in politics that mountains are removed. The Tory member's elder son estimates the political movements of France in an insular spirit which, it may be surmised, has in it something of Mr Tennyson's own feeling:—

Whiff! there comes a sudden heat,
The gravest citizen seems to lose his head,
The king is scared, the soldier will not fight,
The little boys begin to shoot and stab.

Yet to France more than to England the enslaved nations have turned their faces when they have striven to rend their bonds. It is hardly from Mr Tennyson that we shall learn how a heroic failure may be worth as much to the world as a distinguished success. It is another poet who has written thus:—

When liberty goes out of a place it is not the first to
go, nor the second or third to go,
It waits for all the rest to go—it is the last.
When there are no more memories of heroes and
martyrs,
And when all life, and all the souls of men and
women are discharged from any part of the earth,
Then only shall liberty, or the idea of liberty, be
discharged from that part of the earth,
And the infidel come into full possession.

Mr Tennyson's ideal for every country is England, and that is a blunder in politics:

A land of settled government,
A land of just and old renown,

> Where Freedom slowly broadens down
> From precedent to precedent.

That is an admirable verse; but it is nobler to make than to follow precedents; and great emotions, passionate thought, audacities of virtue quickly create a history and tradition of precedents in the lives alike of individuals and of nations. Mr Tennyson loves freedom, but she must assume an English costume before he can recognize her; the freedom which he loves is

> That sober freedom out of which there springs
> Our loyal passion to our temperate kings.

She is

> Freedom in her royal seat
> Of England, not the schoolboy heat—
> The blind hysterics of the Celt.

He cannot squander a well-balanced British sympathy on hearts that love not wisely but too well:—

> Love thou thy land with love far brought
>   From out the storied Past, and used
>   Within the Present, but transfused
> Through future time by power of thought.

What Mr Tennyson has written will indeed lead persons of a certain type of character in their true direction; for those of a different type it will for ever remain futile and false. "Reason," Vauvenargues has said, "deceives us more often than does nature." "If passion advises more boldly than reflection, it is because passion gives greater power to carry out its advice." "To do great things, one must live as if one could never die." England can celebrate a golden wedding with Freedom, and gather children about her knees; let there be a full and deep rejoicing. But why forbid the more unmeasured joy of the lover of Freedom who has dreamed of her and has fought for her, and who now is glad because he has once seen her, and may die for her?

Mr Tennyson's political doctrine is in entire agreement with his ideal of human character. As the exemplar of all nations is that one in which highest wisdom is united with complete self-government, so the ideal man is he whose life is led to sovereign power by self-knowledge resulting in self-control, and self-control growing perfect in self-reverence. The golden fruit which Here prays for, promising power, which Aphrodite prays for, promising pleasure, belongs of right to Pallas alone, who promises no other sovereignty, no other joy than those that come by the freedom of perfect service,—

> To live by law,
> Acting the law we live by without fear.

Mr Tennyson has had occasion to write two remarkable poetical *eloges*— one on the late Prince Consort, the other on the great Duke. In both, the characters are drawn with fine discrimination, but in both, the crowning virtue of the dead is declared to have been the virtue of obedience, that of self-subjugation to the law of duty. In both the same lesson is taught, that he who toils along the upward path of painful right-doing

> Shall find the toppling crags of Duty scaled
> Are close upon the shining table-lands
> To which our God Himself is moon and sun.

Even Love "takes part against himself" to be at one with Duty, who is "loved of Love." Through strenuous self-mastery, through the strong holding of passion in its leash, Enoch Arden attains the sad happiness of strong heroic souls. But it is not only as fortitude and endurance that Mr Tennyson conceives the virtue of noble obedience; it flames up into a chivalric ardour in the passionate loyalty of the Six Hundred riders at Balaclava; and Cranmer redeems his life from the dishonour of fear, of faltering and of treason, by the last gallantry of a soldierlike obedience to the death:

> He pass'd out smiling, and he walk'd upright;
> His eye was like a soldier's, whom the general
> He looks to, and he leans on as his God,
> Hath rated for some backwardness, and bidd'n him
> Charge one against a thousand, and the man
> Hurls his soil'd life against the pikes and dies.

Self-reverence, self-knowledge, self-control, the recognition of a divine order and of one's own place in that order, faithful adhesion to the law of one's highest life,—these are the elements from which is formed the ideal human character. What is the central point in the ethical import of the Arthurian story as told by Mr Tennyson? It is the assertion that the highest type of manhood is set forth in the poet's ideal king, and that the worthiest work of man is work such as his. And what is Arthur? The blameless monarch, who "reverenced his conscience as a king;" unseduced from his appointed path by the temptations of sense or the wandering fires of religious mysticism; throughout the most passionate scene of the poem "sublime in self-repression":—

> I wanted warmth and colour, which I found
> In Lancelot,—now I see thee what thou art,
> Thou art the highest, and most human too,
> Not Lancelot, not another.

Arthur's task has been to drive back the heathen, to quell disorder and violence, to bind the wills of his knights to righteousness in a perfect law of liberty. It is true that Arthur's task is left half done. While he rides forth to silence the riot of the Red Knight and his ruffian band, in his own court are held those "lawless jousts," and Tristram sings in the ears of that small, sad cynic, Dagonet, his licentious song:—

> Free love—free field—we love but while we may.

And thus were it not that a divine order overrules our efforts, our successes, and our failures, we must needs believe that the realm is once more reeling back into the beast.

Disorder of thoughts, of feelings and of will is, with Mr Tennyson, the evil of evils, the pain of pains. The Princess would transcend, through the temptation of a false ideal, her true sphere of womanhood; even this noblest form of disobedience to law entails loss and sorrow; she is happy only when she resumes her worthier place through the wisdom of love. In "Lucretius" the man who had so highly striven for light and calm, for "the sober majesties of settled, sweet Epicurean life," is swept by a fierce tempest in his blood back into chaos; there is but one way of deliverance, but one way of entering again under the reign of law,—to surrender his being once more to Nature, that she may anew dash together the atoms which make him man, in order that as flower, or beast, or fish, or bird, or man, they may again move through her cycles; and so Lucretius roughly wooes the passionless bride, Tranquillity. And may we not sum up the substance of Mr Tennyson's personal confessions in "In Memoriam," by saying that they are the record of the growth through sorrow of the firmer mind, which becomes one with law at length apparent through the chaos of sorrow; which counts it crime "to mourn for any overmuch;" which turns its burden into gain, and for which those truths that never can be proved, and that had been lost in the first wild shock of grief, are regained by "faith that comes of self-control."

Notes

1. S. Teresa, *Life*, ch. xvi.
2. So in the *In Memoriam* when the "light is low" and the heart is sick, Time appears not as a wise master-builder, but as a "maniac, scattering dust."

—Edward Dowden, from "Mr Tennyson and
Mr Browning," 1867, *Studies in Literature*,
1878, pp. 195–211

J. HAIN FRISWELL "MR. ALFRED TENNYSON" (1870)

This scathing extract by the critic J. Hain Friswell vehemently challenges Tennyson's reputation as a poet. Friswell recognizes that Tennyson's poetry is polished and well-suited for the general public, but these are faults in the critic's eyes. He believes that future ages will remove Tennyson from the pantheon of great poets and claim that he has not one poem to match the greatest writings of Percy Bysshe Shelley, John Keats, Samuel Taylor Coleridge, and William Wordsworth. Friswell says that Tennyson's work lacks both sublimity and profundity, that it is well-crafted but lacks true power. Readers might contrast Friswell's opinions with earlier extracts where it is precisely Tennyson's ability to excite his audiences with the power of his verse that is praised. Quoting from the poet's work, Friswell attacks the tepid feelings and the half-hearted convictions revealed in them, saying that Tennyson is perfect as the poet laureate, as none can better him in his capacity to manufacture a verse on demand.

Yes, Tennyson is a greatly successful, but he is not a great poet. The next age will surely reverse the verdict of this. He is sugar sweet, pretty-pretty, full of womanly talk and feminine stuff. Lilian, Dora, Clara, Emmeline—you can count up thirty such pretty names, but you cannot count any great poem of the Laureate's. Shelley has his "Ode to the Skylark," Keats his to the Grecian Urn, Coleridge his "Genevieve," his weird *Ancient Mariner,* Wordsworth that touching, yea, aching sublimity on the "Intimations of Immortality"—where is there one thing of Tennyson which can approach that? He has kept himself aloof from men; he has polished his poems till all are ripe and rotten; he has no fire and no fault; he has never lifted one to Heaven nor plunged us to the lower depths. He has no creed, no faith, no depth. When another poet would bare his heart he talks of his pulses:

> My *pulses*—therefore beat again
> For other friends that once I met;
> Nor *can it suit me to forget*
> The mighty hopes that make us men.

What a grand line is that last, and what a feeble beast crawls on its belly before it! Can we forgive a poet "suiting to forget" Heaven, Hell, Christ and His Death upon the Cross, His agony and bloody sweat?—Heavens, that a Christian poet should be found lisping out *that!*

No, he is no great poet. Mr. Tennyson has been very discreet, and a very good Court poet,—for a manufactured article really none better; but he is like the lady who did not want to "look frightful when dead," and so put on the paint and the fucus, and he will take no deep hold of the world. What did sweet Will Shakespeare do? Did he not say that he had

> *gored* mine own thoughts;
> Sold cheap what is most dear,
> And made myself a motley to the view.

Did he not give us blood and passion with his poetry? But what says Tennyson: "Nor can it suit me to forget" that I am admired by all young ladies, and am a Laureate. Further he adds,

> I count it crime
> To mourn for any overmuch.

And posterity will count it folly to place a half-hearted and polished rhymster amongst her shining great ones who were fellows with poverty and disrespect in this life, and who learnt in suffering that they might teach in song.

—J. Hain Friswell, "Mr. Alfred Tennyson,"
Modern Men of Letters Honestly Criticised,
1870, pp. 155–56

HIPPOLYTE TAINE (1871)

Hippolyte Taine was a highly influential French literary critic and historian. In the following extract, Taine suggests, in less vehement fashion than J. Hain Friswell in the preceding passage, that Tennyson is often too "proper" to succeed in his choice of poetic subject. Tennyson's best-known and most celebrated poem, *In Memoriam A. H. H.*, is criticized by Taine as lacking passionate feeling, as being "arranged." He suggests that some poets are dilettantes, deploying their poetry as a means of escaping the vulgarities and sordid realities in life. Taine focuses on the world of chivalric romance as a perfect example of this dilettante-artist's type of subject matter, an obvious reference to Tennyson's *Idylls of the King*, the Arthurian cycle of 12 poems that the poet published between 1856 and 1885.

The great task of an artist is to find subjects which suit his talent. Tennyson has not always succeeded in this. His long poem, *In Memoriam*, written in praise and memory of a friend who died young, is cold, monotonous, and often too prettily arranged. He goes into mourning; but, like a correct gentleman, with brand-new gloves, wipes away his tears with a cambric handkerchief, and displays throughout the religious service, which ends the ceremony, all the compunction of a respectful and well-trained layman. He was to find his subjects elsewhere. To be poetically happy is the object of a dilettante-artist. For this many things are necessary. First of all, that the place, the events, and the characters shall not exist. Realities are coarse, and always, in some sense, ugly; at least they are heavy; we do not treat them at our pleasure, they oppress the fancy; at bottom there is nothing truly sweet and beautiful in our life but our dreams. We are ill at ease whilst we remain glued to earth, hobbling along on our two feet, which drag us wretchedly here and there in the place which impounds us. We need to live in another world, to hover in the wide-air kingdom, to build palaces in the clouds, to see them rise and crumble, to follow in a hazy distance the whims of their moving architecture, and the turns of their golden volutes. In this fantastic world, again, all must be pleasant and beautiful, the heart and senses must enjoy it, objects must be smiling or picturesque, sentiments delicate or lofty; no crudity, incongruity, brutality, savageness must come to sully with its excess the modulated harmony of this ideal perfection. This leads the poet to the legends of chivalry. Here is the fantastic world, splendid to the sight, noble and specially pure, in which love, war, adventures, generosity, courtesy, all spectacles and all virtues which suit the instincts of our European races, are assembled, to furnish them with the epic which they love, and the model which suits them.

—Hippolyte Taine, *History of English Literature*,
translated by H. Van Laun, 1871, book 5, chapter 6

Henry Wadsworth Longfellow "Wapentake: To Alfred Tennyson" (1873)

Henry Wadsworth Longfellow was an American educator and poet, known primarily for his lyrics. In the following sonnet, Longfellow praises Tennyson's skill as a poet, saying that he is paying homage to the greater poet's ability and his mastery of their art. The metaphor of knights touching lances is no doubt a reference to Tennyson's Arthurian cycle of poems, *Idylls of the King*, and readers might contrast Longfellow's opinion of Tennyson's poetry with those of J. Hain Friswell and Hippolyte Taine, laid out in the two extracts preceding this one. Longfellow praises Tennyson for not being a "howling dervish" in his poetry, for not leaving his audience with "crazed" brains because of the "delirious" music and subjects contained in his verse. It is this lack of fever and chaotic passion in Tennyson's poetry that Longfellow specifically states as earning the Englishman the "laurel-leaves" that were the traditional symbol of victory in the poetic competitions of the classical world.

Poet! I come to touch thy lance with mine;
Not as a knight, who on the listed field
Of tourney touched his adversary's shield
In token of defiance, but in sign
Of homage to the mastery, which is thine,
In English song; nor will I keep concealed,
And voiceless as a rivulet frost-congealed,
My admiration for thy verse divine.
Not of the howling dervishes of song,
Who craze the brain with their delirious dance,
Art thou, O sweet historian of the heart!
Therefore to thee the laurel-leaves belong,
To thee our love and our allegiance,
For thy allegiance to the poet's art.

—Henry Wadsworth Longfellow, "Wapentake: To
Alfred Tennyson," *A Book of Sonnets*, 1873

R. C. Jebb "Alfred, Lord Tennyson" (1880)

Richard Claverhouse Jebb was a British politician and one of the nine-teenth-century's foremost classical scholars. In the following extract, Jebb is in no doubt that Tennyson will maintain his reputation as one of the finest English poets. In contrast to several of the preceding excerpts in this volume, Jebb's seemingly balanced approach praises Tennyson for the musicality of his verse and its "self-restraint" when, presumably, other poets have given way to the passionate outbursts that Henry Wadsworth Longfellow in the preceding extract identifies Tennyson as avoiding. The poet's subtle spirituality, the balance and symmetry of his art, and his abil-ity to work in so many varied poetic forms, make him, for Jebb, one of the greatest writers of verse in any language.

Jebb introduces an unusual line into his appreciation of Tennyson, viewing him within the context of his time. Jebb states that in Tennyson's youth, the industrial and imperial progress of Great Britain seemed to augur a golden age, but that by the middle years of the century, this feeling had given way to doubts and concerns that something was being lost, that all was not as well as it seemed. Jebb does not see Tennyson, like William Wordsworth in the previous generation, as being a philosopher or a great thinker, but acting rather as one who taught his time a liberal faith in religion and society, soothing doubts and ennobling the spirit of his troubled contemporaries in the later nineteenth century. Jebb's conclusion that Tennyson was a latter-day Socrates, maintaining values and a sense of community that many feared were disintegrating, is a novel critical perspective. Those readers interested in Tennyson's role as poet laureate or the cultural influence that a poet is able to wield might consider Jebb's statement from a political perspective. Jebb himself was a politician and a member of Great Britain's governing elite. Might Tennyson be seen as a conservative who helped to maintain the status quo in Victorian Britain? Is his lack of radicalism something that earlier extracts imply when they speak of the poet's verse as bereft of passion and depth of feeling? Is poetry that "soothes" something that should be praised? Is Hippolyte Taine correct in the previous extract in this section, when he critically suggests that Tennyson is a "dilettante-artist"? Is this precisely what Jebb is praising in the following passage? The extract following Jebb's, written by Walt Whitman, takes on these questions of the poet's political and cultural role.

The gifts by which Tennyson has won, and will keep, his place among the great poets of England are pre-eminently those of an artist. His genius for vivid and musical expression was joined to severe self-restraint, and to a patience which allowed nothing to go forth from him until it had been refined to the utmost perfection that he was capable of giving to it. And his 'law of pure and flawless workmanship' (as Matthew Arnold defines the artistic quality in poetry) embraced far more than language: the same instinct controlled his composition in the larger sense; it is seen in the symmetry of each work as a whole, in the due subordination of detail, in the distribution of light and shade, in the happy and discreet use of ornament. His versatility is not less remarkable: no English poet has left masterpieces in so many different kinds of verse. On another side the spiritual subtlety of the artist is seen in the power of finding words for dim and fugitive traits of consciousness; as the artist's vision, at once minute and imaginative, is seen in his pictures of nature. By this varied and consummate excellence Tennyson ranks with the great artists of all time.

This is the dominant aspect of his poetry. But there is another which presents itself as soon as we take the historical point of view, and inquire into the nature of his influence upon his age. Tennyson was not primarily, like Wordsworth, a philosophical thinker, who felt called upon to be a teacher. But from the middle of the century onwards he was the accepted poet, in respect to thought on religion and on many social questions, of that large public which might be described as the world of cultivated and moderately liberal orthodoxy. Multitudes of these readers were imperfectly capable of appreciating him as an artist: have not some of them been discussing who is 'the Pilot' in 'Crossing the Bar'? But at any rate they heard a voice which they could generally understand; they felt that it was beautiful and noble; and they loved it because it soothed and elevated them. They cherished a poet who placed the centre of religion in a simple reliance on the divine love; who taught that, through all struggles and perplexities, the time was being guided towards some final good; who saw the results of science not as dangers but as reinforcements to faith; who welcomed material progress and industrial vigour, but always sought to maintain the best traditions of English history and character. Now, this popular element in Tennyson's fame—as it may be called relatively to those elements which sprang from a full appreciation of his art—was not due to any conscious self-adaptation on his part to prevailing currents of thought and feeling. It arose from the peculiar relation of his genius to the period in which he grew up to manhood. His early youth was in England a day of bright dreams and confident auguries; for democracy and steam, all things were to be possible. Then came the reaction; doubts and difficulties thickened; questions started up in every field, bringing with them unrest, discouragement, or even despair. At such a season the poet who is pre-eminently an artist has a twofold opportunity; by creating beauty he can comfort the weary; but a yet higher task is to exercise, through his art, an ennobling and harmonizing influence on those more strenuous yet half-desponding spirits who bear the stress of the transition, while new and crude energies are threatening an abrupt breach with the past. It is a great work to do for a people, to win the popular ear at such a time for counsels of reverence and chivalry; to make them feel that these things are beautiful, and are bonds of the national life, while the forces that tend to disintegration are also tending to make the people sordid and cynical. This is the work that Sophocles, in his later years, did for Athens, and this is what Tennyson did for the England of his prime.

—R. C. Jebb, "Alfred, Lord Tennyson," *The English Poets*, ed. Thomas Humphry Ward, 1880, 1894, vol. 4, pp. 755–57

WALT WHITMAN "A WORD ABOUT TENNYSON" (1887)

Walt Whitman was an American poet, essayist, and journalist. In the following extract, Whitman casts a critical eye on the role Tennyson had played in British and American society. While Tennyson's artistry is recognized and his immense popularity in the United States is appreciatively granted, Whitman sees the English poet as a reactionary force in the face of democratic progress. Whitman was a fervent political democrat, and his poetry maintains a rugged, free style and tone that is far removed from the polished phrases of Tennyson's work. Despite these differences, Whitman values Tennyson as a poet and his opinions as a marker against which he, and those like him, can measure themselves and can consider their own convictions. Whitman recognizes the genuineness of Tennyson's character and perspective and how his nondemocratic ideologies are natural and sincere to him. The extract presents a remarkably honest and balanced critical appreciation of Tennyson by a fellow poet who, in both his art and political beliefs, was decidedly different from the English laureate. Readers must decide whether Whitman's position can be maintained, as he himself hints at in the extract's opening lines, because the development of democracy is considered by him to be unstoppable at the time. That democrats can "well afford" the conservative warnings of Tennyson or Thomas Carlyle because the rate of progressive change is sometimes excessive makes Whitman's generous and sympathetic position perhaps more easily understood.

The course of progressive politics (democracy) is so certain and resistless, not only in America but in Europe, that we can well afford the warning calls, threats, checks, neutralizings, in imaginative literature, or any department, of such deep-sounding and high-soaring voices as Carlyle's and Tennyson's. Nay, the blindness, excesses, of the prevalent tendency—the dangers of the urgent trends of our times—in my opinion, need such voices almost more than any. I should, too, call it a signal instance of democratic humanity's luck that it has such enemies to contend with—so candid, so fervid, so heroic. But why do I say enemies? Upon the whole is not Tennyson—and was not Carlyle (like an honest and stern physician)—the true friend of our age?

Let me assume to pass verdict, or perhaps momentary judgment, for the United States on this poet—a remov'd and distant position giving some advantages over a nigh one. What is Tennyson's service to his race, times, and especially to America? First, I should say—or at least not forget—his personal character. He is not to be mention'd as a rugged, evolutionary, aboriginal force—but (and a great lesson is in it) he has been consistent throughout with the native, healthy, patriotic spinal element and promptings of himself. His moral line is local and conventional, but it is vital and genuine. He reflects the upper-crust of his time, its pale cast of thought—even its *ennui*. Then the simile of my friend John Burroughs is entirely true, 'his glove is a glove of silk, but the hand is a hand of iron.' He shows how one can be a royal laureate, quite elegant and 'aristocratic,' and a little queer and affected, and at the same time perfectly manly and natural. As to his non-democracy, it fits him well, and I like him the better for it. I guess we all like to have (I am sure I do) some one who presents those sides of a thought, or possibility, different from our own—different and yet with a sort of home-likeness—a tartness and contradiction offsetting the theory as we view it, and construed from tastes and proclivities not at all his own.

To me, Tennyson shows more than any poet I know (perhaps has been a warning to me) how much there is in finest verbalism. There is such a latent charm in mere words, cunning collocations, and in the voice ringing them, which he has caught and brought out, beyond all others—as in the line,

And hollow, hollow, hollow, all delight,

in 'The Passing of Arthur,' and evidenced in 'The Lady of Shalott,' 'The Deserted House,' and many other pieces. Among the best (I often linger over them again and again) are 'Lucretius,' 'The Lotos Eaters,' and 'The Northern Farmer.' His mannerism is great, but it is a noble and welcome mannerism. His very best work, to me, is contain'd in the books of *The Idyls of the King*, and all that has grown out of them. Though indeed we could spare nothing of Tennyson, however small or however peculiar—not 'Break, Break,' nor 'Flower in the Crannied Wall,' nor the old, eternally-told passion of 'Edward Gray:'

> Love may come and love may go,
>> And fly like a bird from tree to tree.
>>> But I will love no more, no more
>>>> Till Ellen Adair come back to me.

Yes, Alfred Tennyson's is a superb character, and will help give illustriousness, through the long roll of time, to our Nineteenth Century. In its bunch of orbic names, shining like a constellation of stars, his will be one of the brightest. His very faults, doubts, swervings, doublings upon himself, have been typical of our age. We are like the voyagers of a ship, casting off for new seas, distant shores. We would still dwell in the old suffocating and dead haunts, remembering and magnifying their pleasant experiences only, and more than once impell'd to jump ashore before it is too late, and stay where our fathers stay'd, and live as they lived.

May-be I am non-literary and non-decorous (let me at least be human, and pay part of my debt) in this word about Tennyson. I want him to realize that here is a great and ardent Nation that absorbs his songs, and has a respect and affection for him personally, as almost for no other foreigner. I want this word to go to the old man at Farringford as conveying no more than the simple truth; and that truth (a little Christmas gift) no slight one either. I have written impromptu, and shall let it all go at that. The readers of more than fifty millions of people in the New World not only owe to him some of their most agreeable and harmless and healthy hours, but he has enter'd into the formative influences of character here, not only in the Atlantic cities, but inland and far West, out in Missouri, in Kansas, and away in Oregon, in farmer's house and miner's cabin.

Best thanks, anyhow, to Alfred Tennyson—thanks and appreciation in America's name.

> —Walt Whitman, "A Word about Tennyson,"
> 1887, *Prose Works,* ed. Floyd Stovall, 1964, vol. 2,
> pp. 570–72

J. M. Robertson "The Art of Tennyson" (1889)

In the following extract, J. M. Robertson gives a detailed analysis of Tennyson's verse from his early poetry to the later dramas at the end of the century. Robertson from the outset states his preference for the art of the poet's younger years and provides numerous examples from the works themselves to justify his position. Readers will have noted in many extracts that the majority of critical opinions favor the earlier poetry over the later works, and those fewer critics who attempt to see a strain of development connecting the elderly poet of the late nineteenth century with the youth of the early years of Victoria's reign, often themselves find that something of value had to be set aside to allow the poet's progress toward a more refined art.

Robertson begins the extract by considering "Locksley Hall Sixty Years After" (1886), a sequel to Tennyson's "Locksley Hall" written in 1835 and published in 1842. The later poem Robertson finds to be weighed down by didacticism and accusatory cant against the modern age, and the critic suggests that to find anything worth redeeming in the poem its art must be considered apart from its teaching. This is essentially what Robertson proceeds to do for the remainder of the extract.

Examining first Tennyson's earliest work and comparing it to the verse of Swinburne, Robertson claims that the former, through careful working upon his craft, surpassed the latter poet's more natural gifts in both his lyricism and his thought. Remarking upon Poe's, Coleridge's, and Swinburne's criticism of the younger Tennyson's verse for lapsing metrically on occasion, Robertson claims that the young poet soon overcame these flaws through an assiduous attention to editing and revision and by learning from his earlier mistakes. The extract proceeds to examine several early poems and lines of Tennyson's to show how the poet's craft was improved and bettered. Robertson highlights *Maud* and "The Lotus-Eaters" as the greatest of the poet's works, the former for its sustained passion and lyrical voice, the latter as the finest example of the formal excellence that Tennyson's verse ultimately achieved.

Robertson says that Tennyson is and was no philosopher, and it is when he is moralizing, as in "Locksley Hall Sixty Years After," or, in different manner but amounting to the same thing, in *Idylls of the King*, that the poet is a failure. He is described as being a cultured man considering what all cultured men might think upon, and it is rather in the presentation of these thoughts than in the thoughts themselves that Tennyson's vocation as a poet should be found. *Idylls of the King* is described as being a "Euphuism," an attempt to renovate an archaism in the modern age. The critic finds it sentimental and affected, as did Thomas Carlyle, whom Robertson quotes, in his criticism of the poem (see the extract contained later in this volume). Tennyson's characters and thought are finest when matched naturally to his lyrical gifts, rather than when they are forced by the tale he attempts to tell. Again, Robertson finds the earlier verses greatest where the poet provides such a synchronicity, highlighting *Idylls of the King* as an example of the unnatural delineation of character and of Tennyson's affected philosophizing.

Readers are provided with a detailed analysis of Tennyson's art in this extract. Robertson examines individual lines in the poet's catalog, comparing different editions and revisions of the same poems, and with them tracing a sense of development in the poet's career. His comments on Tennyson's drama might be compared to the later reviews of *Queen Mary*, *Becket* and *Harold* included in this volume, and this critical overview of the poet's long career should be beneficial to readers when compared to those others seeking to trace a common thread throughout Tennyson's works.

Laying down the new 'Locksley Hall' and taking up the solider volume that contains the old; turning over the familiar leaves, noting many a well-known strain and scanning anew some only half-remembered, one is moved to ask some grave questions concerning the poet who has woven all that divers-coloured web of song. It is not wonderful, considering all he must have heard of the lofty function of the poet and of his own lofty performance, that he should in these latter years assume so frequently as he has done the guise of the prophet: it is not wonderful, but it becomes a little trying. For one thing, the ermine of the peer *will* trail its ceremonious length below the seer's exiguous mantle; and an ancient echo about kind hearts and coronets seems to lend itself malignly to fantastic variations. But there are graver grounds of question. These last outcries over human hopes and human strivings, these raging indictments against to-day's life as compared with yesterday's, how do they ring beside some dozen of the different notes we recall from the older music? By the last account, with its rhymed recapitulation of the bad-blooded objurgations of gout-stricken Toryism, we moderns, having 'risen from out the beast', are lapsing 'back into the beast again,' what with Atheism, Zolaism, Radicalism, extension of the franchise, and disestablishment. That being so, we must needs take what pensive satisfaction we can in those earlier musings of the time when, the laureate being young instead of old, and poor instead of rich in publishers' royalties, the universe so accommodatingly taught such a different lesson. And even as we con the earlier song, there rise up before us a few merely prosaic contrasts between the lyric organism and its environment. They are almost as piquant in their way as the poet's own more inspired visions of to-day. A quarter of a century or more ago, there is painful reason to believe, there was 'incest in the warrens of the poor', prostitution, impurity, murderous misery, and all the rest of it; and about those times our poet was inditing, among other things, welcomes to Alexandra, hallelujahs to the Queen, and hosannas to the Duke of Wellington *in excelsis*. One year the admiring world would have a snatch on the higher Pantheism; in another, such a product of the higher Jingoism as 'The Third of February, 1852', in which the singer is so patriotically successful in proving that the laureate of England can at a pinch beat any *poseur* of anarchic France at his own weapons of newspaper fustian and hustings braggadocio. If his lordship's career as a publicist could only be reviewed by an equally gifted *vates sacer*, in a temper something like that which has inspired his latest efforts, it might furnish a very tolerable companion-piece. The lofty and other sentiments of the young lover of the first 'Locksley Hall', with the commentary which represents the personal element in the poem to have included the vulgarly malignant vituperation by a rejected lover of a better man than himself; the chronic hysterical war-whoop of the muse which achieved the definition of 'this French God, the child of Hell, wild War'; the operose heroics over that undertaker's apotheosis, the funeral of the Duke; the general inculcation of high-mindedness, and the interludes of assiduous incense-burning before that imposing piece of upholstery, the British throne:—a prose-writing Swift, in the absence of another Tennyson, might make a very pretty picture of human imbecility out of it all. And if good is to be done in this world by unpacking our mouths with words and falling a-cursing over the teachings we cannot agree with, it ought to be somebody's business to do for the Laureate what he does with such a will for his contemporaries in general.

Alas! the situation is poignant enough without any splenetic or dithyrambic comment. We need no pessimist to point for us the moral of these murky utterances of the grey-haired singer, the sting of these acrid taunts at the high hopes of his own youth. His mere self-expression, as such, will go as far as any item in his catalogue of ills to create among the fit audience the impression he has so eagerly sought to convey; and if anything can obviate a sense of bitterness in the recipients it will be their perception of the bitterness of the poet's own self-consciousness. No critic can exult over such a demonstration of the fallacy of the inveterate habit of viewing poets as teachers with a clearer and further view of things than other men. It is no satisfaction to have such a proof that the miraculous singer can be as weak and unmagnanimous as any of those he affects to scorn, as far as they from the white light of truth, as false as they to his own ideals. Nor, when we have weighed his teaching in the balances and found it so wofully wanting, can we afford to hold him in the mere contempt in which he so lavishly enfolds his generation; for these very flaws of his are in a manner a penalty attaching to the work he has done for us. It has been half-jestingly half-sadly said that actors and some others are to be regarded as suffering in their own personalities for the sake of those they entertain; and so it is with the poet in his degree. He too must 'go here and there, and make himself a motley to the view, gore his own thoughts, sell cheap what is most dear, make old offences of affections new'. Most flattered of all the artist tribe, he must dree his weird like the rest. We say he is no authoritative teacher, but yet it is in his destiny that the impulse to teach is his highest inspiration, recognizable as such both by himself and his listeners. His song must be beautiful if it is to conquer men; yet if he seeks only beauty his search will never lead him to beauty of the highest kind; which he is doomed to attain only in striving after that moral truth which he is not fated to reach. He is part of the 'riddle of the painful earth', not its unraveller. We shall gain nothing by turning on him a lowering brow; and we shall accordingly do well to deal with the vices of Tennyson's teaching as we might deal with the vices of other poets' lives, as something to be considered apart from his art, if at all, the art being, when all is done, his net performance and our clear gain.

For Tennyson is a great artist, let him now rack his voice and his theme as he will. It must surely have been the constraint of the etiquette of criticism in regard to contemporaries that made Mr. Lowell the other year say of Gray that 'he was the greatest artist in words that Cambridge has produced'. Gray is indeed the most consummate artist, properly speaking, in English poetry down to Tennyson's time, but even Mr. Lowell may safely be defied to draw up such a case for the finished craftsman of last century as can be made out for the one of to-day. Making all due allowance for the amount of artistic cerebration that went to the doing of such work as the 'Elegy'—an allowance apt to be unfairly withheld by critics who dwell on the various sources of the material which the poet has built into his structure—Gray's performance can bear no comparison with Tennyson's, whether in point of range, power, charm, finish, or masterly ease. His best work is not more pregnant than Tennyson's best; there is much less of it; and it is always less perfectly melodious. The later singer came into a heritage of song such as the earlier had not known: he found a tradition of freshness and freedom, where the other came under a burden of scruple and formality. In sheer devotion to art, however, Tennyson stands out even more notably from his contemporaries than did Gray; his bias being made only the more obvious by his early shortcomings. Mr. Swinburne has indicated these with, as usual, all imaginable emphasis.

> There are whole poems of Lord Tennyson's first period which are no more properly to be called metrical than the more shapeless and monstrous parts of Walt Whitman; which are lineally derived as to their form—if form that can be called where form is none—from the vilest example set by Cowley, when English verse was first infected and convulsed by the detestable duncery of sham Pindarics. At times, of course, his song was then as sweet as ever it has sounded since; but he could never make sure of singing right for more than a few minutes or stanzas. The strenuous drill through which since then he has felt it necessary to put himself has done all that hard labour can do to rectify this congenital complaint; by dint of stocks and backboard he has taught himself a more graceful and upright carriage.[1]

I do not remember that Mr. Swinburne has ever thought it necessary to speak of *Queen Mab* with a judicial fervour proportionate to the above; but, allowing for the dialect, the central judgment as to Tennyson's early need and practice of drill is sufficiently well founded; Mr. Swinburne's verdict having important though verbally inadequate support in the opinions long ago independently expressed on Tennyson's metre by Coleridge and Poe,[2] of whom the first was not unfriendly to Tennyson, while the second admired him intensely. Coleridge said:—

> The misfortune is that he [Tennyson] has begun to write verses without very well understanding what metre is. Even if you write in a well-known and approved metre, the odds are, if you are not a metrist yourself, that you will not write harmonious verses; but to deal in new metres without considering what metre means and requires, is preposterous. What I would, with many wishes for success, prescribe to Tennyson—indeed without it he can never be a poet in act—is to write for the next two or three years in none but one or two well-known and strictly defined metres, such as the heroic couplet, the octave stanza, or the octo-syllabic measure of the Allegro and Penseroso. He would, probably, thus get imbued with a sensation, if not a sense, of metre without knowing it, just as Eton boys get to write such good Latin verses(!) by conning Ovid and Tibullus. As it is, I can scarcely scan his verses.[3]

Poe in his essay on 'The Poetic Principle' says of Tennyson: 'In perfect sincerity, I regard him as the noblest poet that ever lived'; but in another passage, after expressing and elaborating a similar opinion, he writes:

> Tennyson's shorter pieces abound in minute rhythmical lapses sufficient to assure me that—in common with all poets living or dead(!)—he has neglected to make precise investigation of the principles of metre; but, on the other hand, so perfect is his rhythmical instinct in general, that, like the present Viscount Canterbury, he seems *to see with his ear*.[4]

The closing qualification is to Poe's critical credit. After all, far too much is made by all three censors of the faults of Tennyson's juvenile work; metrical laxity belonging in more or less degree to the early compositions of the great majority of poets. Tennyson's 'first period', be it remembered, was a very youthful period indeed, and it is to this that Coleridge's criticism must apply. He cannot have been speaking of the poems published in 1833, the best of which show, to say the least, as strong a sense of metre as his own; and when he animadverts as he does on the first volume, issued in 1830, he must have been thinking of what Mr. Swinburne calls the sham Pindarics, which bulk very largely in it. And even of these it is only fair to say that they show rather an early proclivity to wandering measures than an incapacity for strict metre. There are, no doubt, metrical lapses in 'A Dirge', but 'The Sleeping Beauty' is flawless, sufficiently showing that Coleridge's *de haut en bas* suggestions were not needed. At all events, they were not taken; the young poet discarding his Pindarics, but choosing other metres than Coleridge had prescribed. What is really proved, however, by his early sowing of his wild oats and his speedy reformation, is the immense part that may be performed by careful art in the production of the very finest poetry. There is no more remarkable lesson to be learned from a comparison of Tennyson's work with Mr. Swinburne's than this, that the element of inspiration or cerebral excitement, which as it were gives flight to the poet's song, may be possessed in unfailing abundance without securing real poetic success, while a muse that is lacking on that side, to the point even of occasional serious discomfiture, may yet by stress of patient art produce a mass of work that is entirely lovely. Such at least is the fashion in which I am fain to figure to myself the explanation of the fact that Mr. Swinburne, while apparently incapable of such lapses into crass prose as are undeniably committed at times by Tennyson, yet so generally turns out what is to me but tortured verbiage, while Tennyson, despite his 'congenital infirmity'—very real in this regard—so often yields me golden song. There is, indeed, this to be said for the elder poet, that almost from the first he has grappled with artistic difficulties which the younger has from first to last avoided. There is much significance in Mr. Swinburne's attack on Mr. Arnold for taking as poetic themes ideas which are 'flat' and uninspiring. While praising Mr. Arnold's *Empedocles*—in part at least—Mr. Swinburne[5] remarks that 'elsewhere, in minor poems, Mr. Arnold . . . has now and then given signs of sweeping up dead leaves fallen from the dying tree of belief'; in objecting to which practice Mr. Swinburne ostensibly follows a French critic who appears to insist that poetry can only arise out of emotions of a positive or violent order. Further on he appears to reiterate the same doctrine thus: 'This alone I find profitless and painful in his [Mr. Arnold's] work; this occasional habit (sic) of harking back and loitering in mind among the sepulchres. Nothing is to be made by an artist out of scepticism, half-hearted or double-hearted doubts or creeds; nothing out of mere dejection and misty mental weather. Tempest or calm you may put to use, but hardly a flat fog.' I confess I can make nothing out of an antithesis of this kind, in which a fog is treated as something negative and a calm as something positive; and my difficulty is only deepened when Mr. Swinburne goes on to say that 'Deep-reaching doubt and "large discourse" are poetical, so is faith, so are sorrow and joy; but so are not the small troubles of spirits that nibble and quibble about beliefs living or dead; so are not those sickly moods which are warmed and weakened (sic) by feeding on the sullen drugs of dejection,' &c. All that can distinctly be gathered from such a deliverance is that Mr. Swinburne does not like verse that is vaguely melancholy, preferring either joy or black despair: of reasoned justification for the judgment there is none. We have no canon to enable us to distinguish even between 'deep-reaching doubt' and 'sickly moods', to say nothing of the more recondite distinction between such doubt and 'scepticism' pure and simple, or 'half-hearted or double-hearted doubts or creeds': we are simply driven to the conclusion that Mr. Swinburne, disliking the sentiment of certain verses, relieved his mind in some appropriate rhetoric which pretended to be technical criticism, but possessed no such character. Such an utterance is the more surprising as coming from a writer who, however questionable may be some of his technical judgments—notably in the case of the poetry of Mr. Rossetti—is in general so catholic in his recognition of the scope of poetic art and of the artistic values of verse. Such a criticism is fitly followed by the extravagantly unsound dictum that 'When the thought goes wrong, the verse follows after it,'—as if poetry were a matter of propositions. It will never do thus to make our sympathy with or antipathy to a poet's philosophical attitude a ground for deciding that his poetry is not poetical. It is certainly not clear which of Mr. Arnold's poems Mr. Swinburne has in view, as he seems to praise in one place verses which would be thought to come under his ban in another;

but, taking his hostile dicta as they stand, they are once for all refuted by Mr. Arnold's production of fine verse on the very motives interdicted. The truth is, of course, that different poetic idiosyncrasies yield different kinds of verse; that Mr. Arnold is after all, more of a thinker than Mr. Swinburne; and that he can find a lasting dynamic quality in ideas to which Mr. Swinburne instinctively gives a wide berth. These he transmutes into poetry just because he has been profoundly impressed by them. And so, in a different way, Tennyson is capable of poetically transfiguring themes which Mr. Swinburne never thinks of handling, such as those of 'The Miller's Daughter', 'The May Queen', 'Enoch Arden', 'The Gardener's Daughter', 'The Talking Oak', 'Sea Dreams': at least, if the younger singer were to take up such motives, he would infallibly denaturalize them in order to get his due poetic elevation. When Mr. Swinburne goes about to praise anybody in prose, he raises, as a journalist said the other day, a tumulus of laudatory adjectives and substantives; and he does the same sort of thing in all his verse. Simple pregnancy is as far from him as the gift of surrounding an every-day subject with beauty by an 'imperceptible heightening' of the every-day tone. Turning over his volumes, you find a constant hankering after themes that are either antique, or mediŒval, or abnormal; and when they are modern without being abnormal, there is still a constant reliance on the device of archaic diction—one of the easiest methods of being unprosaic, but perhaps also one of the surest signs of a want of the highest poetic originality. Now in Tennyson you will find in general a reaching towards modern naturalness of speech, a preference for simple constructions, similar to that shown and argued for by Wordsworth; though a sense of Wordsworth's frightfully precarious fortune in applying his principle evidently caused the pupil to swerve from the rule of the master. As compared with Swinburne, he is for the most part a realist both in choice of poetic subject and in poetic style, his language having, with certain exceptions, a bias to naturalism even when he treats what would be called elevated themes; while Mr. Swinburne, as has been said, brings to bear on all his subjects alike a style of inordinate and artificial magniloquence; securing elevation indeed without fail, but leaving a critical reader fatigued and nauseated with his waste of sound and fury, and at bottom psychologically untouched. He may move many readers by the sheer contagion of his sibylline excitement; but the piercing power of chosen and welded words, the high art of making a line so eternally living that it can in an instant, at the twentieth coming, clutch our very hearts and stir the deepest wells of unshed tears—this is beyond him, or at least is hardly attained by him once in a thousand pages. If, then, Tennyson falls at times into mere bathos and Swinburne never does, it is to be remembered that the former runs the extra risk by, so to speak, sailing much more closely in the wind's eye than the other; and that the latter secures his immunity by such an exclusive cultivation of the orotund as makes the bulk of his work a mere weariness of the flesh, or at best a marvel of futile fecundity, to the initiated lover of verse; raising, to take a late instance, such a pother of vocables by way of suggesting the fragile personalities of children, as to fatally recall Goldsmith's anticipation of how Johnson would make the little fishes talk like the whales. Tennyson's very mishaps, in short, are found to involve a proof that he has by far the wider artistic range. All this being so, however, it will still hold that his excellences are emphatically the outcome of patient workmanship; that he is, as has been said, above all things an artist.

One of the prominent proofs of the constant care the Laureate has taken to perfect himself in his art is the extent to which he has suppressed the weaker work of his young days, and from time to time retouched for the better very many of his more successful performances. It is probably not generally known that out of the 154 pages of his first volume of *Poems, Chiefly Lyrical*, he afterwards withdrew from his works as much as 61 pages, or two-fifths of the book. There can be no doubt that the suppressed pieces on the whole deserved their fate, being with hardly an exception unimpressive in conception and unsuccessful in execution; though the variety of rhythmical experiment is, it should be said, sufficiently remarkable as coming from a youth of barely twenty. But, as Mr. Swinburne admits, some of the successful poems in the first volume are as finely turned as anything he has done since. The 'melody' which now, as then, stands first in the collection of his poems, is practically perfect to the extent of two-thirds—the only emendation found necessary in the first two stanzas being the change of 'bee low hummeth' to 'wild bee hummeth'—though the awkward succession of dentals in the last stanza makes a feeble finish. And in the middle stanza there may be found, I think, an interesting proof of the care which the young poet was already capable of exercising in his work, though he was not yet grown circumspect enough all round. It runs, as most readers will remember:

> At eve the beetle boometh
> Athwart the thicket lone;
> At noon the wild bee hummeth
> About the mossed headstone;
> At midnight the moon cometh
> And looketh down alone.

Here the proper order of time is departed from—eve coming before noon—probably in order that the rhymes shall fall to the best advantage. I have no information on the subject, but I have an intuition that the poet at first put the third and fourth lines first and second, and then wrote, 'At eve the beetle *drummeth*'; but that, rightly deciding that 'drummeth' would spoil the whole stanza, and having no nearer sound than 'boometh' left him, he decided to put eve before noon in order to have the proper rhyme value of 'hummeth' and 'cometh,' which would be in large part lost if 'boometh' came between. Similarly, in the later poem, 'The Lotos-Eaters,' one strongly suspects that it was only after some trouble that the author was content to make the first and third lines both end in 'land': he probably tried at first some such locution as 'pointed with his hand,' deciding, perhaps for once a little lazily, to use 'land' twice because he could not bring in 'hand' satisfactorily. But the finest samples of the poet's 'prentice-work are, I think, the admirable poem, miscalled a song, beginning 'A spirit haunts the year's last hours'; the three stanzas of 'The Sleeping Beauty,' which were later embodied in 'The Day Dream', but appeared as a separate poem in the volume of 1830; and 'Mariana'; and in these there is little alteration. The first remains unchanged, needing no improvement; and in the second there are just a few differences in the later version, as 'She lying on her couch alone' for 'The while she slumbereth alone'; 'Across' for 'Over' in the third line; and 'broider'd' for 'braided.' Its music was thus substantially perfect, well deserving the fervent praise bestowed on it by Poe. Here, and in 'Mariana', was seen that gift of close observation, the power of the 'seeing eye', so warmly commended by Mr. Swinburne; and in the short piece on 'The Kraken', too, we have the earnest of a fresh kind of achievement in our literature, that weaving of the ideas or the fancies of science into harmonious poetry without loss of the scientific outline, in respect of which Tennyson stands apart from those poets, like Shelley, who have paraphrased such ideas into allegories, as well as from those who, like Mr. Swinburne, steadfastly leave science alone.

Not, however, till the publication of the volume of 1833 could the most clear-sighted reader have seen that the new singer's endowment was really great. Within the three years he had produced a body of work which left his first collection far behind; which indeed included a greater number of short pieces destined to become classic than are to be found in any other volume of English verse, of similar size, ever published. Now it was that English readers were first charmed by the rich chords and the novel modulations of 'The Lady of Shalott'; the tender music of 'The Miller's Daughter'; the new and masterly blank-verse of 'Œnone'; the incomparable blending of form and colour in 'The Palace of Art' and 'A Dream of Fair Women'; and the absolutely unmatchable beauty of 'The Lotos Eaters'. Here was art such as the generation of Wordsworth, Coleridge, Byron, and Shelley, had not yet seen. Art for art's sake indeed might seem to be the object of the poet's pursuit when he appended to 'The Palace of Art' footnotes explaining what his plan had been, giving specimens of excluded sections of the poem, in which he had given other views of the palace than those in the text, and intimating how hard it was to design statues in verse.[6] In 'A Dream of Fair Women' again, where, speaking of Chaucer, he tells how 'for a while *the knowledge of his art held me above the subject*', there is a material inconsistency which the poet has never remedied, much as he has retouched his earlier work, and which, there can be no doubt, he introduced and allowed to stand just because the inconsistent segment was by itself such a perfect piece of workmanship. It is the song of the daughter of Jephthah. Thus he introduces it, after the glowing picture of Cleopatra:

> Slowly my sense undazzled. Then I heard
>   A noise of someone coming thro' the lawn,
> And singing clearer than the crested bird
>   That claps his wings at dawn.

I hardly dare to ask myself, on this stanza, whether 'the crested bird', so admirably named whoever he be, is he that was erst hight Chanticleer; and, assuming him to be that familiar fowl, I am as loth to decide honestly whether the figure is or is not bathetic. But one thing is obtrusively plain, that the verbal music of the virgin's song, thus heralded, should be lyrically incomplex, implying by its simplicity and spontaneity of flow a vocal solo, whose charm lies in its soprano silveriness and beauty of outline. But what have we here—

> The torrent brooks of hallow'd Israel
>   From craggy hollows pouring, late and soon,
> Sound all night long, in falling thro' the dell
>   Far-heard beneath the moon.

> The balmy moon of blessed Israel
>   Floods all the deep-blue gloom with beams divine:
> All night the splinter'd crags that wall the dell
>   With spires of silver shine.

—? Harmony of the very richest kind: hardly a noun without its choicely-fitted adjective: the entire strain packed with tone and colour, stroke upon stroke and chord upon chord, till the whole throbs with music like the charmed thunder of a noble organ. Jephthah's daughter could hardly sing an orchestral andante! The poet knows perfectly the structure and the effect of his interlude, for he goes on:

As one that museth where broad sunshine laves
The lawn by some cathedral, thro'the door
Hearing the holy organ rolling waves
Of sound on roof and floor . . .
     so stood I—

a rather different account from the preliminary parallel of the crested bird of dawn. The incongruity is complete; and yet I fancy we can most of us pardon it for the music's sake, though indeed it might have been averted by the simple sacrifice of the bird, and by, say, making the singer accompany herself on a stringed instrument. An artist who can give us such work is not to be quarrelled with for a trifle; and there are a hundred perfect touches in the same poem to atone for a solitary perversity. We cannot now well conceive what were the feelings of the competent readers of fifty years ago when they turned over the pages of that second volume; but it seems as if there must have been something ecstatic in the sensations of the more tasteful over such a succession of beauties as make up each of the great poems in the book.

A critic enamoured of the past has somewhere complained that our literature is poor in 'gnomic phrases' as compared with those of Greece and Rome; citing among others, if I remember rightly, a phrase of Apuleius—'inevitabiles oculos magnae Veneris', 'great Venus's inevitable eyes'—as a sample of what we cannot do; but one might cite a dozen equally fine coinages from Tennyson's second volume alone. Take 'the maiden splendours of the morning star'—not pure gold perhaps, but still a fine phrase; or 'the star-like sorrows of immortal eyes'; or 'the spacious times of great Elizabeth'—a doubtful proposition certainly, but again a mighty line; or 'brow-bound with burning gold'; or 'the tearful glimmer of the languid dawn'; or even 'those dragon eyes of anger'd Eleanor'—all out of 'A Dream of Fair Women'. So far from there being any suspicion of a lack of 'sense for metre' here, the metre and the sense, in the best lines, are perhaps more thoroughly interpenetrative than in any previous verse in the language. Let one passage be conned as proof:

There was no motion in the dumb dead air,
  Not any song of bird or sound of rill;
Gross darkness of the inner sepulchre
  Is not so deadly still

As that wide forest. Growths of jasmine[7] turn'd
  Their humid arms festooning tree to tree,
And at the root thro' lush green grasses burn'd
  The red anemone.

I do not think it is possible to get anything more perfectly canorous, and at the same time more simply forceful, in English poetry than these lines, especially the two last. And almost as adroit a sequence of words occurs in a descriptive stanza of a more difficult kind, though here the adroitness lapses into noticeable artifice:

Squadrons and squares of men in brazen plates,
  Scaffolds, still sheets of water, divers woes,
Ranges of glimmering vaults with iron grates,
  And hush'd seraglios.

The close is perfect, but 'divers woes' is a too palpable patch. How masterly, however, is this:

'Moreover it is written that my race
  Hew'd Ammon, hip and thigh, from Aroer
On Arnon unto Minneth.' Here her face
  Glow'd, as I look'd at her.

She lock'd her lips: she left me where I stood;
  'Glory to God,' she sang, and past afar,
Thridding the sombre boskage of the wood,
  Toward the morning star.

With an artist who can electrify language so, I suppose we must infer a certain touch of indolence when we find him leaving in such a poem, after all these years, two such lines as these:

The times when I remember to have been
  Joyful and free from blame.

But against that one unredeemedly weak stroke in the 'Dream', there are to be gratefully reckoned some emendations so extensive and decisive as to make the remaining blemish seem a small thing to complain of.

It is the Rev. Mr. Fleay who, in dedicating his *Shakspere Manual* to Tennyson, declares that the Laureate, 'had he not elected to be the greatest poet of his time, might easily have become its greatest critic'. This and other praises of Tennyson's judgment in connection with Shaksperology[8] I doubtless proceed upon personal knowledge; but while outsiders are not in a position to endorse such a conclusion as Mr. Fleay's—while, indeed, they will incline to gravely suspect it of extravagance—they can find data enough in the poet's revision of his own work to satisfy them that his critical power is indeed high. No poet, I believe, has rewritten so much as he; and probably none has ever retouched with anything like such perfect judgment. Wordsworth, for instance, can in no case be safely assumed to have improved his work when he altered it. His well-known but generally misquoted[9] line in the 'Elegiac Stanzas' on a picture of Peele Castle—'the light that never was on sea or land',—stood so in the first appearance of the poem in 1807; but in the edition of 1820 we have:

> a gleam
> Of lustre known to neither sea nor land;

and in that of 1827 the slight modification of 'the gleam, the lustre'; and as it was only in 1832 that Wordsworth had the wisdom to restore the matchless original, some non-copyright editions, as the Chandos, have the tasteless intermediate reading. In 'The Solitary Reaper', again, one line has been changed twice and another thrice, and in each case it may well be doubted whether the first form was not best. It will be found impossible to convict Tennyson of any such unprosperous second thoughts. His more important revisions are always happy, and there is no more striking achievement of the kind in our literature than the extensive emendation he has made on the first cast of 'The Lotos-Eaters'—now, to my judgment, the masterpiece of all English poetic art, strictly considered as such. A few alterations, always judicious, have been made in single lines and phrases; the line 'Full-faced above the valley stood the moon' being a substitution for 'Above the valley burned the golden moon', where the cadence made a monotony with the context which the spondee 'full-faced' dissolves; and 'Three silent pinnacles of aged snow' having taken the place of the too ambitious 'Three thunder-cloven thrones of oldest snow'. Then we have 'watch' for 'hear', before 'the *emerald-colour'd* water falling'; and 'barren peak' for 'flowery peak'; and even a finikin excision of the plural in 'eyelids still', and of the possessive in 'river's seaward flow', in accordance with a view on which the poet has acted in several other cases, that a final and an initial sibilant should not come together. But the great improvement in the revised poem—in addition to the gain of the present sixth section, an exquisite piece which did not appear in the volume of 1833—is the insertion of the noble passage from 'We have had enough of action and of motion we' to the end, in the place of forty lines of irregular and entirely boyish versification, possessing neither dignity nor adequate melody. It is nothing short of startling to compare such facile jingle as this—

And the dark pine weeps,
And the lithe vine creeps,
And the heavy melon sleeps
On the level of the shore—

with the glorious harmony of those immortal later lines in which, shifting his key and his measure, the poet so strangely and so finely rises from the perfect loveliness of the lotos-eaters' self-regarding song to a strain of intense and thrilling brilliance, pitched at as high a level of moral inspiration as the great poets of the world have ever reached. Magistral as Milton at his greatest, but subtle beyond his scope, and informed with even a richer art than his, the strain that limns the life of the Olympian Gods is one of the supreme possessions of the English tongue; and it exists for us as the amends made by the poet for an ill-planned piece of youthful composition which his mature judgment could not tolerate.

Certainly the change makes good anything that Mr. Swinburne or any of his predecessors has said on the all-importance of form and measure. The enduring beauty of 'The Lotos-Eaters' rests as a whole on its rigorous regard to metrical law; the deleted passage being one of those early experimental performances in loose-flowing verse, of which the 1833 volume furnishes another ineffectual sample in 'The Hesperides', which, a reader feels, might have been a fine poem if only the singer had resolutely bitted and reined his wandering fancy as he did in the great poems he published at the same time. For in the face of these it is clear that Mr. Swinburne's theory of a constitutional weakness of spine which only the back-board could cure, is one of the most gratuitous of that authority's rhetorical flights. We are dealing with a case in which a poet set out with an equipment of splendid artistic gifts in company with one or two vicious propensities, which last, when he saw whither they led him, he speedily and entirely discarded. And this was but one exhibition of a capacity of artistic self-criticism which asserts itself in other ways than in the abandonment of a mistaken theory of versification. There were other errors of taste in these first poems. Thus in 'A Dream of

Fair Women', in Iphigenia's account of her death, we have in the first version, which was still allowed to stand in the edition of 1842, this unpleasant and awkward passage:

> One drew a sharp knife thro' my tender throat
>   Slowly,—and nothing more;

now supplanted by the every way happier lines:

> The bright death quiver'd at the victim's throat;
>   Touch'd; and I knew no more.

Then, in Cleopatra's reverie on Mark Antony, in place of the two stanzas beginning, 'The man, my lover', there originally stood three, in which were these lines:

> The glories of great Julius lapse and wane
>   And shrink from suns to stars—

(that cheap conceit being of course begot by the need of a rhyme to 'Mars')—

> That man of all the men I ever knew
>   Most took my fancy;

> What sweet words, only made
> Less sweet by the kiss that broke 'em, liking best
> To be so richly stayed—

the last about as insufferable a piece of Elizabethanism as any modern has turned out. At the beginning of the poem, too, there originally stood four stanzas, embodying an ill-chosen figure in which 'the Poet' was vaingloriously enough presented as 'self-poised' like a man in a balloon, 'hearing apart the echoes of his fame'; the deletion of which youthfully self-sufficient prologue allows the poem to begin much more naturally and efficiently, as it now stands. Again, there is quite a multitude of alterations in 'The Lady of Shalott' since the first version, the reason for the changes being not so much inferiority of technique in that as an apparent re-conception of the theme in the poet's mind. There are, however, some curious re-arrangements of the rhymes, of which I give a few samples:

First Version.

The little isle is all inrailed,
With a rose-fence, and overtrailed
With roses; by the marge unhailed,
The shallop flitteth silken-sailed.
   * * * *

She lives with little joy or fear;
Over the water, running near,
The sheep-bell tinkles in her ear;
Before her hangs a mirror clear,
Reflecting towards Camelot.
And, as the mazy web she whirls,
   * * * *

Till her eyes were darkened wholly,
And her smooth face sharpened
slowly.
   * * * *

Present Version.

By the margin, willow-veil'd,
Slide the heavy barges trail'd
By slow horses; and unhail'd
The shallop flitteth silken-sail'd.
   * * * *

And moving thro' a mirror clear
That hangs before her all the year,
Shadows of the world appear.
There she sees the highway near,
Winding down to Camelot.
There the river eddy whirls
   * * * *

Till her blood was frozen slowly,
And her eyes were darken'd
wholly.
   * * * *

But the most decisive transformation is that made in the last stanza:

First Version.

They crossed themselves, their stars
they blest,
Knight, minstrel, abbot, squire, and
guest,
There lay a parchment on her breast,
That puzzled more than all the rest,
The well-fed wits at Camelot.
'*The web was woven curiously,*
The charm is broken utterly,
Draw near and fear not—this is I,
The Lady of Shalott.'

Present Version.

Who is this? and what is here?
And in the lighted palace near
Died the sound of royal cheer;
And they crossed themselves
fear,
All the knights at Camelot:
But Lancelot mused a little space;
He said, 'She has a lovely face;
God in his mercy lend her grace,
The Lady of Shalott.'

The deepening and heightening of the later finish is too obvious to need comment. I can conceive, however, that some readers, following such a process of technical, or, as it might be put, mechanical elaboration, will exclaim that this is surely not the method of the true poet, the 'inspired singer' of literary tradition. Assuredly the actuality does not correspond with the myth; but it is just so much the worse for the myth. The notion of a poet as a semi-divine personage who gets his rhymes and rhythms from heaven, as it were, and whose function is to convey a superior form of truth to a world whose part it is to listen to him with reverence and allude to him as 'the Poet' with a capital P—this view of the matter is no doubt very agreeable to 'the Poet', and has naturally received much support from his own deliverances on the subject; but a more rational analysis simply sets such transcendentalism aside, and reckons up the inspired one as an artistic organism of a particular kind, whose very constitution partly incapacitates him for steadiness, solidity, or real depth of thought, but whose work it is to put such ideas as he comes by into the perfectest form he can attain. He may often think soundly and nobly, if not originally; but such wisdom and elevation will avail him little as poet if he cannot charm them into the shape of beautiful speech. And the beauty of his speech is a matter of manipulation of words, just as the painter's art is a matter of handling pigments. When he strikes such a chord of rhymes as this:

> All in the blue unclouded weather,
> Thick jewell'd shone the saddle leather,
> The helmet and the helmet-feather
> Burn'd like one burning flame together,
> As he rode down to Camelot,

any one can see that he must have reckoned up the chimes at his disposal; that it must have cost him some calculation to introduce 'leather' without being absurd; and that the whole musical effect is thus no outburst of one who 'sings because he must'—that is a professional affectation which, cherishing it as he does in common with prophets and Christian warriors and other self-esteeming personages, we must be content to forgive him—but the carefully adjusted performance of a man of culture with a delicate taste in words and cadences. And he is just as much fulfilling the poetic function when he charms us with an old-world concord like that picture of Sir Lancelot, as when he weaves a larger harmony to tell of the heartless Gods of ancient song:

> For they lie beside their nectar, and the bolts are hurled
> Far below them in the valleys, and the clouds are lightly curled
> Round their golden houses, girdled with the gleaming world.

There are only four or five rhymes to 'world', and the poet's moral lesson here must needs adopt the vocables 'curled' and 'hurled', or else 'furled' and 'whirled', or 'purled'. Is it supposed that his inspiration gave him the right words without his having to stop to think? And if his specialty is admitted thus to lie in the exquisite expression of ideas rather than in the study of human problems, how shall he rank as any more of a 'teacher' than any other thoughtful man of fair thinking power who seeks to teach his fellows in speech or printed prose? The poet's propositions, as such, if they strike the reader favourably, do so because they are of a kind already made more or less common property by non-artistic means; and to credit him with pre-eminence as a thinker for thus working in intellectual material is no more reasonable than to credit with pre-eminent mental power a painter who puts into a picture a view of life that appeals to many ordinary people who have not the power to paint. In three lines in 'The Two Voices' we have a rhymed and cadenced expression of the pathos of the grave, simple but forceful:—

High up the vapours fold and swim:
About him broods the twilight dim:
The place he knew forgetteth him.

There is nothing here—no idea, that is—that has not been thought and said one way or another a thousand times: it is the utterance of a universal sentiment. But the poet chances to put it into a shape of mournful beauty, and his tercet henceforth haunts us like a profound phrase of Beethoven; and, whatever we may say about the matter, we can see perfectly well that the effect is psychologically traceable to the sheer throb of the rhythm and the climax of the consonances; that the effect, in short, is subtly aesthetic, and physiologically akin to that produced by music. And when, at the close of the early poem beginning 'My life is full of weary days', we con the stanza—

Then let wise Nature work her will,
And on my clay her darnel[10] grow;
Come only, when the days are still,
And at my headstone whisper low,
And tell me if the woodbines blow

—we become sensible of that indescribable transmutation of mood, the working of which in us is the triumph of tragic art; but here too we shall find that it is the culminating movement of the verse in the closing lines that is the added something without which the triumph had not been.

But this very finish, as it happens, is the success it is because the poet has had the judgment to discard two other stanzas which in the first version followed that quoted; stanzas good in themselves, but constituting an anti-climax to its noiseless intensity and effortless poignancy of strain. That particular revision is one of many proofs of a gift he has in perhaps a unique degree among poetic artists—the eye for an ending. I can think of no one but Keats who had previously shown a sense of the technical importance of a 'perfect close'; and even he has not always proved himself alive to it; the last stanza of the 'Ode to a Nightingale', for instance, being a partial falling away from the level of the rest of the poem. We have, however, examples of perfect success in the 'Ode to Melancholy'; in the closing line of the sonnet on Chapman's Homer:

Silent, upon a peak of Darien;

and in the even finer sonnet that ends

And faithful Petrarch, gloriously crowned.

The effect here is one of cessation while still on the wing, so to speak, as compared with the so general poetic practice of conscientiously dismounting from Pegasus in order to take leave of the reader. That Tennyson had the fullest appreciation of this secret in technique would, I think, be decisively proved, if in no other way, by the fact of his retaining in his collected poems the piece entitled 'The Captain'. That is a performance at best melodramatic in conception, and quite third-rate in execution—a rhymed story which, save for a few phrases, might have been by an average workman like Whittier. But one line, the last, is admirably perfect; and it can hardly be doubted that the poet has allowed the piece to stand mainly for the sake of that.

There the sunlit ocean tosses
  O'er them mouldering,
And the lonely seabird crosses
  With one waft of the wing.

If we must needs read a rhymed moral tale—including such a line as 'Years have *wander'd by*'—to light on such a masterly touch as that, we can afford the sacrifice. The presence of the weak elements must, of course, be put to the poet's debit, with a due protest against what one feels, in his case, to be a falling short of attainable perfection. Something must indeed be set down to 'judicial blindness' in many cases of unredeemed sins in verse; as when Wordsworth, after all his anxious alterations on 'The Solitary Reaper', left unnoticed to the last the weak tautology, 'I listened motionless and still'. So we must assume that Tennyson has somehow missed seeing the metrical and other flaws in a number of the lines of 'Aylmer's Field', and the pedestrian character of a number of the phrases in *In Memoriam*, as, 'kill'd in falling from his horse', 'the noble letters of the dead' and such a *banal* attempt at serious humour as this:

> These mortal lullabies of pain
> May bind a book, may line a box,
> May serve to curl a maiden's locks.

He duly repented of the line 'She lit white steams of dazzling gas' in the first version of 'The Palace of Art', recognizing how domestic use had pre-empted past hope of elevation the illuminant in question; and perhaps there is not for every reader, what there is for some of us, a prosaic ring in the legal phrase 'portions and parcels', which has been allowed to stand in 'The Lotos-Eaters'; or a clink as of machinery in the inapposite 'dew'd with showery drops', or in the lines about the dews on waters between walls of granite 'in a gleaming pass'—the only hints of flaw that I can discover in the poem after dreaming myself to sleep with it a thousand times. But there can be few right-thinking people who have not shuddered over that unspeakable intimation at the end of 'Enoch Arden':

> And when they buried him the little port
> Had seldom seen a costlier funeral.

Here—such is human imperfection—we have perhaps Tennyson's very worst line employed as an ending. Such an offence against the commonest sanctities of song and taste, not to say syntax, can hardly be dismissed as an artistic oversight: it must be held to point to a certain strain of commonness, of Beaconsfieldian tawdriness of sentiment, so to say, in the Laureate, which makes itself specially felt in his attitude towards the royal family, and, as Mr. Swinburne has not unjustly argued—though here the vice is less crude in its manifestations—in the morality of the *Idylls of the King*. It is a vein of clay which runs here and there through the fine gold of his art. We cannot overlook such a blemish in reckoning up his personality: it is as real as his better elements. But in a critical study of his art we can do no more than resignedly or bitterly recognize it; turning with a sense of relief, in this matter of poem-endings, to the happier closes of so many of his works, getting rid of the flavour of undertaker's sentiment in a study of the perfect judgment he has shown in rounding off so many of his other things; and winding up, say, with such an artistic *bonne bouche* as the stanza, at the end of 'The Talking Oak', on that 'famous brother-oak',

Wherein the younger Charles abode
Till all the paths were dim,
And far below the Roundhead rode,
And humm'd a surly hymn.

Only less felicitous than such endings is the poet's art of lyric beginnings, shown in so many a musical reduplication, as in 'Tears, idle tears', 'Turn, fortune, turn thy wheel', 'Low, low, breathe and blow', 'Low, my lute, breathe low, my lute', 'Sun, rain, and sun', 'Late, late, so late'—an artifice arising out of the very psychological instinct of song. Sheer bad taste, in matters of feeling, must needs spoil a poet's verse whatever be his skill; but against the few purely artistic vulgarities in Tennyson's poetry we can at least set more master-strokes of unprecedented felicity than any other man's work will yield us.

Our study has dealt, thus mainly with the earlier portions of Tennyson's work, for the sufficient reason that it is in connection with that we can most closely trace the decisive workings of his artistic faculty. His later volumes were, practically, fully smelted before issue, and we can but trace in them the line of his development. A few alterations there are in these; indeed, the 'Ode on the Duke of Wellington' has been very much retouched since its first appearance; but one does not find many changes in the rest of the poet's work; the substitution of 'great world' for the original 'peoples' in the well-known line in 'Locksley Hall'—

Let the great world spin for ever down the ringing grooves of change—

being one of the few that have much importance. *Maud*, which represents the high-water mark of the poet's lyrical achievement, has undergone almost no verbal alteration, though a number of passages have been added to the first version, as—stanzas 14, 15, and 16 in Part I, section i; numbers 4 and 6 in section x; the whole of section xix; section iii in Part II; and the closing number. These additions, it will be seen, are calculated to give greater continuity and completeness to the poem as a narrative whole—a form of improvement which the poet had not neglected in revising his earlier work. Thus 'The Miller's Daughter' has been not only very much retouched, but the stanza which now stands fourth is an addition, as are likewise those three which describe the share of the lover's mother in the episode, and the two which stand third last and second last; and the second of the two songs is a complete substitution, while the first has been altered. The total effect is to add weight and solidity to the whole; the process indeed showing that the poet altered his tale at his pleasure, but being none the less a gain. And so in 'The Palace of Art' there has been an extensive re-arrangement of the stanzas, as well as a re-casting of some, the logical scheme of the first version having evidently failed to satisfy the author on re-reading. While, however, his progress has thus not been merely one of skill in the choice and concatenation of words, but has, as was natural, involved a certain ordering and reconsidering of his general thought, the nature of the latter development will be found to negate once more the theory that a poet's special endowment or inspiration, as such, is moral or intellectual, in the sense of a prompting and a capacity to teach men truth of any kind. This at least, I should be prepared to maintain in the face of such poems as 'The Two Voices', 'The Palace of Art', taken either as a final whole or in respect of the modifications made on the first form, and *In Memoriam*. Any careful reader who will take the trouble to analyse these productions for their didactic significance will find that they only group loosely a number of quasi-philosophical reflections of a sufficiently familiar order, and that the poet has really no connected system of thought of his own. Professor Masson indeed stoutly maintains, in his book on *Recent British Philosophy*, that it is a gross oversight to exclude from such a survey as he professes to make, the names and teachings of such writers as Tennyson, the Brownings, and Clough. But we do not find that the Professor indicates what contributions the poets have actually made to philosophy, and such an omission is rather fatal to the claim. The truth is, Tennyson, like Browning, has passed with many people as a philosophical teacher because he raises philosophic questions in his verse; and it may be said for the Laureate that, with less metaphysical subtlety than his friend and rival, he contrives much the oftener to 'drop into poetry' in the course of his disquisitions. It is, I think, the Duke of Argyll who has pronounced *In Memoriam* a great storehouse of poetic thought and feeling for these generations, and in this form the claims made for that work by its admirers need not be disputed. What it does is to give us, in verse almost constantly good and often admirable in its sad dignity and grave harmony, a train of reflections such as occur to a cultured poet in common with other men of culture whose thought is mostly coloured by feeling, in connexion with a sorely-felt bereavement. And the feeling is in general so vital and so freshly phrased that the total effect is decisively poetic; so that, fatally as fashions of 'poetic thought' tend to pass away—witness the proved mortality of *The Excursion* and *The Prelude*—we cannot well conceive that Tennyson's many-toned lament for his friend will ever take its place in the limbo of disestablished classics. None the less confidently may we maintain, however, that the means by which it will hold its place will be the artistic charm of phrase and cadence in its parts in detail, and not their philosophic import whether singly or together. And the truth of this, if it need further enforcement, will be apparent to most readers from a consideration of the merits of *Maud* in its two aspects of an ethical contention and a sustained lyric rapture. That any one in these days will defend the final political or social doctrine deducible from that poem, I shall not believe until I am definitely challenged. Even the author has shown some misgivings about his thesis; for the added closing stanza has a certain deprecating ring in comparison with what went before; and one of the few alterations in the diction of the work is in the preceding stanza, where the 'peace, that I deem'd no peace' has been substituted for the more uncompromising 'long, long canker of peace', of the first edition. The prescription to society conveyed in the final section—a prescription fitly summed up in the formula 'go to the Crimea and thou shalt be saved'—is a piece of sanguinary sentiment too crude and too puerile to be worth getting indignant over at this time of day, though it might well exasperate rational people at the time of publication. If this is to be taken as a sample of the element of inspirational value in the teaching of poets, the discussion need not go far. But just as obvious as the crudity of the teaching, to an impartial critic, is the exquisite perfection of the style of the song. To me, at least, such lines as these—

And the cobweb woven across the cannon's throat
Shall shake its threaded tears in the wind no more—

are as entirely admirable in point of poetic art as they are repulsive in their moral intention. To share in such an exultation we must be pestilent citizens; to miss the felicity of the expression we must be dull readers. Clearly we cannot reckon the poet a teacher.

Maud I venture to repeat, is Tennyson's high-water mark as a lyrist or singer of passion; as 'The Lotos-Eaters' may be reckoned his masterpiece in sheer form and the loveliness of repose. And in studying the former work we are able to see the trend of Tennyson's artistic movement as it relates to and affects the development of our poetry in general. He is in his own way a realist or naturalist; that is, he has tended on the whole, in the works under review, towards naturalness of speech and away from old convention; which is the sum of the whole matter as regards the realistic spirit in any art. We shall not go far wrong in saying that the note of originality, and therefore of permanence, is mainly traceable, in the case, of modern poets whom we esteem, to a faculty of saying things, however finely, more straightforwardly, more plainly, more unaffectedly, more in the fashion in which, rhyme and cadence apart, they might be said singly in prose, than did their predecessors. I need only refer to the critical gospel of Wordsworth for the first explicit statement of the theory. As to the practice, one instance can suffice; and we may take that of Poe's poem 'For Annie', where it will be found that, in respect of mere accidence or arrangement of terms and clauses, the writing goes on about as inartificially, and with about as few inversions, as would a prose statement of the same ideas; the reiterations being the chief element of difference. Now, this reaching towards freedom of verbal movement concurrently with the fullest circumspection, is strikingly apparent in *Maud*; where there is perhaps more of the air of spontaneity than in any contemporary verse, not excepting that of Mr. Browning, whose rhymes are too often far-fetched to permit of any such illusion. In this poem Tennyson has finally attained, without sacrifice of metrical coherence, that ease of cadence which he seems to have been aiming at in his early 'sham Pindarics', where the effort was too much for his hold of metre. To give the full proof would involve sampling every metre in the poem, with its extraordinary wealth of various melody, where each transition seems to be a new triumph of easeful beauty, which is yet as constantly virile as the early experiments were lax and emasculated. Just to show what entire freedom of form may be obtained in strict obedience to fundamental law, let us take one passage, which is indeed 'irregular' to the eye and the finger, but which is all the same metrically perfect to the last pulse of its flow:

O, art them sighing for Lebanon
In the long breeze that streams to thy delicious East,
Sighing for Lebanon,
Dark cedar, tho' thy limbs have here increased
Upon a pastoral slope as fair,
And looking to the South, and fed
With honey'd rain and delicate air,
And haunted by the starry head
Of her whose gentle will has changed my fate,
And made my life a perfumed altar-flame;
And over whom thy darkness must have spread
With such delight as theirs of old, thy great
Forefathers of the thornless garden, there
Shadowing the snow-limb'd Eve from whom she came.

The very simple reasons why this versification is entirely delightful, while such things as 'The Hesperides' leave us wearied and uncharmed, are that, in the first place, the pace or beat is never ruptured, but throbs lullingly through the continuously varied rhyme-lengths, exactly like the tempo of music that, wedded to no meted lengths of speech, proceeds by its own rhythmic law— or, to take another instance, like the movement of a *danseuse* who carries beauty of motion far beyond the narrow limits of ordinary dancing without once giving us the idea of jolt or hiatus; while, again, the poet has of course attained a much more perfect judgment in words and a much clearer sense of what he wants to say, and gives us a rounded period in which not a word is strained or misused, in place of the old thin-spun tissues of wilful fantasy.

But if we thus praise the supple freedom of the verse of *Maud*, I fear we are committed to a somewhat different attitude towards the *Idylls of the King* and the tragedies which the author has been producing of late years. The having previously ventured a detailed commentary[11] on *Becket* is a sufficient reason why I should not here offer more than a summary judgment on these dramatic experiments, to the effect that while the great and various mass of the poet's rhymed verse represents a constant advance in poetic technique, his work in drama has been radically unhappy, in that he has held to a worn-out form, to which he has quite failed to give any new life. He has, in fact, stuck to the old fallacy that the drama is a branch of poetry, and has in consequence sought to fuse together two literary arts which were indeed once in constant combination, but which have in this country for three hundred years been more and more differentiating; and which Tennyson has himself done a vast deal to differentiate further by the very advance he has made in one of them. The function of the dramatist in these days, it cannot be too often repeated, is not to say things finely—the poet's task—but in all seriousness to 'hold as 'twere the mirror up to nature.' Now, the mere harking back to the far-gone past for dramatic subjects instead of showing the 'body of the time his form and pressure', is in itself a sign of an unvital variety of the dramatic instinct—a habit of mind in which, instead of seizing and presenting genuine characters in whom the actor's art may become incarnate, the artist sees everything in a medium of inherited convention, and accordingly prefers instinctively to take his personages from periods over which convention has always reigned, that he may be disturbed by no air of disobedience in his puppets. It stands to reason that if verse-form has modified since Shakspere's day, drama-form ought to have modified too; but whereas Shakspere wrote little non-dramatic verse, and therefore did not overshadow the 'heaven of poetic invention', his magnificent dramatic product has daunted the whole literature of England,

and in large part that of Germany, down to these days. Whom Shakspere daunts may be well daunted, to parody—is it Goethe's?—line on the God-deluded; but the fact remains that the thrall is thrall, and no free 'maker'. And in any case, the habit of producing poetry proper clearly tells against soundness of dramatic method, and *vice versa*. It cannot, indeed, be doubted that if Tennyson had devoted himself to the dramatic form from the first he might have been original and masterly in that as he has been in lyrism. All along he has given striking proofs of a power to seize and portray character in phases and wholes, as in his youthful masterpiece 'The Two Sisters', 'Lady Clara Vere de Vere', the 'English Idylls' generally, the 'Enoch Arden' group, and a number of shorter pieces. That the writer of all these poems could both group characters and project situations is abundantly clear; and the author of 'The Grandmother' and the two versions of 'The Northern Farmer' might even claim, so far as these pieces went, to be abreast of the best English fiction of his time, so fresh and masterly is their realistic 'nudity', as Zola would call it. But while these latter performances have barely as much poetic flavour as will keep them in the poetic category, verse as they are, the dramas constitute an absolute relapse into convention. They are methodistic and formal, as they needs must, in respect of their historical motives, where the character-poems are subtly and freely original; and the scrupulous attempt to make them realistic in the Shaksperean fashion only serves to emphasize the more their artistic insincerity. *The Promise of May* where the poet has at last attempted a modern subject, is the final evidence of his failure as a dramatist; a failure absolutely inevitable, as we can now see, in the nature of the case, and, perhaps we should add, something of a fine failure in its way. The attempt has all along amounted to an exhibition of superior—indeed, very superior—dilettantism; and when, as is natural, the effort at a modern play is found to show most decisively the fallacy of the method employed, with its primitive transitions from verse to prose and its crude grouping of impossible abstractions beside thinnish actualities, we can only hope that the old poet will be content to leave drama alone for the rest of his days.

But if this criticism be admitted to hold good against the dramas, it is to be feared a similar judgment will ultimately be come to in regard to the *Idylls*. 'Superlative lollipops', Carlyle called them, in prompt resentment of their sentimental didacticism; going thus nearer the truth than did Dickens, whose first sensation on conning them was that of the blessedness of reading a man who could write. The whole question between those of us who sum up against the *Idylls* and those who adhere to Dickens's position, is as to whether the poet's art here, highly developed as it undoubtedly is, wealthy as it is in resource, and consummate as is its conduct, has moved on the lines of healthy evolution, or has diverged on a line of impermanent variation; whether, in short, these poems, pleasant as they have been to the sophisticated palate of the generation now passing away, will be pronounced successes a generation or more hence. In such a matter it is perhaps prudent not to prophesy; but on the other hand it is well to have the courage of our opinions; and I venture for my part[12] to lay it down that, lacking as they do those artistic virtues of naturalness and sincerity which vitalize other portions of Tennyson's work, they must in time be classed among his mistakes. And the cause and manner of the failure are I think apparent. He had succeeded in those character studies where his artistic volition played freely, either entirely creating or working on the actual; but to take the naïf old Arthurian stories and pinch and lace them into so many superfine moral commentaries for the present day, adding the hothouse sentiment of the nineteenth century to the quaintly childish idealism of the original, and grafting on the old romance a mawkish cultus which seemed to take its rise or have its end in a nauseous adulation of a living personage—this was to place art in a fatally false position, where no acquired resource could finally avail it. The poet is writing to fill a given scaffolding, and as a result we have a constant and laboured archaism of style instead of the telling simplicity and robust modernness of his best rhymed verse; a delicate and charming Euphuism in its way, but still a Euphuism, and therefore a doomed development. This might seem to be a case justifying Mr. Swinburne's dictum that when the thought goes wrong the verse follows it; but it is not the wrongness but the fashion of going wrong that is at the bottom of the matter. There is all the difference in the world between affectation and sincere wrong-headedness and the thesis here maintained is that while the wrong-headed artist may give us fine poetry, he who gives way to an affectation cannot, for the reason that that is a vice striking directly at his art; that, in brief, the *Idylls* as a whole amount to a masquerade, which cannot succeed in creating the right illusion. Only a lengthened analysis, however, could give the full justification of such a judgment; and it must be left for the present in its summary form.

It remains but to say a word on Tennyson's latest performances on what may be termed his normal lines; the verdict here again being necessarily summary. To put it bluntly, these productions seem to prove that while he largely retains his old faculty of tragic and humorous characterization, his power of creating 'rhythmical beauty' is for the most part gone; the old-time Tennyson giving us his swan-song, a worthy one indeed, in the nobly beautiful lines 'To Virgil'. Than these, indeed, he has done nothing more happily inspired and achieved. While, however, 'Rizpah' and 'The Spinster's Sweet-Arts' may be taken to prove the retention of his other powers—though some pieces, as 'The Flight', tell for an opposite view; the sequel to 'Locksley Hall' and the 'Epilogue' in the 'Tiresias' volume furnish positive proof, so far as positive proof will go, of the decline in his general sense of beauty. To some perhaps this will not amount to saying that there has been any substantial falling off in the Laureate's work. Mr. Swinburne has set the fashion of treating 'Rizpah' as his greatest achievement, on the strength, not so much of its poetic workmanship, as of the tragic impressiveness of its motive and the dramatic intensity of some of its expressions. These are indeed powerful and memorable enough; but those to whom poetry, as such, is a matter of beauty of speech, can hardly let Mr. Swinburne coerce them into giving the palm in Tennyson's work to a piece which, as a little reflection will show, might have been made about equally powerful in prose. Realism of character representation, as distinguished from naturalism in the structure of non-dramatic phrases, obviously tends towards prose as being the natural utterance of real persons, true poetic values lying rather in the direction of a beauty of speech which is utterly beyond actual use, though its triumph lies in seeming natural at its topmost flight, as the finished athlete's most strenuous feat seems done with joyous ease. If this be granted, 'Rizpah' must rank as a powerful study in an intermediate literary form rather than as belonging to the higher poetry; and this is of course entirely consistent with the view that the artist's cunning for that other work is now as good as gone. The 'Epilogue' was presumably meant to be beautiful—was, however, commonplace; and, splenetic as is the later 'Locksley Hall', the poet cannot but have meant to give it some of the dower of beauty that he bestowed on the earlier poem. Spleen, however, remains uppermost, and only a few lines here and there break mellowly on the strident invective of what is as much a self-impeachment as an arraignment of the world. As in the couplet picturing a perfected earth:

Robed in universal harvest, up to either pole she smiles,
Universal ocean softly washing all her warless isles.

But, to say nothing of the epithet-stringing, the new poem contains some outrages in the way of padding such as the Laureate never before committed, as when, in order to get a rhyme, he speaks of the dead wife as

Feminine to her inmost heart and feminine to her *tender feet*.

Mr. Browning, certainly, has padded as brazenly as this for many a long day; but then Mr. Browning does it to the philosophic end of making out that whatever is, is right, and is thus apt to be more easily forgiven than one who employs such devices in an outpouring of scorn against mankind. Padded denunciation is too powerfully suggestive of infirmity. In fine, we must go back to the poetry of the poet's earlier days if we would have what is best in his art; and indeed this is but what has always been in the service of the Muses. What is song but one of the ways of birth to the urging force of all things, a flower of the vernal blood or the summer-nourished brain, finding their fulfilment like every other cosmic energy? And though spring and summer rain and blast yield thrilling interludes of radiant storm, and autumn many a wondrous harmony and grave magnificence of ripened meaning, how shall the sun-forsaken winter tell of aught but the ebb of the eternal tide, the passing of the protean spirit that is only to return in other lives? In all of us, says the great critic, there is or was a poet whom the man survives. Even so is it with *the* poet. Or, if the waning pulse is ever to chime into the old music, it is to the spell of a passion that recreates the past, not to the bitter musings of frost-nipped eld. It is reviving youth in the poetic heart that sings here:

Landscape-lover, lord of language
more than he that sang the Works and Days;
All the chosen coin of fancy
flashing out from many a golden phrase;

Thou that singest wheat and woodland,
tilth and vineyard, hive and horse and herd;
All the charm of all the Muses
often flowering in a lonely word;

Chanter of the Pollio, glorying
in the blissful years again to be,
Summers of the snakeless meadow,
unlaborious earth and oarless sea;

I salute thee, Mantovano,
I that loved thee since my day began,
Wielder of the stateliest measure
ever moulded by the lips of man.

In some such temper, borrowing his own melodious acclaim, let us to the last salute that singer of our youth who is the Virgil of our time.

Notes

1. 'Miscellanies', p. 255.
2. There are several curious points of agreement between Coleridge and Poe in criticism. Both, for instance, had a boundless admiration for Fouqué's *Undine*, and they expressed themselves in almost identical terms. See the *Table Talk*, under date May 31st, 1830, and compare Poe's works (Ingram's ed.) iii, 388, 461; iv. 132, 369.
3. *Table Talk*, under date April 24th, 1833.
4. *Marginalia*, cxcvi.
5. *Essays and Studies*, p. 133.
6. Since this was written, an interesting account of the development of the poem in question has appeared in the *Princeton Review* (1887 or 1888) under the title 'The Vicissitudes of a Palace'.
7. 'Clasping jasmine' in the first edition.
8. It was he, it appears, who first suggested to Mr. Spedding that Fletcher's hand was apparent in the *Henry VIII*, and Mr. Spedding pronounced him 'a man of first-rate judgment on such a point'. See Furnivall's Introduction.
9. Twice, for instance, by Mr. Lowell, who gives it 'land or sea' in his essay on Pope (*My Study Windows*, 6th ed. p. 283, *n*), and in his essay on Wordsworth ('Camelot' vol. of Essays, p. 208).
10. Originally 'darnels', which was perhaps better.
11. *Our Corner*, February 1885.
12. But indeed I venture little. The more powerful impeachment of Mr. Swinburne (*Miscellanies*, pp. 247–253), which was not in my recollection when I wrote mine, goes much further, and, barring some characteristic exaggeration, is unanswerable. And since I wrote there has appeared in a newspaper article on 'Fifty Years of Victorian Literature', bearing the mark of a certain fine Roman hand, this corroborative judgment:—'Lord Tennyson, before he moralized Malory, had given the world an inestimable amount of pleasure, merely by virtue of that beauty which made Poe regard him as the greatest of all poets. His blank-verse sermons, on the other hand, are of no avail, and only disturb his narrative' (*Daily News*, June 22, 1887). Yet Clough on their publication wrote: 'I certainly think these Idylls are the best thing Tennyson has done' (*Prose Remains*, ed. 1888, p. 250). The old order changeth.

—J. M. Robertson, "The Art of Tennyson," *Essays Towards a Critical Method*, 1889, pp. 233–82

ANDREW LANG "INTRODUCTORY: OF MODERN ENGLISH POETRY" (1889)

Andrew Lang was a literary critic who, in the following extract, maintains that Tennyson's place among the greatest English poets is assured. He recognizes that the poet's verse is not without flaws, occasionally affected in style and mannered in feeling. But Lang believes these faults are occasional and negligible when set against that which is most valuable in Tennyson's long career. The poet's versatility in writing in differing forms, his imagination, and his learning are all singled out for praise.

Let us attempt to get rid of every bias and, thinking as dispassionately as we can, we still seem to read the name of Tennyson in the golden book of English poetry. I cannot think that he will ever fall to a lower place, or be among those whom only curious students pore over, like Gower, Drayton, Donne, and the rest. Lovers of poetry will always read him as they will read Wordsworth, Keats, Milton, Coleridge, and Chaucer. Look his defects in the face, throw them into the balance, and how they disappear before his merits! He is the last and youngest of the mighty race, born, as it were, out of due time, late, and into a feebler generation.

Let it be admitted that the gold is not without alloy, that he has a touch of voluntary affectation, of obscurity, even an occasional perversity, a mannerism, a set of favourite epithets ('windy' and 'happy'). There is a momentary echo of Donne, of Crashaw, nay, in his earliest pieces, even a touch of Leigh Hunt. You detect it in pieces like 'Lilian' and 'Eleanore', and the others of that kind and of that date.

Let it be admitted that *In Memoriam* has certain lapses in all that meed of melodious tears; that there are trivialities which might deserve (here is an example) 'to line a box', or to curl some maiden's locks, that there are weaknesses of thought, that the poet now speaks of himself as a linnet, singing 'because it must', now dares to approach questions insoluble, and again declines their solution. What is all this but the changeful mood of grief? The singing linnet, like the bird in the old English heathen apologue, dashes its light wings painfully against the walls of the chamber into which it has flown out of the blind night that shall again receive it.

I do not care to dwell on the imperfections in that immortal strain of sympathy and consolation, that enchanted book of consecrated regrets. It is an easier if not more grateful task to note a certain peevish egotism of tone in the heroes of 'Locksley Hall', of *Maud*, of 'Lady Clara Vere de Vere'. 'You can't think how poor a figure you make when you tell that story, sir,' said Dr. Johnson to some unlucky gentleman whose 'figure' must certainly have been more respectable than that which is cut by these whining and peevish lovers of Maud and Cousin Amy.

Let it be admitted, too, that King Arthur, of the *Idyls,* is like an Albert in blank verse, an Albert cursed with a Guinevere for a wife, and a Lancelot for friend. The *Idyls,* with all their beauties, are full of a Victorian respectability, and love of talking with Vivien about what is not so respectable. One wishes, at times, that the 'Morte d'Arthur' had remained a lonely and flawless fragment, as noble as Homer, as polished as Sophocles. But then we must have missed, with many other admirable things, the 'Last Battle in the West.'

People who come after us will be more impressed than we are by the Laureate's versatility. He has touched so many strings, from 'Will Waterproof's Monologue,' so far above Praed, to the agony of 'Rizpah,' the invincible energy of 'Ulysses,' the languor and the fairy music of the 'Lotus Eaters,' the grace as of a Greek epigram which inspires the lines to Catullus and to Virgil. He is with Milton for learning, with Keats for magic and vision, with Virgil for graceful recasting of ancient golden lines, and even in the latest volume of his long life, 'we may tell from the straw,' as Homer says, 'what the grain has been.'

> —Andrew Lang, "Introductory: Of Modern
> English Poetry," *Letters on Literature,* 1889,
> pp. 4–8

EDMUND GOSSE "THE INFLUENCE
OF DEMOCRACY" (1891)

Edmund Gosse was an English poet, author, and literary critic. In the following extract, Gosse reflects on the relationship between Tennyson and the English public, the poet and popular opinion. Tennyson, for Gosse, never deliberately sought to flatter his readership and always wrote for himself and not to please others. It is only due to the course of his long life and poetic career that Gosse believes Tennyson might be misunderstood as seeking to play to the gallery. Rather, the poet altered popular taste to the point that the general public could more fully and ably appreciate his writings. In line with the prevailing aesthetic perspective of the 1890s, Gosse proclaims that life follows art, not vice versa: Tennyson created the literary tastes of late Victorian Britain. Readers might again consider just how much power a poet can wield in maintaining the status quo or in radicalizing his audience. A valuable contrast in perspectives on Tennyson and democracy might be gained by considering Gosse's views alongside those of Walt Whitman, as presented in a previous extract in this section.

If, then, we might take Tennyson as an example of the result of the action of democracy upon literature, we might indeed congratulate ourselves. But a moment's reflection shows that to do so is to put the cart before the horse. The wide appreciation of such delicate and penetrating poetry is, indeed, an example of the influence of literature on democracy, but hardly of democracy on literature. We may examine the series of Tennyson's volumes with care, and scarcely discover a copy of verses in which he can be detected as directly urged to expression by the popular taste. This prime favourite of the educated masses never courted the public, nor strove to serve it. He wrote to please himself, to win the applause of the "little clan," and each round of salvos from the world outside seemed to startle him in his obstinate retirement. If it grew easier and easier for him to consent to please the masses, it was because he familiarised them more and more with his peculiar accent. He led literary taste, he did not dream of following it.

—Edmund Gosse, "The Influence of Democracy,"
1891, *Questions at Issue*, 1893, p. 40

Aubrey De Vere "To Alfred Tennyson" (1893)

Aubrey De Vere was an Irish poet and in the following poem states that the worlds depicted in Tennyson's verse are more lovely than those in reality and speak to a sense of both the benign and the values that other critics have pointed out in previous extracts. De Vere's sonnet implies that there is something distinctly "British" about Tennyson's poetry, beyond the simple subject matter, that, perhaps in a similar sense to what Edmund Gosse mentions in the preceding extract, Tennyson has "created" what it means to be a Briton at the end of the nineteenth century. Also like Gosse, De Vere is speaking from the *fin de siècle* aesthetic position, which maintained that art is considered to be superior to life and capable of fashioning life into something more beautiful that it actually is. Readers might contrast John Ruskin's perspective, as contained in another extract in this section, which is much more critical of Tennyson's subject matter and the utility of his poetry than De Vere's and Gosse's assessments written at the end of the nineteenth century.

The land whose loveliness in verse of thine
Shows lovelier yet than prank'd on Nature's page
Shall prove *thy* poet in some future age,
Sing thee—*her* poet—not in measured line
Or metric stave, but music more benign;
Shall point to British Galahads who wage
Battle on wrong; to British maids who gage,
Like Agnes, heart and hope to love divine.
Worn men like thy Ulysses, scorning fear,
Shall tempt strange seas beneath an alien star;
Old men from honored homes and faces dear
Summoned by death to realms unknown and far
Thy "Silent Voices" from on high shall hear;
With happier auspice cross the "Harbour Bar."

—Aubrey De Vere, "To Alfred Tennyson," *Century Magazine*, May 1893, p. 37

MAX NORDAU (1895)

Max Nordau was a Hungarian author, controversial social critic, physician, and, along with Theodor Herzl, one of the co-founders of the World Zionist Organization. In his book *Degeneration*, from which the following short excerpt is taken, Nordau railed against modern culture and many of his contemporary thinkers and artists. The Pre-Raphaelites were a group of British artists and authors that Nordau singled out for particular condemnation, and the "lily-bearing mystics" is a reference to his perception of them as fey, unmanly, degenerate, and irrational. That Nordau eulogizes Tennyson is hardly welcome praise to modern readers, but the critic's view was an influential and not unrepresentative one in the last years of the nineteenth century.

. . . if the whole of English poetry is not to-day unmitigatedly pre-Raphaelite, it is due merely to the fortunate accident that, contemporaneously with the pre-Raphaelites, so sound a poet as Tennyson has lived and worked. The official honours bestowed on him as Poet Laureate, his unexampled success among readers, pointed him out to a part at least of the petty strugglers and aspirants as worthy of imitation, and so it comes about that among the chorus of the lily-bearing mystics there are also heard other street-singers who follow the poet of the *Idylls of the King*.

—Max Nordau, *Degeneration*, 1895, p. 99

George Saintsbury "Tennyson" (1895)

George Edward Bateman Saintsbury was an English author and literary critic, and in the following extract, he analyzes his own impressions of Tennyson throughout the poet's career and examines his reputation a few years after his death. Saintsbury confesses from the beginning of the extract that he is and always has been a fervent admirer of Tennyson's poetry, remembering how impressed he was in his youth after reading the poet's early work. He is not too biased a eulogist, however, to add that it was possibly because of his youth that he enjoyed Tennyson's verse, but upon considering this possibility, Saintsbury insists it was not the case. He remembers his disappointment after reading *Enoch Arden* for the first time and is not altogether unsympathetic to the critical assessment of Tennyson's friend Edward FitzGerald, who claimed that, after 1842, the poet's verse never reached the heights it had once achieved. Nevertheless, Saintsbury believes that Tennyson was always capable of not only achieving those levels again in later years but that his work maintained its capacity to charm. It is with a consideration of this quality of "the charming" that the extract concludes. Saintsbury references Samuel Taylor Coleridge's critical view of the young Tennyson's work (part of which criticism is contained in an extract in this volume) and gives an example of a youngster's similar, contemporary perspective. The capacity that Tennyson's verse has to "charm" is, the extract suggests, perhaps its greatest quality. While some may grow into appreciating his poetry, there will always be others who simply are not capable of finding anything in it to appreciate.

I do not think that any one can ever have had and maintained a greater admiration for the author of "The Lotos-Eaters" than I have. This admiration was born early, but it was not born full grown. I am so old a Tennysonian that though I can only vaguely remember talk about *Maud* at the time of its first appearance, I can remember the *Idylls* themselves fresh from the press. I was, however, a little young then to appreciate Tennyson, and it must have been a year or two later that I began to be fanatical on the subject. Yet there must have been a little method in that youthful madness,—some criticism in that craze. A great many years afterwards I came across the declaration of Edward FitzGerald, one of the poet's oldest and fastest friends, to the effect that everything he had written after 1842 was a falling off. That, of course, was a crotchet. FitzGerald, like all men of original but not very productive genius who live much alone, was a crotcheteer to the nth. But it has a certain root of truth in it; and as I read it I remembered what my own feelings had been on reading *Enoch Arden,* the first volume that came out after I had enrolled myself in the sacred band. It was just at the end of my freshman's year; and I bought a copy of the book (for which there had been some waiting, and a tremendous rush) on my way home from the prize-giving of my old school. To tell the truth, I was a little disappointed. For *Enoch Arden* itself, as a whole, I have never cared, despite the one splendid passage describing the waiting in the island; nor for "Aylmer's Field"; nor for divers other things. "The Voyage" was of the very best, and "In the Valley at Cauterets," and one or two other things. "Boadicea" was an interesting experiment. But on the whole one was inclined to say, Where is "The Lotos-Eaters"? Where is the "Dream of Fair Women"? Where is "The Palace of Art"?

Perhaps they were nowhere; perhaps only in the very best of the *Ballads* of 1880, and once or twice later, did the poet ever touch the highest points of his first fine raptures. But he never failed, even to his death day, to show that he was the author of these raptures, and that he could still go very near, if not absolutely up to them, when he chose. It has, however, been a constant critical amusement of mine to try to find out if possible whether this impression was a mere fallacy of youth, and if so how far. And some of the results of the inquiry which has been going on more or less ever since I turned through the Marble Arch into Hyde Park, and took *Enoch Arden* out of my pocket on that summer day, may not improperly form the subject of this and another of these papers. For the inevitable post-mortem depreciation has set in in reference to this great poet already, and it may not be uninteresting to others to see how it strikes a contemporary who had prepared himself for it......

We have all heard of the strange objections which even Coleridge, who might have been thought most likely of all living men to appreciate Tennyson, made (though he did not fail wholly in his appreciation) to the new poet's manner. I knew a much lesser but even more curious and far more recent instance myself. A boy of eighteen or nineteen, altogether average except that he had, I think, some Eurasian strain in him, neither a dunce nor a genius and decidedly fond of reading, once took out of a library the *Poems,*—THE *Poems,* that is to say, the volume containing everything before the *Idylls* except *Maud, The Princess,* and *In Memoriam.* After a day or so he returned it, saying sadly to the librarian that "he could not read it. It was just like prose." Had he been Dr Johnson he would probably have said that "the rhymes were harsh and the numbers unpleasing," just as the Doctor did of "Lycidas."

To us, of course, on the other hand, the whole or the greatest charm of Tennyson comes from the fact that he affects us in exactly the opposite way. But I think there is a certain excuse for the laughers of 1830, for Coleridge, and for my Eurasian schoolfellow. I am sure at least that I myself read

Tennyson and liked him (for I always liked him) for several years before his peculiar and divine virtue dawned upon me. It has never set or paled since, and I am as sure as I can be that if I were to live to be a Struldbrug (which Heaven forbid) one of the very last things of the kind that I should forget or lose my relish for would be this. But comparatively few people, I think, have ever fully recognised how extremely original this virtue of his is. The word "great" is most irritatingly misused about poets; and we have quite recently found some persons saying that "Tennyson is as great as Shakespeare," and other people going into fits of wrath, or smiling surprise with calm disdain, at the saying. If what the former mean to say and what the latter deny is that Tennyson has a supreme and peculiar poetic charm, then I am with the former and against the latter. He has: and from the very fact of his having it he will not necessarily be appreciated at once, and may miss appreciation altogether with some people.

—George Saintsbury, "Tennyson,"
Corrected Impressions, 1895

LESLIE STEPHEN "LIFE OF TENNYSON" (1899)

Sir Leslie Stephen was an English author and critic and the father of Virginia Woolf and Vanessa Bell. He was the first editor of the *Dictionary of National Biography*, and in this extract, Stephen begins by remarking on the impossibility of apprehending how Tennyson's mind must have worked. Not even poets, let alone regular "mortals," would have been able to understand the thought processes of such a man. His remarks are personal and self-deprecating, open and honest and, as such, afford the reader a glimpse into a man growing older with Tennyson and his verse through the nineteenth century. Stephen recounts his youth and the fact that all his schoolfellows were "Tennysonian," that the name of the poet was, at the time, synonymous with the profession itself. He gives thanks for the communion and the fellow feeling that he and his friends were given by their devotion to the poet and his verse in his early career.

Turning to the *Idylls of the King*, Stephen quotes several of the mixed responses to its publication in 1859, saying that for many of his friends, as well as for him, this was the beginning of a less ardent regard for Tennyson's verse. Stephen recognizes that it was very much a case of the poet's philosophy, his replies to the crises of his age, that left the younger devotees of his work cold and that this might well be regarded as a shortcoming on the part of those earlier admirers. Stephen says it was not philosophy per se, nor the allegory in *Idylls of the King* that he and others like him were disinclined to accept; it was rather the belief that the questions of the age required a much more strident response than those they felt were suggested by Tennyson's poem. Stephen excuses himself by saying that it was, quite possibly, his own aesthetic failure to appreciate the poem, but he certainly approved of those other works, such as *In Memoriam*, in which he felt Tennyson's philosophy was more forcefully asserted.

Stephen finds it tempting to consider Tennyson's upbringing, so few details being provided in the poet's biography. He recognizes, sensibly, that to hazard wild assumptions about what produced a man of genius like Tennyson, what aspect of his childhood or background afforded him the type of early life from which genius springs, is a pointless exercise. It does not stop Stephen, though, from speculating on what might have been if Tennyson had attended Oxford rather than Cambridge and become involved in the religious controversies there (the Tractarian movement and Cardinal Newman's sermons affecting a generation of Oxford undergraduates). Stephen defends Tennyson's *In Memoriam* from the attack made on it by Hippolyte Taine (those passages are included previously in this section), stating that all British people who had read the poem responded to the poet's depths of emotion. The extract is fair but scathing of Taine's attitude to Tennyson as being the position of a refined effete uninterested in the realities of his world and the common person. It is an opinion that Stephen finds impossible to comprehend.

Stephen again bemoans the lack of information about the poet's life, now between his departure from Cambridge and his settling in Farringford 20 years later. He touches on Tennyson's consideration of the earlier generation of romantic poets, of Wordsworth and Keats in particular, his sensitivity to critical rejection, and his early struggles as a poet, along with his political attitudes, specifically to the reform movement in England in his early adulthood. The conclusion of the extract details some of Thomas Carlyle's criticisms of Tennyson's later work in contrast to the "heroic" aspects of the poet's earlier writings. Stephen broadly agrees that Tennyson's delicate nature and his sensitivity to the doubts and the problems of the later Victorian period left the philosophy of his later verse too vague, too insubstantial, and simply lacking the vigor and force that the crises of the age required. He concludes that he cannot class Tennyson with the "great sage poets": Aeschylus, Shakespeare, Dante, and Goethe; but that is not to say he does not wholeheartedly appreciate the beauty of the emotions, no matter what philosophy is attached to them, and the refined music always expressed in the poet's art.

Every one, I presume, has read the deeply interesting volumes in which Lord Tennyson has paid most appropriate homage to the memory of his father; and the life has probably suggested to most of us some comments upon the familiar poetry. A remark reported by Tennyson's old friend, Jowett, is a useful warning against overambitious attempts in that direction. 'There was,' said Tennyson, 'one intellectual process in the world of which he could not even entertain an apprehension—that was' (the process which created) 'the plays of Shakespeare.' If Tennyson could not imagine the Shakespearean intellect, it is impossible for people who are not poets even to guess at the Tennysonian. The most obvious of his merits is the most tantalising to a would-be explainer. It is especially difficult, as he observes, and as other people have observed before him, to be 'at once commonplace and poetical'; to find the one incomparable and magical phrase for the thought which has been trying to get itself uttered for centuries. There are interesting accounts in these volumes of the way in which some of Tennyson's most perfect passages sprang from accidental phrases, 'rolled about' in his mind; but phrases may roll about in some minds for a very long time to very little purpose. Leave a phrase to simmer in your memory; brood over it, let it crystallize into form in your mind, and the feat will be done. It will, that is, if your mind is Tennysonian; but there is the mystery. One trivial example comes home to the Alpine traveller. He has seen and tried for years to tell how he is impressed by his beloved scenery, and annoyed by his own bungling whenever he has tried to get beyond arithmetical statements of hard geographical facts. And then Tennyson, who was never in his life more than 7000 feet above the sea, just glances at the Monte Rosa from the cathedral at Milan, and in a four-line stanza gives the whole spirit of the scene to perfection. It does not seem fair, but if justice supposes an equal distribution of abilities, the world is not remarkable for fairness. Tennyson's superlative skill in this art is too conspicuous and too universally acknowledged to justify more than a passing recognition of an undeniable truth. And, perhaps, criticism of really great and familiar poetry should be mainly reserved for the select few who may without arrogance claim to be more or less of the same spiritual order. One may, however, say something upon various points suggested by this biography, and especially as to the audience which first listened to the new poetical revelation.

I will begin with a few words as to my own experience in regard to that matter. Tennyson had already made his mark when I was a schoolboy; and when I was at college all youths who professed a literary turn knew the earlier poems by heart. Ebullient Byronism was a thing of the past. There was no longer any need for the missionary zeal which had taken Cambridge men of an earlier generation to propagate the worship of Shelley at Oxford. 'Chatter' about that luminary was already becoming commonplace; a mere repetition of accepted poetical orthodoxy. Admiration of Browning, though it was distinctly beginning, implied a certain claim to esoteric appreciation. But Tennyson's fame was established, and yet had not lost the full bloom of novelty. It was delightful to catch a young man coming up from the country and indoctrinate him by spouting 'Locksley Hall' and the 'Lotus Eaters.' *In Memoriam* had just appeared when I was a freshman—Tennyson became Poet Laureate in my first term—and *Maud* came out the year after I had graduated. Any one who cares to know by contemporary evidence how Tennyson's poetry affected the young men of that period may turn to the essays of George Brimley, a man of fine taste, who died prematurely, and who, as librarian of Trinity, gave utterance to the correct sentiment of Tennyson's old college. Tennyson, he declares, is doing for us of the nineteenth century what Shakespeare and Chaucer did for the England of their own days. Brimley spoke for the civilised part of University society: Tennyson's friends, Thompson (afterwards master) and W. G. Clark, the editor of Shakespeare, were conspicuous in that exalted region; and the younger generation all accepted the Tennysonian faith as that becoming enlightened persons. I only followed my companions when I tacitly assumed that 'poet' was a phrase equivalent to 'Tennyson.' The enthusiasm no doubt was partly obligatory; to repudiate it would have been to write oneself down an ass; but it was also warm and spontaneous. For that one owes a debt of gratitude to the poet not easily to be estimated. It is a blessing to share an enthusiasm, and I hope, rather than believe, that modern undergraduates have some equally wholesome stimulus of the kind. I do not think that we of the older generation have changed our estimate of Tennyson's merits, even though our 'enthusiasm' may have subsided into a more temperate warmth of approval. I mean, however, our estimate of the old poems. One could love them without putting the later works on the same level. Some readers were sensible of a considerable difficulty in that matter. The first series of *Idylls of the King* appeared in 1859. This volume at once extended Tennyson's popularity beyond all previous limits. Ten thousand copies were sold in the first week; hundreds went off monthly; Tennyson made such a success in the merely bookselling sense as to rival Scott, Macaulay, and Dickens. The success, too, was as marked if judged by some higher tests. Thackeray wrote in 'a rapture of gratitude' to acknowledge the greatest delight that had ever come to him since he was a young man. The Duke of Argyll reported that even Macaulay had been conquered, and predicted, truly enough, that many would appreciate the new poems who had failed to appreciate the old. Mr. Gladstone welcomed the *Idylls* in the *Quarterly*, and Jowett wrote as enthusiastically as Thackeray. These judgments, too, are still repeated, and Mr. Stopford Brooke's recent volume upon Tennyson contains a long commentary, which, if more discriminative, is still cordially reverential. I have conscientiously tried to enlighten myself by studying it, but even a knowledge that one ought to be enthusiastic is a different thing from enthusiasm. Not to recognise the wonderful literary skill and the exceeding beauty of many passages would, of course, imply more stupidity than any one would willingly admit; but I am afraid that from the publication of the *Idylls* I had to admit that I was not quite of the inner circle of true worshippers. I am glad to shelter myself to some extent behind higher authorities. Edward FitzGerald confessed when the *Holy Grail* appeared (in 1870) that he was inclined to prefer the old 'Lady of Shalott' method of dealing with the Round Table to the elaborated epic poem. He supposed that a bit must be wanting in the map of his brain, but anyhow, while feeling 'how pure, noble, and holy' the work was, he passed on to where the old Lincolnshire farmer drew tears to his eyes. He got back to 'substantial rough-spun nature,' and felt that the 'old brute' was 'a more pathetic phenomenon' than the Knights of the Round Table. This is only, as he explains, one of 'old Fitz's crotchets' (and it may be said incidentally that FitzGerald's letters, crotchety or not, are among the best things in these volumes). Mr. Ruskin, on the appearance of the first *Idylls*, puts virtually the same point in more formal language. He thinks that 'the true task of the modern poet' should be to 'give the intense, masterful, and unerring transcript of an actuality.' He is not sure, he confesses, that he does not 'feel the art and finish in these poems a little more than he likes to feel it.' Upon this Lord Tennyson makes an interesting remark. The *Idylls*, he tells us, were not carefully elaborated. "Guinevere" and "Elaine" were each written in a few weeks, and hardly corrected at all.' The poet, of course, had been long brooding over them; and many phrases had come to him from accidental suggestions, and gone through a slow incubation; but the actual execution was rapid. This, however, does not quite meet the criticism. It is not a question, I fancy, of the elaboration of the language, but of the vividness and spontaneity of the thought to be elaborated. The art becomes obvious, because Tennyson seems not so much to be inspired by an overmastering idea as to be looking about for appropriate images to express certain ethical and religious sentiments. He has obviously seen the Northern farmer with his own eyes; he has only contrived his knights, who never seem to me to be clothed in real flesh and blood. Jowett remarks that the 'allegory in the distance greatly strengthens, also elevates, the meaning of the poem.' To me, I humbly confess, 'allegory,' rightly or wrongly, means nuisance. The 'meaning' which it sticks on to a poem is precisely what the poem cannot properly 'mean.' The old 'Morte d'Arthur,' as it appeared with the charming old setting, was one of the poems which we all knew by heart. One of the charms was surely that the behaviour of the persons was delightfully illogical and absurd. Rather, perhaps, it took one to the world in which true logic demands illogical behaviour. Things take place there according to a law of their own, which is the more attractive just because it is preposterous and apparently arbitrary. When Sir Bedivere throws Excalibur into the lake, the whole proceeding is, as indeed Sir Bedivere very properly perceives and points out, contrary to all commonsense. His reluctance gives us warning that we have got into the world governed by phantastic laws. Throwing a sword into a lake does not, within ordinary experience, produce a barge occupied by three queens with crowns of gold; just as shooting an albatross does not, as a rule, produce a dead calm and death of a ship's crew by thirst. But though things of dreamland follow laws of their own, even dreamland has laws, and they ought to be observed when once you get there. The 'Ancient Mariner' was ridden by a nightmare, and all things happened to him according to the genuine laws of the nightmare world. Arthur's Round Table was a dream of the mediaeval imagination, and the historian of its adventures should frankly put himself in the corresponding attitude of mind. It lends itself admirably to represent the ideals which were in the minds of the dreamer, and therefore unconsciously determined the constitution of the imaginary world. But when the personages, instead of obeying the laws of their own world, are converted into allegory, they lose their dream reality without gaining the reality of ordinary life. The arbitrariness especially ceases to be delightful when we suspect that the real creatures of the fancy have become the puppets of a judicious moralist. The question, What is the meaning? throws one's mind out of gear. When Sir Bedivere made his second appearance somebody asked Tennyson whether the three queens were not Faith, Hope, and Charity. The poet replied that they were, and that they were not. They might be the Virtues or they might be the Three Graces. There was, he said, an 'allegorical, or perhaps rather a parabolic, drift,' in the poem; but he added there was not a single fact or incident in the *Idylls* which might not be explained without any mystery or allegory whatever. This explanation may be very satisfactory to some readers, and if they are satisfied, their state is the more gracious; but I humbly confess that so soon as genuine inhabitants of Fairyland can be interpreted as three virtues or three graces, they cease to fascinate me. In the *Holy Grail* the mystical purpose is most distinctly avowed. We are told to learn what it means by studying the visions of Sir Percival, and his 'subsequent fall and nineteenth century temptations.' The result of my study is that the visions are turned into waking shams, and leave a residuum of edifying sermon. The intrusion of the nineteenth century is simply disenchantment. If I want to be moral, I should get much more instruction out of *Mme. Bovary* or some other 'masterful transcript of actuality' than out of Tristram and Iseult, and if I want to be romantic, the likeness of King Arthur to the Prince Consort takes all the vigour out of the prehistoric personage. The Prince Consort, no doubt, deserved Tennyson's profound respect; but when we find him masquerading among the Knights of the Round Table, his admirable propriety of behaviour looks painfully like insipidity and incapacity for his position.

This line of criticism is, of course, very obvious; and, I admit, may be simply a proof of the critic's unsuitability. I desire simply to state the historical fact that the publication of the *Idylls* marks the point at which some disciples were sensible of a partial refrigeration of their zeal. The old Tennysonian power was not extinct; many of the poems up to the last had all the old exquisite charm, and the older poetry never lost it. But from this time a certain class of admirers—perhaps the duller class—felt that they dwelt in the outer court, and that they could not enter the inmost shrine with befitting reverence. There was not, I must add, in my case at least, any objection to the combination, as it is called, of philosophy with poetry. 'Your poetry,' as Jowett said to Tennyson, 'has an element of philosophy more to be considered than any regular philosophy in England.' 'It is,' he adds, 'almost too much impregnated with philosophy,' although this again 'will be to some minds its greatest charm.' Tennyson himself was amused by discovering that he had been talking Hegelianism without knowing it. The fact is, I take it, that poetry in a mind of great general power, not only may be, but cannot help being, philosophy. Philosophy itself, it may be plausibly urged, is in reality nothing but poetry expressed by the cumbrous methods of dialectical formulas. It labours painfully to put together ostensible reasons for the truth of the conceptions of life and the world which are directly presented in the poetic imagery. Tennyson's philosophy would have been present, though not consciously indicated, if he had simply recast the Arthurian legends in the spirit of the original creators. Nor will I argue that dislike to allegory is anything better than a prosaic prejudice, or, perhaps, an application of some pretentious aesthetic canon. Perhaps, indeed, the allegorical form was not so much the stumbling-block as the philosophical or ethical system itself which was meant to be adumbrated. Or rather, for that, I think, is the true account, we who fell off disliked a philosophy which required to be insinuated through an allegorical clothing. We were going through an intellectual crisis;

and if we exaggerated its importance, Tennyson at least, as many other
utterances prove, and as his memoirs show most convincingly, was equally
impressed by the greatness of the issues. But for that reason, we (I repeat that
by 'we' I only mean the wicked) wanted something more downright and
dogmatic. A religious philosophy which hides itself behind mythical figures
and vague personifications of abstract qualities; which can only be shadowed
forth and insinuated through a rehabilitated romance, seemed inadequate
and even effeminate. We fancied that if it ventured into broad daylight it
would turn out to be mere commonplace disguised or made of moonshine
and flimsy sentimentalisms. Or, possibly, we were not distinctly aware that
there really was any mystical meaning at all, and simply felt that when such
vital questions were being raised, we could not be really interested in this
dim poetic land of unsubstantial shadows. When, a little later, we began to
know what Omar Khayyam had said some eight centuries before, we felt the
power of a direct and intensely powerful utterance of one mode of treating
the eternal problem. All this, it may be replied, is to explain that a certain
class of young men were partially alienated from Tennyson's poetry because
they did not like his philosophy; which is a proof that they were aesthetically
dull and philosophically grovelling. I will not dispute the inference; I think,
indeed, that there is much to be said for it; and as I have admitted my
tendencies that way, I am obviously disqualified from speaking as an
impartial judge. I only wish to urge, by way of extenuation at any rate, that
we were still accessible to other Tennysonian influences, and, indeed, to
poems in which his doctrine finds a more direct utterance. I love *In
Memoriam,* and should be sorry if I were forced to admit that I could not
understand the true secret of its extraordinary beauty. Professor Sidgwick
contributes to this volume a most interesting account of its influence upon
him. For certain reasons, I could not adopt all that he says, and my intellectual
dissent from Tennyson begins, I may say, at an earlier stage; but I decline to
admit that I am for that reason incapable of feeling the emotional power.
Therefore, without attempting to argue the aesthetical canons, I return to the
purely historical question suggested by these volumes. Froude, in a letter to
the author, says that in his estimate, Tennyson stands 'far away, by the side of
Shakespeare, above all other English poets, with this relative superiority even
to Shakespeare, that he speaks the thoughts and speaks to the perplexities
and misgivings of his own age.' Froude adds characteristically that Tennyson
came before the world had become inflated 'with the vanity of progress, and
there was still an atmosphere in which such a soul could grow. There will be
no such others for many a long age.' It is rash, I think, to prophesy about 'long
ages,' but Froude is at any rate a good witness as to the facts. Froude had

known better than most people the doubts and perplexities by which Tennyson's contemporaries were distracted; and though Froude's own view remains rather a mystery, the impression made upon a man so alive to many sides of modern thought is no small proof of Tennyson's power. Now the memoirs ought to show us how Tennyson was prepared for the office of prophet. It has become common, as Mr. Palgrave remarks in his reminiscences, to treat of a poet as though he were 'evolved by a natural law'; and he gives an amusing instance in Taine's *a priori* speculations as to the evolution of Tennyson. Tennyson, as Taine suggested in a conversation, must have been brought up in luxury, and 'surrounded with things of costly beauty.' Mr. Palgrave was able to upset this theory, so far as concerned Tennyson's personal history. There is, of course, one absolute limit to any such speculation. No human being can presume to guess what are the conditions which determine the innate qualities of a man of genius. No one can say why such a plant, or a whole family of such plants, should have suddenly sprung up in a Lincolnshire vicarage, or why, a few years after, a similar phenomenon should have presented itself at Haworth. One can only ask how far the genius was influenced by its 'environment'? In both cases it might seem at first sight to be most unfavourable. The Brontës had an even less congenial atmosphere in Yorkshire than the Tennysons among the rough farmers of Lincolnshire. And yet in both cases there is this much similarity in the result, that, as the Brontës became even fanatical admirers of the cross-grained, hard-fisted York-shireman, Tennyson acquired at least a keen imaginative sympathy with the race of 'Northern farmers.' It would be as easy as absurd to deduce from these instances a general theory about the advantage of a bracing atmosphere for sensitive plants. In the case of Tennyson it must be admitted that the scantiness of details in the earlier parts of the memoir is rather tantalising. When Tennyson had become famous, materials of course became abundant, and Lord Tennyson tells us that he has had to make selections from forty thousand letters. For the early years, in which the mind and character were being formed, he had had little beyond a few recollections of his parents' talk. One would gladly know more of the crusty old grandfather who disinherited his eldest son; and of the stalwart son himself, six feet two in height, famous for social geniality and yet given to fits of despondency, and capable of being something of a tyrant in his family. His soul, we are told, was 'daily racked by bitter fancies, and tossed about by stormy troubles.' He had strange adventures in Russia and on the Continent. From the age of eleven the son had this father for his sole instructor, and must have profited, and also, one guesses, have suffered from the 'dominating force' of the paternal intellect. Then there is only a glimpse of the charming aunt, who would 'weep for hours' over the infinite goodness of God. He had damned most of her friends, and 'picked out for eternal salvation,' her who was 'no better than her neighbours.' One would like again to know more even of the cook, who declared that if you 'raaked out hell with a smaall tooth coamb' you wouldn't find the likes of her master and mistress. Was this characteristic of the cook or of her employers? It might conceivably be interpreted as confirming a later statement that Tennyson's mother, being an angel, was undiscoverable in the lower regions, and she appears to have been in fact a most charming old lady, with a strong sense of humour. There are hints enough here for a hypothetical biography, with any number of remarks about 'heredity' and 'environment.' All that can be safely said is that Tennyson was obviously a born poet, writing verses of unmistakable promise at the age of fourteen and fifteen; even getting, at the age of seventeen, £20 from a singularly discriminative country bookseller for the volume (written with his brother); and accumulating at least the materials for other poems, including the 'Ode to Memory,' which, we are told, he considered to be one of the best among his 'very early and peculiarly concentrated Nature poems.' Personally, I have always been grateful to it for one of those life-giving touches which went far to reveal or justify for me the charm of fen scenery. Whatever the influences, Tennyson came up to Cambridge as a poet, and even, it seems, as a man already set aside for poetry. At Cambridge, at any rate, he was contented to stand aside from the ordinary competitions. Like other men of poetical genius, he felt little respect for the regular studies of the place; and melodiously complained that the authorities 'taught us nothing, feeding not the heart.' The heart, indeed, cannot be fed upon Newton's *Principia*. There might, I think, be some reply to the charge of 'lethargy' made against the University of that time: the place was really waking up under the influence (among others) of Julius Hare and Thirlwall and Whewell; but, undoubtedly, the influence of his own contemporaries was the really important matter for Tennyson. There may be, in many ways, better official teaching now; but the existing generation must be congratulated if it includes any large admixture of young men so keenly interested in intellectual pursuits as were Tennyson's special circle. The Union had just ceased to be thrilled by the eloquence of Charles Austin and Macaulay and Praed, and their rivals who supplied recruits to the 'philosophical Radicals,' and sought glory in the Reform Bill agitation. Charles Buller, the most beloved by his friends the Radicals, left college soon after Tennyson came up; Maurice, who had already founded the 'apostles,' with Sterling, the most attractive of men, represented the other school of Liberalism, which regarded Coleridge as its oracle. Among Tennyson's intimates and warm friends in later life were such men as

Spedding, and Monckton Milnes, and Trench, and many others keenly interested, at least, in the literature of to-day. Edward FitzGerald, though a contemporary, was not as yet known to Tennyson; but Lord Houghton seems to have been fully justified in saying that the Cambridge of those days could boast a body of young men such as had been rarely surpassed in promise. Chief among them, in Tennyson's opinion, and in that of many good judges, was Arthur Hallam. Whatever might be the dreariness of the lecture-room, a young man of genius could have no reason to complain that his lot was cast in barren places. Tennyson in later years always looked back with affection to those 'dawn-golden times'; and, indeed, his memory inspired phrases too familiar for more than a passing allusion. To students of the might-have-been, it might be tempting to ask what would have happened if Tennyson had gone to Oxford and come under the influence of Newman and Hurrell Froude. The Dean of Westminster tells us how, when he first met Tennyson among his intimates, in 1841–2, he was startled by their indifference to the Tractarian Controversy, and to the questions which interested the disciples of Arnold. Would an Oxford-bred Tennyson have written another *Christian Year,* or achieved that poem which Clough never succeeded in writing?

Anyhow, the retrospective view of Tennyson's college life might suggest some melancholy reflections. Death cut short some promising careers; some, though they did good work, failed to make a public mark: they have left an impression upon their personal friends, but an impression of which even the tradition will expire in the next generation; and others, perhaps for want of some quality of mind or character, eventually dropped behind the real leaders of the time, and compounded with the commonplace world. Why did not Tennyson fall to the rear? Such a catastrophe must at one time have seemed not improbable to an outside observer. His friends, indeed, seem to have fully recognised his abilities. He was, briefly, one of the 'mighty of the earth,' said Blakesley. 'He was,' says Fanny Kemble, whose brother John was a college friend, 'the great hero of the day.' His tall, powerful figure, his 'Shakespearian' head, finely poised, 'crowned with dark, wavy hair,' made him look the character of the 'coming poet' as well as could be desired by a painter. The striking point about him, then as afterwards, was the 'union of strength with refinement.' And yet one imagines that the college dons, the 'lion-like' Whewell, for example, also conspicuous for physical as well as intellectual prowess, must have shaken their heads when Tennyson not only declined to enter the Senate House competitions, but apparently decided to become a mere looker-on at life, and passed years in a quiet Bohemian company; smoking pipes at intervals with Carlyle and joining friends at the Cock; but mainly vegetating in the country with no very obvious prospects, and apparently surrendering his mind a little too unreservedly to a 'wise passiveness,' though he might be slowly secreting a few exquisite poems.

That, no doubt, represents one aspect of Tennyson. Mr. Lecky remarks that 'nature evidently intended him for the life of the quietest and most secluded of country gentlemen, for a life spent among books and flowers and a few intimate friends,' sheltered from all outside shocks. And at the period to which the recollection refers (late in the 'sixties) this was an obvious, though, as Mr. Lecky of course recognises, very far indeed from an exhaustive, judgment. The house at Farringford, the Mecca of many future generations of Tennysonians, looks as if it had been secreted, like the shell of a mollusc, by the nature of the occupant. The sweet English scenery, which no one ever painted so well, and the sea, which he loved like a true Englishman, show themselves through the belt of wood, calculated to keep the profane vulgar at a distance. It seemed a providential *habitat* for a man so very open to even petty irritations. 'A flea will annoy me,' as he said to Tyndall; 'a fleabite will spread a square inch over the surface of my skin. . . . I *am* thin-skinned, and I take no pains to hide it.' And, indeed, though the fact is fully admitted, it is perhaps less conspicuous in these volumes than it was to casual observers. They were apt to carry away the impression that Tennyson must spend an unreasonably large part of his time in fretting over the wounds made by trumpery critics. The absolute simplicity of the man, indeed, which was equally obvious, suggested pity instead of contempt for what must be regarded as an infirmity. No poet since Pope was so sensitive to the assaults of Grub Street; though happily he was altogether incapable of condescending to Pope's miserable methods of retort. It is, however, easy to understand the view which commended itself to Taine. His theory was that Tennyson was a kind of refined epicurean; a man lapping himself in British comfort against all disagreeable sights and painful truths; averting his eyes as much as possible from harsh contrasts and harrowing doubts; and enveloped in a panoply made from the soothing creeds of political and religious opportunists, with only just enough of the light of reason filtered through a screen of tradition to pass for being at once liberal and respectable. Though Taine had to give up his theory as to Tennyson's personal environment, he still draws a picture of English country life as seen from the railway—its well-ordered parks and neat country houses embowered in well-ordered gardens—and contrasts it with the stimulating, though rough realities of Parisian life, among which his favourite De Musset penetrated the true secret of life. Taine naturally prefers De Musset, and his criticism, though it is obviously from a partial outsider, hits off one view which cannot be overlooked. Matthew Arnold, as I have observed elsewhere, introduces the 'great, broad-shouldered genial

Englishman' of the 'Princess' as a type of British 'Philistinism,' and intimates his opinion that the creator is too much in sympathy with the type.

It is equally true that no lover of Tennyson's poetry could admit Taine's scornful account of the *In Memoriam* as the mourning of a correct gentleman, wiping away his tears with a cambric pocket-handkerchief. I can subscribe, on the contrary, without hesitation, to the commonplace British opinion that no poet has ever shown such depths of tenderness or such skill in interweaving the most delicate painting of nature with the utterance of profound emotion. And this brings us back to the biographical problem. Over twenty years intervened between Tennyson's departure from Cambridge and the settlement in Farringford. Here again, through no fault of Lord Tennyson, we feel the want of a few more documents. No doubt a reader may be content with what is expressed or can be inferred from the poetry. Yet the matter-of-fact personal history, if it could have been told, would surely have had a deep interest. In the first place, one would like to know, if a purely prosaic person, something about the bare pounds, shillings, and pence. Tennyson, as we discover from a remark of Carlyle's, inherited a 'small annuity on his father's decease' (1831), and chose to 'club with his mother and sisters,' and so to 'live unpromoted and write poems.' This may be all very well for a bachelor; and we are glad to discover that from 1850 his copyrights were producing five hundred pounds a year, which, considering the small bulk of his publications, shows that he was doing remarkably well for a poet. In 1845, however, he had still been in need of a pension; and the smallness of his income was of serious importance. He had met his future wife in 1836; he had become engaged to her apparently in 1837, and felt the need of making a livelihood. It was from the vagueness of his expectations in that direction that the correspondence between him and Miss Sellwood was forbidden in 1840, and they apparently did not meet again for ten years. Meanwhile all his independent property was lost about 1844, together with part of his brothers' and sisters', in an unfortunate speculation, and distress caused 'real hardship,' and even an attack of illness. He must, therefore, have gone through a period of trial, affecting not only his pocket, but his hopes of domestic happiness, of which one would have liked to know a little more. That he took his troubles bravely, whatever they may have been, is proved by his literary history. Whatever else he did, he never condescended to lower his aims or the perfection of his workmanship. He allowed his poetry to ripen in his mind, as though he had been in possession of Taine's hypothetical luxuries; and, it would seem, he kept his feelings, whatever they may have been, to himself. His extreme sensibility led him to seek for the utmost possible perfection; not to court immediate popularity. The years of comparative nonrecognition must have been trying, and the relative slightness of the personal record of these twenty years is the more regrettable. Fuller materials, had they been accessible, must have brought out more distinctly the real strength which lay beneath the morbidly sensitive outside. His 'sensitiveness,' as Mr. Lecky observes, 'seemed to me,' as it did to others, curiously out of harmony with 'his large, powerful frame.' Whether there is any real incompatibility between athletic vigour and delicacy of nervous organisation is a problem which I must leave to physiologists. Another instance of the same combination may be found, for example, in Hawthorne; and, I dare say, in plenty of other instances. Generally speaking, we are inclined, with whatever reason, to anticipate from an athletic giant more of the rollicking vigour of a Christopher North than of the exquisite workmanship which makes 'jewels five words long'—the power, as Johnson put it, of hewing a colossus from a rock, not of carving figures on cherry-stones. Tennyson, no doubt, though this side of his character is a little in the background, could have taken his part in one of the jovial 'Noctes,' if he had been sure that no reporters were present. But the massive physical framework seems to be indicated by a certain slowness which might pass into indolence. Your giant may be sensitive, but he carries too much ballast to be easily stirred to utterance. He is contemplative or dreamy rather than impetuous and excitable. If Shelley had put on more flesh, he might have been equally poetical, but he would not have indulged in the boyish explosions which imply an excessive mobility of the nervous system. Byron's extraordinary alternations between corpulence and thinness induced by starvation appear to be clearly connected both with his power and his weakness, and might be considered at length in the essay which ought to be written upon the relation between fat and poetry. But I must not be led into such a digression here. One sees in Tennyson's portraits the deep, dreamy eyes under the noble brow, and recognises the man predestined to be a thoughtful spectator of the battle of life, rather than an active participator in the superficial contests.

And here, of course, we have the obvious remarks about the spirit of his generation. Young men were ceasing to feel the revolutionary inspiration, though they were still accessible to the utterances of the departing period. When Byron died in 1824, Carlyle exclaimed that the news came upon his heart 'like a mass of lead'; he felt a 'painful twinge,' as if he had lost a brother. Tennyson, then only fourteen, felt the same news to be an 'awful calamity,' and rushed out-of-doors to write upon the sandstone, 'Byron is dead.' But Byronism soon followed Byron. Shelley was unknown to Tennyson, till his college days at least, and the successor, though, of course, admiring his predecessor's marvellous powers, admitted that Shelley was 'after too much in the clouds' for him. Keats, on the other hand, he declared, 'would have been among the very greatest of us if he had lived. There is something of the innermost soul of the poet in everything he ever wrote.' 'Wordsworth's very best,' he said, 'is the best in its way that has been sent out by the moderns,' and one is glad to hear that he was once able to express to Wordsworth himself his deep sense of the 'obligation which all Englishmen owed to him.' From various scattered remarks it is clear that Tennyson, like other poets, could be an admirable critic of his brethren; but these sayings are interesting as indicating his own tendencies in early days. How much he actually owed to Keats and Wordsworth must be uncertain. Probably he would have been much the same had he never read a line of either. But one may say that he wished to utter teaching congenial to Wordsworth's in language as perfect as that of Keats's most finished workmanship. The famous hypothetical addition to Wordsworth's poems,

A Mister Wilkinson, a Clergyman,

the authorship of which was claimed both by Tennyson and FitzGerald, indicates the weakness which was naturally avoided by one who could equally appreciate Keats. Like Keats's, at any rate, Tennyson's poetry shows the dying-out of the old fervour which had stimulated Wordsworth's first efforts, made Coleridge and Southey 'pantisocratists,' and inspired Byron and Shelley during the days of the Holy Alliance. The movements of 1830, both in Europe and England, roused some of Tennyson's circle, such as Sterling and Kemble; but, as far as one can infer from the indications, both Tennyson and Arthur Hallam looked at least doubtfully upon the Reform agitation in England. The Tennysons, indeed, set the bells ringing to the horror of the parson at Somersby when the Bill was passed; but Hallam thought that William iv., when he met the 'first assembly of delegates from a sovereign people' (that is, the first Reformed Parliament), would perhaps be the last King of England; and even Tennyson, a little later, hopes against hope that there are still true hearts in old England 'that will never brook the sight of Baal in the Sanctuary, and St. Simon' (the leader of the famous sect) 'in the Church of Christ.' The St. Simonians show what an 'immense mass of evil' is in existence, and are 'a focus which gathers all its rays.' The Reform Bill was not to be a descent of Niagara, but a passage over the rapids into a superficially quiet reach. A judicious friend gives another view. Sterling, he says, had been misled, like Shelley, by the desire to abolish unjust institutions, but had afterwards perceived that the right method was to 'implant a principle with which selfishness cannot coexist.' Reformers would complain that they must wait for a long time if they have first to extirpate selfishness. With this we may associate a criticism of Spedding upon the early poems, which showed, he thought, over indulgence 'in the luxuries of the senses, a profusion of splendours, harmonies, perfumes, gorgeous apparels, luscious meats and drinks,' and so forth, which rather 'pall upon the sense,' and make the outward obscure the inner world. The remark falls in with Taine's criticism. Such a Tennyson might be too easily reconciled to the creature-comforts of the upper classes in England and become a mere dreaming Sybarite. His own view of the situation is apparently given in the 'Palace of Art.' It was a comment, as we are told, upon a remark made to him at college by Trench: 'Tennyson, we cannot live in art.' The poem itself is so marvellous a collection of those felicities of description in which Tennyson is unapproachable, that perhaps it rather raises the question why the architect of the palace should not have stayed there quietly and worshipped 'art for art' for the rest of his days. The conversion comes rather abruptly, but, at least, shows how much Tennyson's mind was occupied with the problem of how the artist is to be also the moralist. I certainly do not quarrel with his solution, which in some sense worked itself out in *In Memoriam*. The moral crisis through which he passed is indicated by the 'Two Voices' or 'Thoughts of a Suicide' (that is, of somebody who decided not to commit suicide), written contemporaneously with the first poems of *In Memoriam*, under a 'cloud of overwhelming sorrow.' All joy, he said, was 'blotted out' of his life and he 'longed for death.' He continued, however, to write, and his writing does not suggest unbroken gloom. He was finally, it would seem, restored to full mental health by the love which was to be the blessing of later years. If we may not call it morbid, it is at least abnormal that the loss of a college friend should cause not only immoderate agony, but such prolonged depression. Arthur Hallam may have deserved all that was said of him, though for us he can only be, like Sterling, a symbol of the virtue of friendship, a type canonised by genius, but, like some other saints, a little wanting in individuality. We cannot define the merits which prompted eulogies in some ways unparalleled in our literature. Lycidas, as Tennyson and others have said, is a test of poetical sensibility. I deny parenthetically that there can be any universal test in such matters, but the meaning is no doubt that it is a test of the appreciation of such poetical merits as are independent of the pathos of the theme. It is a test, that is, precisely because the beauty of the poetry does not imply any very keen sensibility about the person ostensibly commemorated. Milton could be noble and melodious, though one does not suppose that he lost his appetite for breakfast for a single day after hearing of King's death. The sincerity of Tennyson's grief, on the contrary, is implied in every section. He was, we are told, profoundly impressed by Shakespeare's sonnets when he was writing *In Memoriam,* and we can understand why at the time he then thought them even greater than the plays. The intense passion of some of the sonnets ('no longer mourn for me when I am dead,' for example) equals or surpasses in its way anything in *In Memoriam.* But, whatever the solution of their mystery, they do not convince me that Shakespeare was at any time disqualified by his emotions from attending to the interests of the Globe Theatre. As an embodiment of the purest passion of friendship, the *In Memoriam* is, I take it, unapproachable; and, in spite of any reservations upon other points, that must be, to some minds, the great source of Tennyson's power over his readers. Mr. Palgrave ends his reminiscences of Tennyson by saying that forty-three years of friendship made him recognise lovableness' as the 'dominant note' of his friend's character. That, I think, is also the impression, and certainly there cannot be a better one, which is made by the whole of this biography. Tennyson had his weaknesses, which can be divined where filial reverence properly refrains from an articulate statement or a distinct insistence upon them. Nor, as I shall say directly, can I admit without reservations some other claims to our allegiance. But the unsurpassed sweetness and tenderness of character is evident in every chapter. It is impossible to read the book without learning to love the man better. It is needless to speak of the beauty of the domestic life; needless, at any rate, to express more than the sense of satisfaction that, for once, a poet, of abnormally sensitive character even for a poet, was surrounded by an atmosphere of unbroken harmony for so many years. If he lost Hallam, he always preserved the friendship of Carlyle (tempered by an occasional growl); of the inimitable FitzGerald, never less delightful because he could never affect insincere admiration; of the wise and placid Spedding, the 'Pope,' as Tennyson called him, of the young men at Trinity; of Maurice, revered by all who knew him for saintliness of character if not for lucidity of intellect; of the cordial and generous Kingsley, and of Mr. Aubrey de Vere, and others who still live and cherish his memory. If he was over-sensitive to 'fleabites' of petty criticism, the irritation never embittered him; no ungenerous and 'nasty' remark about his contemporaries seems to mar the impression of real dignity of character. He thought a good deal about himself: most people do; but any little vanity he shows is perfectly innocent and consistent with substantial simplicity and modesty. His foibles added a certain piquancy to the sentiment of his friends: it is pleasant to feel that you are petting a tender and childlike nature as well as simply sitting at a great man's feet. Undoubtedly a man might be equally lovable and yet unable to write a line which would not have set Tennyson's teeth on edge. But even Tennyson's astonishing sensibility to the 'music of words,' and his power of compressing into a stanza the quintessence of sentiments or perceptions which other men might dilute into volumes, would have been thrown away without this singular sweetness of character. When I read 'Tears, Idle Tears,' I feel that a man might be forgiven even by a stern moralist for devoting a lifetime to stringing together a few melodious phrases as a perpetual utterance of our better moods. Gray did something of the kind; but Tennyson, though not a voluminous poet, has probably left an unsurpassed number of phrases which will live in the memory both of gentle and simple— the most punctilious 'aesthete' and the reader whose ignorance, better than knowledge, allows him to be charmed without knowing or asking why.

If these volumes contain what we had all more or less divined, they call attention to a claim which may provoke more discussion. Jowett, as we see, regarded Tennyson as a teacher of philosophy. Maurice dedicated his most characteristic volume to Tennyson as to one who has been a great spiritual teacher; and Dr. Martineau, giving an account of the meeting at the 'Metaphysical Society,' speaks of Maurice's fellowship of thought with 'the truest *vates* of his age.' It becomes an outsider to treat these and other weighty testimonies with all respect. And yet the insistence upon this aspect of Tennyson's work strikes one perhaps as a little excessive. There is, of course, no question as to the depth of Tennyson's interest in theological questions. The frequent recurrence of this claim, however, tends, I think, to give an impression that the famous line ought to have been 'A Mr. Tennyson, a clergyman,' and to put a little too much out of sight the fact that he was not always in the pulpit. He could yield himself, it is obvious, to perfectly unsophisticated enjoyment of sensuous impressions; he could talk very effectively and very humorously as a simple man of letters, or even, if we may say so without offence, as a man of this world capable of hearty contempt for clerical as well as other cants and hypocrisies. I have more than once had a similar surprise in reading biographies of men whom I have seen in the flesh; and the explanation is not far to seek. Fuller tells us somewhere of the bishop who used to go down to the cellar with his old friend and chaplain, where they could throw their canonicals aside, pledge each other in a good glass of wine, and refresh their souls in a jolly conversation. No doubt they showed on such occasions a side which did not get into official biographies. Tennyson certainly could doff his 'canonicals'; but, however this may be, it suggests another point which demands some delicacy of handling. Professor Sidgwick thinks that *In Memoriam* expresses with admirable clearness a true philosophical judgment of certain tendencies of modern speculation. I cannot discuss that problem on which Professor Sidgwick speaks with authority as well as sympathy. In any case the poetical merit of a work does not depend upon its philosophical orthodoxy. The orthodox, whoever they may be, can be terribly vapid and the heretics much more inspiring. A man would be a very narrow-minded critic who was unable to admire any of the great men from Lucretius to Dante who have embodied the most radically opposite conceptions of the world. But we must draw a line, as Tennyson is reported to have said, between such poets as Keats, Byron, and Shelley, and the 'great sage poets,' at once thinkers and artists, such as Aeschylus, Shakespeare, 'Dante, and Goethe.' Can we think of Tennyson himself as belonging to the highest class? Did he not only accept the right view, whatever that may be, but express it forcibly and majestically as one of the small class which represents poetry thoroughly transfused with philosophy? I at least cannot see my way to such a conclusion; and the mere comparison seems to me to suggest the real limitations to Tennyson's art. I will only notice what is suggested by many passages in these volumes. Carlyle, we are told, was first attracted to Tennyson by the 'Ulysses.' He quotes in his first letter to Tennyson the noble passage:—

It may be that the gulfs will wash us down:
It may be we shall touch the Happy Isles,
And see the great Achilles, whom we knew.

'These lines,' he says, 'do not make me weep, but there is in me what would fill whole lachrymatories as I read.'[1] Afterwards Carlyle appears to have suggested that Tennyson was wasting his time by scribbling verses. Carlyle, late in life, would occasionally quote the 'Ulysses' by way of contrast with Tennyson's later performances. The old poem, he thought, had the true heroic ring; and Tennyson himself, it may be remarked, says that it was written soon after Hallam's death, and gave his feelings about fighting the battle of life perhaps more simply than anything in *In Memoriam*. Carlyle's criticism came to this, that Tennyson had declined into a comparatively sentimental and effeminate line of writing, mere 'astheticisms' instead of inspiring a courageous spirit of confronting the spiritual crisis. The *Idylls of the King* could not be the epic of the future, but at best a melodious version of conventional and superficial solutions of the eternal problem. King Arthur had (in Carlylese) too much of the 'gigman' to be a great leader of modern men. The average critic, as we are frequently reminded in these volumes, complained that Tennyson was 'morbid.' *Maud*, in particular, gave that offence in spite of irresistible beauties. Tennyson himself argued that the critics confounded the author with his creature. The hero of *Maud* was only a dramatic personage; he was a 'morbid poetic soul,' and the poem was to be taken as 'a little *Hamlet*.' The original *Hamlet* would itself be now criticised, he thought, as 'morbid.' Mr. Gladstone, who first took the poem to represent the worship of Jingo, recanted on further consideration, and discovered that Tennyson had only approved of 'lawful war'—which makes a great difference. *Maud*, I must say in passing, fell in, at any rate, too easily with the curious delusion of the time (embodied also in Kingsley's *Two Years Ago*) that the Crimean War implied the moral regeneration of the country. Necessary or absurd, I don't think that the war can now be credited with that effect. *Maud*, I fancy, will be remembered for the surpassing beauty of the love lyrics, and not from any lively interest in a hero who is not only morbid, but silly. Hamlet may have been morbid—an interview with one's father's ghost is rather upsetting—but at least he was not contemptible. However, we will not for a moment identify the gentleman in *Maud* with Tennyson. Another poem, 'Despair,' provoked, we are told, bitter criticism, 'because the public did not recognise it as a dramatic monologue.' It is, I think—as I believe the most ardent Tennysonians admit—a distinctly inferior specimen of his art; but it expresses something not purely dramatic. Tennyson himself remarked that he would commit suicide if he thought there was no 'future life'; and his hero acts upon that principle. He is equally shocked by the 'horrible know-nothing books,' and by a view of hell such as commended itself to Tennyson's aunt; and the suggestion is natural that the reasonable course for a man equally horrified by both opinions is to put an end to himself. It would not be fair to lay any stress upon an admitted shortcoming, and the 'dramatic monologue' argument may be taken for what it is worth. But this, too, is, I think, clear. When Tennyson is presented to us as giving the true solution of the doubts which beset our time, we should have some positive as well as negative testimony to his merits. We cannot, it is true, expect a full solution. A gentleman is reported to have asked him whether the existence of evil was not the great difficulty. Tennyson certainly could not be expected to throw much light upon Job's difficulties, and seems to have judiciously diverted the conversation by referring to the 'charge of the heavy brigade.' No poet, and indeed no philosopher, can be asked to solve the eternal problems off-hand. What we do see, is that Tennyson, like many noble and deep thinkers, was terribly perplexed by the alternatives apparently offered: by his aversion on one side to certain orthodox dogmas, and by his dread and hatred of some tendencies which claim at least to be scientific. His ideal hero was the man who faced doubts boldly and attained clear convictions of one kind or other. On the other hand, he is always haunted by the fear of depriving your sister of her 'happy views' (a woefully feeble phrase, by the way, for Tennyson), and praises a philosopher for keeping his doubts to himself. The resulting attitude of mind may not be morbid: certainly it may fairly be called pathetic, and even those who do not sympathise with his doctrine will do well to feel for his distress. It may teach them, at least, what is in any case worth knowing: why their teaching is so repulsive to many tender and delicate minds. But I confess to share Carlyle's regret for the loss of the old heroic tone of the 'Ulysses.' Noble poetry, let us admit, may express either faith or scepticism: a conviction that we know or that we can never know; it may be openly pessimistic, or expressive of an enthusiastic faith in the future; but Tennyson, even in the *In Memoriam,* always seems to me to be like a man clinging to a spar left floating after a shipwreck, knowing that it will not support him, and yet never able to make up his mind to strike out and take his chance of sinking or swimming. That may be infinitely affecting, but it is not the attitude of the poet who can give a war-cry to his followers, or of the philosopher who really dares to 'face the spectres of the mind.' He can lay them for the moment; but they are always in the background, and suggest, too often, rather a querulous protest against an ever-recurring annoyance than any such mental victory as issues in a coherent and settled conviction on either side. I merely wish to indicate an impression, and will not attempt to indicate the similar attitude in regard to the great social and political movements. I cannot, though my inability may be owing to my own spiritual blindness, place him among the 'great sage poets,' but I have wished to intimate that such as I am are not therefore disqualified from appreciating his poetry in another capacity: as a document indicating the effect of modern movements of thought upon a mind of extraordinary delicacy and a nature of admirable sweetness; but, far more, as a perfect utterance of emotions which are all equally beautiful in themselves whatever the 'philosophy' with which they are associated. The life, I believe, will help to strengthen that impression, though I have only attempted to notice some of the more obvious remarks which it may suggest.

Notes

1. I remember to have heard Carlyle in his old age speak with equal enthusiasm of this poem.

—Leslie Stephen, "Life of Tennyson," *Studies of a Biographer,* 1899, vol. 2, pp. 196–240

LEWIS E. GATES "NATURE IN TENNYSON'S POETRY" (1900)

In the following extract, Lewis E. Gates sees Tennyson as carrying on the romantic tradition of the treatment of nature in art. That is not to say that

Gates portrays the poet as simply a latter-day romantic: Tennyson has been too thoroughly imbued with the modern Victorian spirit and the belief in scientific progress. The influence of science checks Tennyson anytime he approaches the romantic concept of the transcendent power of nature. As a consequence, Tennyson's deployment of the physical world in his verse is as a symbol of men's emotions and passions, offered in a manner that far surpasses, in Gates's opinion, that of Wordsworth. The extract suggests that the latter poet's portrayal of human temperament is far less nuanced than Tennyson's own.

Gates proceeds to examine Tennyson's spiritualization of nature as evidenced in several of his poems. The critic concludes that, unlike a contemporary such as Browning who moved in style and theme beyond the romantic tradition, Tennyson—in his love of beauty and the imagination, in his lack of sympathy with the real world (a fact that several critics quoted in this volume remark was as much a part of the retiring man himself as it was part of his verse), in his vague portrayal of character, and in the escapist nature of much of his work—was the heir to an earlier generation of poets.

Gates does not express any views of Tennyson's verse that were not also expressed by other critics, but he presents a view of the poet as the inheritor of the romantics' mantle, which allowed him to look back over half a century. Those mid-nineteenth-century critics were still living with several of the romantics as their contemporaries (for example, Wordsworth died in 1850), but Gates, with the benefit of hindsight, views Tennyson as part of a tradition rather than as a new poet on the literary scene.

One of the most important effects of the Romantic movement was the closeness of the relation it established between nature and the human soul. The intense and oftentimes eccentric emotions that tended to throw the Romantic poet out of sympathy with his fellow men and with conventional life became the solvent of the rigid forms of the material universe. The poet's fervid mood proved the very fire necessary to fuse nature once and for all with emotion, to make it coalesce with thought and the inner life of man, and to unite matter and spirit more subtly and intimately than ever before. The Romantic poets subdued nature to spirit; they interpreted nature in terms of human feeling; they sent their imaginations out along countless lines of subtle association, drew all nature into sympathy with their intense experiences, and converted all the facts and forms of nature into "the passion-winged ministers of thought." Nature was no longer to stand apart from man as a system of half-hostile forces, or a mass of dry facts, meaningless except for science: it was not to be as for Pope and the Deists merely a great machine of infinitely ingenious construction, set running once and for all by the great Mechanician and for ever after grinding out effects unerringly and inevitably. For many Romantic poets—notably for Wordsworth, Coleridge, and Shelley—nature was a direct emanation from the one great spiritual force which manifests itself also in the myriad individuals that make up the human race. The countless ideas and feelings that float through the mind of man and the countless shapes and aspects of the world of nature were alike the utterance of one great imaginative Artist, who expressed through these two sets of symbols his thoughts of beauty and truth. Hence the poet who seeks a proper image to stand for his thought has simply to let his imagination guide him through the beautiful forms of nature till he finds a fitting symbol; his thoughts are God's thoughts, and have been already uttered in some fixed shape of beauty, or through some changing aspect, of the outside world. This is really the postulate on which Wordsworth's and Coleridge's theory of imagination depends; imagination, they urge leads to objective truth, while fancy only plays prettily with images; imagination discerns essential analogies between mind and matter, and brings once more into at least transient unity the world of spirit and the world of nature.

Tennyson's poetry carries on with fine loyalty and in some ways with increased effectiveness the Romantic tradition in the treatment of nature. Not that he accepts or expresses extreme transcendental conceptions of the relation of nature to man and of nature and man to God. The scientific spirit is continually imposing its check upon him and compelling him to recognize, at least transiently, the literal meaning of the facts of nature as interpreted by the analytic, positive mind of his day and generation. Yet the Romantic mood of intimacy with nature survives in Tennyson, not simply undiscouraged by the revelations of science, but even quickened and intensified in its delicate susceptibility. He has done more than perhaps any other single poet of this century to spiritualize nature in the sense of making it subservient to the needs of the human soul and of forcing it to become symbolical of human moods and passions. He has done even more than Wordsworth to give a new meaning to nature; for whereas Wordsworth worked continually in the interests of a few simple moods with which many men nowadays cannot fully sympathize, Tennyson has had at his service an exquisitely graduated temperament, varying through an almost limitless range of complex moods, nearly every one of which may be shared by a sensitive reader.

From the outset Tennyson's poetry was noteworthy for its powerful and suggestive use of landscape. "Mariana" in his first volume, and "Mariana in the

South," "Fatima," and "Œnone" in his second volume were experiments after effects not before attempted in English literature. These poems are not studies of different "ways of love," or merely portraits of different types of women; they are immensely imaginative studies of irresistible and all-dominating moods, each of which is symbolized through the figure of a woman portrayed against a sympathetic background of nature. They are studies of landscape as landscape is seen through an atmosphere determined by feeling. Each poem owes its power to the congruity of its details, to the imaginative unity that pervades it and subdues every minutest circumstance of colour and light and shade and motion till they all breathe out one inevitable chord of feeling. The blinding light and the stifling heat of the landscapes in "Mariana in the South" seem the very exhalation of defeated passion; in the other "Mariana," the details of the "lonely moated grange," from the "blackest moss" of the flower-plots to the "glooming flats" and "dark fens," all image "Mariana's" deadly languor and desolation. The poem is a study in black of a passion of melancholy as the other poem is a study in flame-colours of a passion of consuming tenderness and devotion.

Of course, there are not many of the poems that have such absolute imaginative unity. But there is a second group where noticeably similar effects are gained by somewhat similar methods; this group contains most of the other poems that are called by the names of women,—"Lilian," "Isabel," "Madeline," "Eleanore," "Adeline," and "Margaret." Each poem portrays a temperament in terms of look, gesture, bearing, complexion, and form; each is the interpretation of a woman's soul as it reveals itself by means of subtle material symbols. The power of each poem is due to the poet's intuitive appreciation of the value of material facts as the expression of thought and feeling. Two of the poems, "Adeline" and "Margaret," beside portraying typical women, have a symbolical value; the "twin-sisters" symbolize the Romantic spirit as it shows itself now in the fanciful interpretation of nature, and now in the deeply imaginative interpretation of the passionate life of past generations. The less human of the sisters, "shadowy, dreaming Adeline," weaves into bright and tender myths all she sees in the outside world; she dreams childlike dreams over butterflies, bluebells, and "lilies at dawn," and finds all nature instinct with half-fantastic life. Margaret is the type of the Romantic spirit in its more serious moods and its "more human" sympathies; of its passion for "dainty sorrow" and of its ardent reveries over the great deeds and glorious tragedies of history.

What can it matter, Margaret,
    What songs below the waning stars

> The lion-heart, Plantagenet,
> Sang looking thro' his prison bars?
> Exquisite Margaret, who can tell
> The last wild thought of Chatelet,
> Just ere the falling axe did part
> The burning brain from the true heart,
> Even in her sight he loved so well.

Thoughts and images like these are the "feast of sorrow" from which the pale lady of Romance is loath to part. The mood that is suggested is much like that of Keats's more sombre odes; it has much in common with the mood of those verses which in the "Ode to a Nightingale" describe Ruth "amid the alien corn." Both passages send the imagination travelling back along the dark ways of history to the intense passionate experience of an isolated soul; both depend for their effectiveness on the curious modern mood that finds a special charm in the uncertain lights and shades, the mysterious chiaroscuro of the past.

The other poems of this group probably have no symbolical meaning; but they are quite as remarkable for their portrayal of temperament through bodily signs. And the interesting point to be noted with reference to all these poems is that they form one more illustration of the far-reaching sensitiveness to harmonies between matter and spirit which is perhaps in the last analysis the deepest source of Tennyson's power.

Besides the poems of the two general groups already considered, there are, of course, many others in Tennyson's earliest volumes which contain atmospheric landscapes of remarkable beauty and suggestiveness. In the "Ode to Memory" there occurs a series of landscapes which are called up out of the poet's boyhood; and they all have the dewy splendour, the freshness, the brilliancy of the impressions of youth; there rests on all of them the light of early morning. The "Lotos-Eaters" portrays a series of scenes from the land where "it seemed always afternoon"; the poem is a study in yellow and gold and orange; the landscapes are seen through a dreamy mellow haze and in the light of a westering sun; and not one of them could be conceived of as occurring in the "Ode to Memory." Nor could the following landscape be found by any possibility in the "Lotos-Eaters":—

> Pour round my ears the livelong bleat
> Of the thick-fleeced sheep from wattled folds,
> Upon the ridged wolds,
> When the first matin-song hath waken'd loud

Over the dark dewy earth forlorn,
What time the amber morn
Forth gushes from beneath a low-hung cloud.

There breathe through these lines the sense of mystery and the awe and yet the hope and the keen delight that are stirred in the heart of an impressionable boy by the sights and sounds of dawn. The Lotos-Eaters knew no such nature as this.

Nor is it only in Tennyson's early or short poems that this atmospheric treatment of landscape is to be found. His later long narrative poems are full of equally good illustrations of his power to re-create nature in terms of a dominating mood. The action of these poems goes on in the midst of natural scenery which is perpetually varying in tone and colour, and light and shade, in sympathy with the mood of the moment. In *Maud*, this suffusion of nature with passion is especially noticeable; and the hysterics and bad psychology of that poem are made endurable by the beauty of such imaginative sketches as the following:—

I heard no sound where I stood
But the rivulet on from the lawn
Running down to my own dark wood;
Or the voice of the long sea-wave as it swell'd
Now and then in the dim-gray dawn;
But I look'd, and round, all round the house I beheld
The death-white curtain drawn;
Felt a horror over me creep,
Prickle my skin and catch my breath,
Knew that the death-white curtain meant but sleep,
Yet I shudder'd and thought like a fool of the sleep of death.

This should be compared with Wordsworth's "Strange fits of passion have I known"; the mood is substantially the same; but Tennyson's lines are far finer in phrasing, more suggestive in imagery, and more thoroughly atmospheric.

In *Enoch Arden*, too, there are many passages where, with like intensity and imaginative power, nature is subdued to the passion of the moment. What could be finer from this point of view or more inappropriate from the point of view of Enoch's psychology than the famous lines describing Enoch's sense of isolation on the desert island?—

No sail from day to day, but every day
The sunrise broken into scarlet shafts

Among the palms and ferns and precipices;
The blaze upon the waters to the east;
The blaze upon his island overhead;
The blaze upon the waters to the west;
Then the great stars that globed themselves in
Heaven,
The hollower-bellowing ocean, and again
The scarlet shafts of sunrise—but no sail.

In order to bring out more unmistakably the peculiar transformation to which in such descriptions as these nature submits in passing through Tennyson's temperament, it may be well to quote two or three of his simpler descriptions of natural scenery where he merely portrays frankly and delicately some clearly visualized aspect or object of the outside world. Descriptions of this sort also abound, and are wrought out with an exquisite fineness of detail that does not preclude breadth of treatment, and with marvellous felicity of phrase. The first of the following passages is from "Margaret" and the second from *Maud*:—

The sun is just about to set,
The arching limes are tall and shady,
And faint, rainy lights are seen,
Moving in the leavy beech.
I was walking a mile,
More than a mile from the shore,
The sun look'd out with a smile
Betwixt the cloud and the moor,
And riding at set of day
Over the dark moor land,
Rapidly riding far away,
She waved to me with her hand.
There were two at her side,
Something flash'd in the sun,
Down by the hill I saw them ride,
In a moment they were gone.

The lines from "Margaret" show as loving and faithful a study of nature as Wordsworth's, and as great delicacy of phrase in recording unusual or little noticed aspects of the outside world. The passage from *Maud* is a masterpiece of description; the landscape is sketched, in its broad features, with bold, free strokes, and the figures are flashed upon the reader's imagination by a gleam of light and a motion. In both these passages the treatment is sincere and simple; nature is shown under a white light, with no modifying or harmonizing atmosphere. But description of this kind, though attractive enough in its way and bearing witness to the perfection of Tennyson's technique, lacks the specific charm and peculiar power of Romantic description; it is not imaginative in the distinctively Romantic meaning of the term; it does not, to use Lamb's words, "draw all things to one." In the passages earlier considered, the unifying and harmonizing power of imagination pervades every line, phrase, and word, and makes them all eloquent of a single thought and mood. This action of imagination is compared by Wordsworth in a famous passage of the last book of the *Prelude,* to the light of the moon as this light is seen, from the summit of a lofty hill, falling on a widespread landscape, and blending all the infinitely various details into a single harmonious impression of splendour and power.

Such Romantic imagination in dealing with nature Tennyson possessed in a high degree; and indeed, from one point of view, he may be said simply to have carried on to richer conclusions the work which the Romanticists began. As has already been suggested, he has probably been more influential than even Wordsworth, in conveying widely and permanently into the English temperament a delicate and swiftly responsive sensitiveness to the emotional suggestiveness of nature. Wordsworth was, in large measure, preoccupied with the moral meaning of the external world; to quote his own words, he sought "to exhibit the most ordinary appearances of the material universe under moral relations." Tennyson subdues nature still further and makes it eloquent of all our moods and passions. Wordsworth's moods are comparatively limited in variety and in subtlety; their very grandeur and their lofty elevation, when Wordsworth is at his best, prevent great refinement or great subtlety of feeling. His temperament is too simple, and his nature has too great mass, to admit of complex combinations of feelings or of quick and ravishing changes. "Admiration, love, and awe," these are the moods Wordsworth most insists on; and in the service of these cogent but comparatively simple feelings he is fondest of interpreting the great world of nature. Tennyson's moods, on the other hand, run through a very wide range and shade into each other through an infinite series of gradations. He plays on an instrument of far greater delicacy of adjustment and of much greater variety of tone-colour. He was heir to all the rich emotional life of the Romantic poets, and received by way of artistic inheritance a temperament already sensitive to a thousand influences that would have left the men of an earlier century unmoved; and to these inherited aptitudes for feeling subtly and richly were added all the half-tones and minor gradations of feeling that the intense spiritual and intellectual life of the post-Romantic period tended to develop. With this exquisitely sensitive temperament, he looked on the outside world and found everywhere correspondences between his moods and the aspects of nature. To catch and interpret, in all its range and subtlety and evanescent beauty, this emotional suggestiveness of nature was Tennyson's task, just as Wordsworth's task was to catch and register its moral and spiritual suggestiveness. Tennyson's poetry, then, may be regarded as in a very special sense, a continuation of the Wordsworthian tradition, and as carrying still further that subdual of nature to the needs of man's spirit that Wordsworth wrought at so faithfully.

The variety and the subtlety of Tennyson's moods are most noticeable when we turn from his treatment of landscape to his use of natural sights and sounds as symbols. It is, of course, only by the use of these symbols that he could hope to suggest the thousand and one changes of mood he tried to portray. These evanescent moods have no names; there are no conventional signs that the poet can use to place them before his readers; hence for each mood he must find some natural equivalent—some symbol that shall stand in its place, and, by touching secret springs in our minds and hearts, evoke the subtle complex of feeling he aims to suggest. These equivalents and symbols Tennyson finds chiefly in nature; and his use of them is the last means to be noted by which he brings about a closer union between matter and spirit.

This symbolical use of nature, together with its effect in giving a spiritual meaning to the world of the senses, is well illustrated in the lyric, "Tears, idle tears." The mood that the thought of the past calls up is highly complex—a resultant of many strangely blending elements; and the poet uses a series of sensuous images, a series of natural sights and sounds, to suggest the elementary feelings that enter into this mood. The "freshness" of delight with which the past is for a moment restored, the infinite "sadness" with which its irrevocableness forces itself once more on the thought, the "strangeness" of the far-away dim regions of memory,—these are the notes of feeling that go to make up the whole rich chord of the mood; and each has as its symbol, to call it into being, an image from nature:—

Fresh as the first beam glittering on a sail,
That brings our friends up from the under-world,
Sad as the last which reddens over one
That sinks with all we love below the verge;
So sad, so fresh, the days that are no more.

Ah, sad and strange as in dark summer dawns
The earliest pipe of half-awaken'd birds
To dying ears, when unto dying eyes
The casement slowly grows a glimmering square;
So sad, so strange, the days that are no more.

Each of the images in these verses is a symbol charged with feeling. And not only does the series of symbols serve to suggest at the moment of reading the precise mood of the poet, but always thereafter a reddening sail at sunset and the song of birds at dawn mean something more to us than they meant before Tennyson used them as symbols. Nature has taken on a whole new range of spiritual associations.

There are later poets who have surpassed Tennyson in variety and complexity of mood and in suggestiveness and subtlety of symbolic phrasing. In both these respects Dante Gabriel Rossetti was probably Tennyson's superior. But his superiority was gained at great cost. Nature, in his poetry, is broken up into a mere collection of symbolic sights and sounds; we miss the breadth of treatment and the fine open-air quality of Tennyson's work; there is often a sense of artificiality, of exaggeration, almost of violence done to nature to force her into the service of the poet's moods. Moreover, the variety and the subtlety of Rossetti's moods are gained at a like cost. Delight in moods became with Rossetti moodiness, and the study of moods reached the point of morbid introspection: subjectivity became a disease.

Tennyson, then, resembles the Romantic poets in his lack of sympathy with real life. He lived in a dream-world rather than in the world of real men and real women; and it is this dream-world, with its iridescence of beauty and its simplified and intensified characters, that he portrays for us in his poetry, save where he shows us the distorted pictures of life to be found in the minds of men half-mad with disappointed passion. His impatience of conventional life, his lack of interest in concrete character, and his intense subjectivity mark him out as akin to the Romantic poets, and as not having passed so decisively beyond the Romantic point of view and the Romantic mood as Browning, for example, passed beyond them. He was like the Romantic poets, too, in the fact that it was to nature that he turned to find escape from the crude actualities of everyday life; and it is probably through his share in the great Romantic work of spiritualizing nature that he will be most enduringly influential.

—Lewis E. Gates, "Nature in Tennyson's Poetry,"
Studies and Appreciations, 1900, pp. 77–91

G. K. Chesterton "Two Great Victorian Poets: I. Tennyson" (1902)

Gilbert Keith Chesterton was an English polymath of the early twentieth century, a journalist, political philosopher, and author of fantasy
and detective stories, Christian apologetics, and poetry. In this extract,
Chesterton, as always, provides a unique and extraordinary reading. He
begins by examining Tennyson's love of beauty, saying that unlike the
romantic poets of his youth, Tennyson did not triumph in his depictions
and love of beauty in nature but rather excelled in portraying the beauty
already existing in art, presenting his readers with the beauty of buildings,
sculpture, and palaces.

Chesterton, echoing the ancient Greek philosopher Plato, says that
Tennyson thereby became the imitator of an imitation, presenting in
his poetry art rather than life. Chesterton does not conclude at this
point but goes on to examine why Tennyson was more capable as
a poet in his depiction of art. Chesterton sees the poet as a product
of his age, the time in which Darwin's *On the Origin of Species* (1859)
shattered many people's certainties about the world. Chesterton states
that it was not a fear that Darwin's theory would overturn religion that
concerned Tennyson's age (faith and evolution were not incompatible to
Chesterton's way of thinking) but rather that it would overturn morality.
In the eternal battle of humans with sin, the extract states, people
always had the beauty of nature to turn to for solace, but Darwin's view
of the natural world was one of violence and conflict; Tennyson's age
was left with nothing but memories and myths of what nature had once
meant. But the age was also left with art. This is the reason, Chesterton
claims, that Tennyson strove to present the ordered beauty of art in
his own verse and drama, to fight the battle being fought by his age
against the encroachment of corruption. He could no longer, like the
romantics before him, turn to nature to see beauty and to find comfort
in life; thus he turned in his verse to art as all that remained to him in the
great struggle of his age.

Chesterton believes that it is possible that one day Tennyson may be
forgotten as a poet, as he was a product of his period, writing in and for
that time. Still, Chesterton holds that the poet should be remembered and
praised because he followed a call to duty (there is a telling distinction
made at the conclusion of the extract between Tennyson's lack of talent
as a philosophic poet and his vocation, or call, to be a philosophic poet). It
might have been the case that Tennyson would have been a much better

poet if he had ignored this call, this fight against the evil threatening his age, but he did not.

Readers unfamiliar with Chesterton's thought and style may find this extract peculiar in its argumentation, but it is typical of this original and insightful thinker. The fact that Chesterton wrote this extract in the early years of the twentieth century, when the 1890s' aesthetic of the supremacy of art over nature was still influential, should, however, be recalled. In no sense was Chesterton a decadent aesthete; but the aestheticism of his own age would indubitably have influenced his reading of Tennyson's search for beauty not in the natural world but in the world of art. Chesterton's perspective on Tennyson is obviously as much religious as it is aesthetic, and it is one of the peculiarities of this combination that marks the following extract as wholly original for any student examining the poet's verse and thought.

It was merely the accident of his hour, the call of his age, which made Tennyson a philosophic poet. He was naturally not only a pure lover of beauty, but a pure lover of beauty in a much more peculiar and distinguished sense even than a man like Keats, or a man like Robert Bridges. He gave us scenes of Nature that cannot easily be surpassed, but he chose them like a landscape painter rather than like a religious poet. Above all, he exhibited his abstract love of the beautiful in one most personal and characteristic fact. He was never so successful or so triumphant as when he was describing not Nature, but art. He could describe a statue as Shelley could describe a cloud. He was at his very best in describing buildings, in their blending of aspiration and exactitude. He found to perfection the harmony between the rhythmic recurrences of poetry and the rhythmic recurrences of architecture. His description, for example, of the Palace of Art is a thing entirely victorious and unique. The whole edifice, as described, rises as lightly as a lyric, it is full of the surge of the hunger for beauty; and yet a man might almost build upon the description as upon the plans of an architect or the instructions of a speculative builder. Such a lover of beauty was Tennyson, a lover of beauty most especially where it is most to be found, in the works of man. He loved beauty in its completeness, as we find it in art, not in its more glorious incompleteness as we find it in Nature. There is, perhaps, more loveliness in Nature than in art, but there are not so many lovely things. The loveliness is broken to pieces and scattered; the almond tree in blossom will have a mob of nameless insects at its root, and the most perfect cell in the great forest-house is likely enough to smell like a sewer. Tennyson loved beauty more in its collected form in art, poetry and sculpture; like his own Lady of Shalott, it was his office to look rather at the mirror than at the object. He was an artist, as it were, at two removes: he was a splendid imitator of the splendid imitations. It is true that his natural history was exquisitely exact, but natural history and natural religion are things that can be, under certain circumstances, more unnatural than anything in the world. In reading Tennyson's natural descriptions we never seem to be in physical contact with the earth. We learn nothing of the coarse good-temper and rank energy of life. We see the whole scene accurately, but we see it through glass. In Tennyson's works we see Nature indeed, and hear Nature, but we do not smell it.

But this poet of beauty and a certain magnificent idleness lived at a time when all men had to wrestle and decide. It is not easy for any person who lives in our time, when the dust has settled and the spiritual perspective has been restored, to realise what the entrance of the idea of evolution meant for the men of those days. To us it is a discovery of another link in a chain which, however far we follow it, still stretches back into a divine mystery. To many of the men of that time it would appear from their writings that it was the heart-breaking and desolating discovery of the end and origin of the chain. To them had happened the most black and hopeless catastrophe conceivable to human nature; they had found a logical explanation of all things. To them it seemed that an ape had suddenly risen to gigantic stature and destroyed the seven heavens. It is difficult, no doubt, for us in somewhat subtler days to understand how anybody could suppose that the origin of species had anything to do with the origin of being. To us it appears that to tell a man who asks who made his mind that evolution made it, is like telling a man who asks who rolled a cab-wheel over his leg that revolution rolled it. To state the process is scarcely to state the agent. But the position of those who regarded the opening of the *Descent of Man* as the opening of one of the seals of the last days is a great deal sounder than people have generally allowed. It has been constantly supposed that they were angry with Darwinism because it appeared to do something or other to the Book of Genesis; but this was a pretext or a fancy. They fundamentally rebelled against Darwinism, not because they had a fear that it would affect Scripture, but because they had a fear, not altogether unreasonable or ill-founded, that it would affect morality. Man had been engaged, through innumerable ages, in a struggle with sin. The evil within him was as strong as he could cope with—it was as powerful as a cannonade and as enchanting as a song. But in this struggle he had always had Nature on his side. He might be polluted and agonised, but the flowers were innocent and the hills were strong. All the armoury of life, the spears of the pine wood and the batteries of the lightning went into battle beside him. Tennyson lived in the hour when, to all mortal appearance, the whole of the physical world deserted to the devil. The universe, governed by violence and death, left man to fight alone, with a handful of myths and memories. Men had now to wander in polluted fields and lift up their eyes to abominable hills. They had to arm themselves against the cruelty of flowers and the crimes of the grass. The first honour, surely, is to those who did not faint in the face of that confounding cosmic betrayal; to those who sought and found a new vantage ground for the army of Virtue. Of these was Tennyson, and it is surely the more to his honour, since he was the idle lover of beauty who has been portrayed. He felt that the time called him to be an interpreter. Perhaps he might even have been something more of a poet if he had not sought to be something more than a poet. He might have written a more perfect Arthurian epic if his heart had been as much buried in prehistoric sepulchres as the heart of Mr. W. B. Yeats. He might have made more of such poems as "The Golden Year" if his mind had been as clean of metaphysics and as full of a poetic rusticity as the mind of William Morris. He might have been a greater poet if he had been less a man of his dubious and rambling age. But there are some things that are greater than greatness; there are some things that no man with blood in his body would sell for the throne of Dante, and one of them is to fire the feeblest shot in a war that really awaits decision, or carry the meanest musket in an army that is really marching by. Tennyson may even have forfeited immortality; but he and the men of his age were more than immortal; they were alive.

Tennyson had not a special talent for being a philosophic poet, but he had a special vocation for being a philosophic poet. This may seem a contradiction, but it is only because all the Latin or Greek words we use tend endlessly to lose their meaning. A vocation is supposed to mean merely a taste or faculty, just as economy is held to mean merely the act of saving. Economy means the management of a house or community. If a man starves his best horse, or causes his best workman to strike for more pay, he is not merely unwise, he is uneconomical. So it is with a vocation. If this country were suddenly invaded by some huge alien and conquering population, we should all be called to become soldiers. We should not think in that time that we were sacrificing our unfinished work on Cattle-Feeding or our hobby of fretwork, our brilliant career at the bar, or our taste for painting in water-colours. We should all have a call to arms. We should, however, by no means agree that we all had a vocation for arms. Yet a vocation is only the Latin for a call.

In a celebrated passage in *Maud*, Tennyson praised the moral effects of war, and declared that some great conflict might call out the greatness even of the pacific swindlers and sweaters whom he saw around him in the commercial age. He dreamed, he said, that if

The battle-bolt sang from the three-decker out on the foam,
Many a smooth-faced, snub-nosed rogue would leap from his counter or
till,
And strike, were it but with his cheating yard-wand, home.

Tennyson lived in the time of a conflict more crucial and frightful than any European struggle, the conflict between the apparent artificiality of morals and the apparent immorality of science. A ship more symbolic and menacing than any foreign three-decker hove in sight in that time—the great, gory pirate-ship of Nature, challenging all the civilisations of the world. And his supreme honour is this, that he behaved like his own imaginary snub-nosed rogue. His honour is that in that hour he despised the flowers and embroideries of Keats as the counter-jumper might despise his tapes and cottons. He was by nature a hedonistic and pastoral poet, but he leapt from his poetic counter and till and struck, were it but with his gimcrack mandolin, home.

Tennyson's influence on poetry may, for a time, be modified. This is the fate of every man who throws himself into his own age, catches the echo of its temporary phrases, is kept busy in battling with its temporary delusions. There are many men whom history has for a time forgotten to whom it owes more than it could count. But if Tennyson is extinguished, it will be with the most glorious extinction. There are two ways in which a man may vanish—through being thoroughly conquered or through being thoroughly the Conqueror. In the main the great Broad Church philosophy which Tennyson uttered has been adopted by every one. This will make against his fame. For a man may vanish as Chaos vanished in the face of creation, or he may vanish as God vanished in filling all things with that created life.

—G. K. Chesterton, "Two Great Victorian Poets:
I. Tennyson," *Bookman,* New York, October 1902,
pp. 349–51

WORKS

The following section examines various critical reactions to a number of Tennyson's publications, from those produced in the middle years of the century to a consideration of the poet's drama several years after his death. Readers should note those critical attitudes that recur and those that are noticeably inflected by the cultural moment in which they were written. It is as clear in this section as it is in the previous one that shifts in taste and literary fashion are strongly reflected in reviews written over the course of the nineteenth century. There are certainly continuities of opinion within the following critical extracts, but there are many more examples reflecting the alteration of literary and cultural values that occurred throughout Victoria's reign.

THE PRINCESS

HENRY WADSWORTH LONGFELLOW (1848)

In the following extract, the American poet Henry Wadsworth Longfellow describes his first delighted impressions after reading The Princess, praising, as so many critics and readers have done before and since, the music of Tennyson's verse. Unlike those who have admired the harmonies of the poet's work, however, Longfellow has found a discordant note "somewhere," one that he cannot exactly articulate.

Fields came out in the afternoon, and brought me an English copy of Tennyson's new poem, *The Princess*. F. read it in the evening. Strange enough! a university of women! A gentle satire, in the easiest and most flowing blank verse, with two delicious unrhymed songs, and many exquisite passages.

I went to bed after it, with delightful music ringing in my ears; yet half disappointed in the poem, though not knowing why. There is a discordant note somewhere.

—Henry Wadsworth Longfellow, *Journal,*
February 7, 1848, cited in Samuel Longfellow,
Life of Henry Wadsworth Longfellow, 1891,
vol. 2, p. 109

BAYARD TAYLOR (1848)

Bayard Taylor was an American literary critic, poet, and travel writer. In the following extract, the young writer gives Tennyson's poem perhaps the highest praise anyone could: He says that it is so powerful and so beautiful that he fears he can never read the poet again or he himself will be ruined as an author, incapable of any original work, possessed and haunted by Tennyson's own poetic vision.

I had the misfortune to be deeply intoxicated yesterday—with Tennyson's new poem, *The Princess,* which I shall bring to thee when I return home. I dare not keep it with me. For the future, for a long time at least, I dare not read Tennyson. His poetry would be the death of mine, and, indeed, a *pervadence* of his spirit would ruin me for the great purposes of life. His intense perception of beauty haunts me for days, and I cannot drive it from me.

—Bayard Taylor, letter to Mary Agnew,
February 13, 1848, *Life and Letters of Bayard
Taylor,* eds. Marie Hansen-Taylor and Horace E.
Scudder, 1884, vol. 1, p. 119

EDWARD FITZGERALD (1848)

Edward FitzGerald was one of Tennyson's closest friends and a poet in his own right. In the following extract from a letter, FitzGerald describes his feeling that Tennyson is wasting his poetic talent at the very point when he would otherwise be expected to be gleaning the greatest rewards for his mature work. It would seem that FitzGerald has caused some quarrels with others over his opinion that *The Princess* is unworthy of the poet.

I had a note from Alfred three months ago. He was then in London: but is now in Ireland, I think, adding to his new poem, the *Princess*. Have you seen it? I am considered a great heretic for abusing it; it seems to me a wretched waste of power at a time of life when a man ought to be doing his best; and I almost feel hopeless about Alfred now. I mean, about his doing what he was born to do.

—Edward FitzGerald, letter to Frederick
Tennyson, May 4, 1848

IN MEMORIAM A.H.H.

MAX MILLER (1850)

In the following extract, Max Miller writes to a friend to plan a visit during which he hopes to lift his spirits and dispel the despondency and boredom he is currently feeling at Oxford University. He looks forward to being "jollier" and insists that poetry be read on his vacation to cheer him up. As a consequence, Miller requires that he and his friend do not read *In Memoriam* and proceeds to express his opinions on fitting subject matters for poets, to Tennyson's detriment. While Miller recognizes that the poem is beautiful, he finds its expression of emotion an "open grave," unseemly and perhaps embarrassing to view. Miller suggests that death requires from a poet something beautiful to cover up its occurrence or a simple, short statement.

I am thoroughly tired of Oxford, and hope I shall feel jollier again when we sit together on your tower and smoke a weed; but no *In Memoriam*, rather something about airy, fairy Lilians and other sweet creatures without a soul. However, I do not mean to say that Tennyson's last poems are not very beautiful, yet I do not like those open graves of sorrow and despair, and wish our poets would imitate the good Christian fashion of covering them with flowers, or a stone with a short inscription on it

—Max Miller, letter to F. Palgrave, June 18, 1850,
Life and Letters of Max Miller, ed. Georgina Max
Muller, 1902, vol. 1, p. 116

SARA COLERIDGE (1850)

Sara Coleridge was the daughter of the English romantic poet Samuel Taylor Coleridge and an author in her own right. In the following extract

from a letter to the Irish poet Aubrey De Vere, Coleridge thanks him for his
gift to her of Tennyson's poem. She hopes to enjoy it as much as De Vere
has told her he does, seeing Tennyson as a fit heir to Shakespeare and the
best of modern poets excepting, diplomatically, Sara's own father and his
close friend William Wordsworth. Sara's own feelings about Tennyson's
poem can be seen in the following extract from a letter written a week
and a half after this one.

I have just received your kind present of *In Memoriam;* many thanks. What
a treasure it will be, if I can but think of it and feel about it as you do, and as
Mr. T does! You said, "the finest strain since Shakespeare;" and afterwards
that you and Mr. T—agreed that it set the author above all modern poets, save
only W. W. and S. T. C.

> —Sara Coleridge, letter to Aubrey De Vere,
> August 6, 1850, *Memoir and Letters of Sara
> Coleridge,* ed. Edith Coleridge, 1873, vol. 2, p. 287

SARA COLERIDGE (1850)

In this extract from a letter, Sara Coleridge finds Tennyson's poem to be
lacking "truth" and "force." Rather, she finds *In Memoriam* to be at times
suggestive of affectation; at other moments she finds the work to be
forced. Coleridge says that the best poetry flows naturally and, consequently, becomes transparently honest and powerful. It would seem that
she finds some of Tennyson's images and language awkward or grating,
something to be "stumbled over" rather than easily followed.

I agree with Mr. Kenyon and Lady Palgrave, who are not mere friend-
critics, that *In Memoriam* is a highly interesting volume, and worthy to be
compared with the poems of Petrarch. I think it like his poems, both in
the general scheme, and the execution of particular pieces. The pervading,
though not universal, fault, as you, I think, say too, is quaintness and
violence, instead of force, in short, want of truth, which is at the bottom
of all affectation, an endeavour to be something more, and higher, and
better, than the aspirant really and properly is. The Heaven of poetry is not
to be taken by these means. It is like the Elysium, described to Laodamia,
whatever is valuable in that way flows forth spontaneously like the products
of nature, silently and without struggle or noise. How smoothly do all the
finest strains of poetry flow on! the noblest passages in the *Paradise Lost,*

and in Mr. Wordsworth's and my father's finest poems! The mind stumbles not over a single word or image.

—Sara Coleridge, letter to Edward Quillinan,
August 15, 1850, *Memoir and Letters of Sara Coleridge*,
ed. Edith Coleridge, 1873, vol. 2, pp. 292–93

CHARLOTTE BRONTË (1850)

Charlotte Brontë was a popular English novelist, the author of *Jane Eyre* and *Villette*. In the following extract, she expresses her feelings after reading Tennyson's poem; or rather, half of it as it seems she cannot finish it in its entirety. Brontë states that her problem with *In Memoriam* is that, while she knows the emotions the poem contains are real, she finds in their worked, measured expression something that rings false. She suggests that her opinion might change over time but that true and deep sorrow cannot be expressed in verse. Presumably, the contention is that grief is wild and chaotic, whereas verse is structured and articulated. Brontë's perspective on Tennyson's expression of emotion in the poem seems to be akin to that of Sara Coleridge in the preceding extract.

I have read Tennyson's *In Memoriam,* or rather part of it; I closed the book when I had got about halfway. It is beautiful; it is mournful; it is monotonous. Many of the feelings expressed bear, in their utterance, the stamp of truth; yet, if Arthur Hallam had been somewhat nearer Alfred Tennyson—his brother instead of his friend—I should have distrusted this rhymed, and measured, and printed monument of grief. What change the lapse of years may work I do not know; but it seems to me that bitter sorrow, while recent, does not flow out in verse.

—Charlotte Brontë, letter to Elizabeth Gaskell,
August 27, 1850

HENRY HALLAM (1850)

Henry Hallam was the father of Tennyson's friend Arthur Henry Hallam, whose death inspired the poet to compose *In Memoriam*. In this extract from a letter to Tennyson, Hallam expresses his gratitude for the "monument" to his son's death, recognizes the grief Tennyson feels as being akin to his own, and praises the verse as an "enduring testimony" to the memory of Arthur.

I know not how to express what I have felt. My first sentiment was surprise, for, though I now find that you had mentioned the intention to my daughter, Julia, she had never told me of the poems. I do not speak as another would to praise and admire: few of them indeed I have as yet been capable of reading, the grief they express is too much akin to that they revive. It is better than any monument which could be raised to the memory of my beloved son, it is a more lively and enduring testimony to his great virtues and talents that the world should know the friendship which existed between you, that posterity should associate his name with that of Alfred Tennyson.

—Henry Hallam, letter to Alfred, Lord Tennyson, 1850, cited in Hallam Tennyson, *Alfred Lord Tennyson: A Memoir*, 1897, vol. 1, p. 327

VIDA D. SCUDDER (1895)

In the following extract, Vida D. Scudder closely reads Tennyson's poem as an expression of his turbulent emotional struggle, which she describes as a "soul-epic." Scudder's reading strikes to the heart of the human condition when confronted by pain: Questions about despair, the anguish of the spirit, the will, truth, trust, hope, fortitude, the conflict between reason and experience, the challenge to faith, and above all, the enduring power of love are all considered. "The mystery of sub-consciousness" mentioned at the end of the extract sets off Scudder's perspective as distinct from those that have come before, the new psychoanalytic term adding a depth of analysis that earlier assessments necessarily lacked. While it would be incorrect for readers to question the judgments of Sara Coleridge or Charlotte Brontë in their letters above, for each woman honestly responded to her immediate impression of Tennyson's verse, Scudder is writing a consideration of a poem famous for half a century, and writing after the great wave of doubt and the questioning of the old certitudes of faith and belief that had occurred in the latter half of the nineteenth century. All the considerations of *In Memoriam A.H.H.* extracted in this volume are products of their time, as they could only ever be. Readers should consider the cultural moments that inflect each author's opinion and how tastes regarding the feelings expressed by Tennyson have altered in the course of 50 years.

In Memoriam is a poem of triumph, but of triumph overcast. The pall of gloom that broods heavily above the soul at the beginning is indeed soon broken by far, sad regions of light. Towards the end the sun itself streams forth, illumining the sorrow to beauty; but it is an English sunlight, white, not golden, still filtered through a veil of pensive mists.

It is difficult to conceive a poem wider and more subtle in rendering the possible sufferings of a soul shaken free from all convention by the shock of pain. Problems of the mind, the conduct, and the heart blend and break, one against the other, with the pathetic inconsistency, the alternations of fervor and stupor, of sorrowful life itself. In the Prelude, Cantos 1–28, the forces, stunned by sorrow, gather themselves together for conflict. In the first Cycle, Cantos 28–78, sometimes called the Cycle of the Past, are concentrated the most poignant problems of thought; in the second, the Cycle of the Present, Cantos 78–104, are faced the problems of the life of feeling and action which the soul, on earth, cannot escape; while in the Cycle of the Future, Cantos 104–119, the outlook is mainly towards an ideal social order, and the humanity to be. The concluding poems give the summary and interpretation, in the light of faith won at last, of the great problem. From the very beginning, the personal grief is taken up into a larger sorrow. The problem that confronts the poet is to find a witness to eternal life in the presence of that vast witness to perpetual death seemingly given by nature and our human fears. The great question is viewed, now from the side of emotion, now from that of thought, and at times the shore of assurance seems far away. In the fluctuating motion that tosses the bitter foam of doubt over most dear and sacred desires, one firm fact alone remains, giving to the poem the necessary coherence of structure. It is the constancy of human love on earth, to which from the beginning the poet desperately and blindly clings. Before the end of the great soul-epic, this constancy, gathering to itself all of thought and feeling that can minister to faith, becomes to him the calm revealer of a love beyond the grave.

In Memoriam, taken as a whole, has a tone profoundly Christian, it advances towards a triumphant and Christian end. Yet, if we regard not conclusion but method, we find the poem in essence skeptical. Its agnosticism lies intellectually though not spiritually as deep as its Christianity, its very faith is of the agnostic type. For this faith is held by effort of the will, not by demonstration of reason. From the first awakening of volition when the fumes of sorrow roll away, to the final apostrophe:—

O Living Will that shalt endure
When all that seems shall suffer shock,

choice, not conviction, determines creed. There is much meditation suffused with thoughtful argument, but the arguments do but circle around the central problem, disposing of minor difficulties but never touching its gloomy heart. Next to the will, feeling is the great champion of faith. The heart in wrath gives to the cruel suggestions of reason the reiterated answer: "I have felt." They are lame hands of faith indeed that the poet stretches out. The final triumph won is that of simple trust: trust adequate to console and even to nerve to conduct, not adequate to create even the illusion of knowledge. Reason, Tennyson emphasizes again and again with calm and sad assurance, can never attain to truth. We must "faintly trust the larger hope," "believing where we cannot prove;" and as this sad phrase confronts us in the Prologue, we find it once more at the very end, where once more we are bidden to trust "with faith that comes *of self-control*" "the truths that never can be proved" on earth.

The intellectual problems are indeed hardly met, much less answered; and yet, before the end, reason in a sense is satisfied. The movement of the poem is close to that of experience, far from that of pure thought, and hence comes its very vitality and power. Facts of nature and of the soul come to the poet whose love is clasping grief with desperate instinct, as mocking, hideous, serene denials of the spiritual truth for which he longs. Tortured, but touchingly sincere, the soul again and again faces and voices with unflinching completeness the message of despair: it then turns away, exhausted by the very intensity of thought-sorrow, and sinks for rest into the healing and normal sorrow of the heart. Long after, when much new experience has been entered, when the spirit has been strengthened by courageous endurance and the conquest of practical solutions, the same face will recur: and behold! it is no longer dark with insidious denial, but the radiant witness to faith. In the mystery of sub-consciousness, the great change has been wrought.

Thus, for instance, the first hint of wider thought that comes to the dazed spirit is the terrible conception of nature as a great phantom, hollow and unsubstantial, the mere mocking image of man. The conception is languidly dropped; for at first the pathetic hints at thought of the bruised spirit are lame and broken, and it is long before they have strength to gather themselves into consecutive sequence. But far later, in the triumphant conclusion, the idea reappears, and how different is its aspect! Once it forced the soul into the very solitude of death: now it is the joyous witness of perfect idealism. The world is shadow indeed, but the shadow of immortal spirit. The solid lands may melt like mists, like clouds may shape themselves and go: the poet knows that they exist as symbol only of eternal love.

—Vida D. Scudder, *The Life of the Spirit in the Modern English Poets*, 1895, pp. 284–88

MAUD AND OTHER POEMS

GEORGE BRIMLEY "TENNYSON'S POEMS" (1895)

In the following extract, George Brimley defends Tennyson's *Maud* from the charge made by several critics that in its depiction of a hysterical, melo-dramatic character in love, the poet has offered the public an immoral individual they are then expected to imitate. Brimley states that all of Tennyson's verse before the publication of *Maud* has demonstrated only the most noble of feelings, the purest of passions, and images and narra-tives that strengthen readers' spirits and wills. If this poem depicts another type of individual entirely, it is not because Tennyson desires his readers to emulate his thoughts, emotions, and actions but rather because such a type exists in England, whatever the rights or wrongs of his character.

Brimley derides those critics who have sought to track this presumed morbid strain through earlier Tennyson's poems, saying that the sales figures for the poet's prior publications make it clear that the English public certainly does not seem to agree with such an opinion. Tennyson, Brimley claims, has with *Maud* presented a tragedy. The critical point that no one would blame Shakespeare for being immoral because Othello commits suicide, nor accuse Goethe of cynicism because of his Mephistopheles, is forcefully made at the extract's conclusion. Readers interested in the mid-nineteenth-century critical view of the relationship between art and life, or the question of the "moral purpose" of poetry, will find much to consider in the following extract.

The general characteristic (of Tennyson's poetry) is, that the passion there shown in operation is a purifying, strengthening, sustaining power; that it allies itself with conscience and reason, and braces instead of debilitating the will. The small poem called 'Fatima' is the only instance in which Mr. Tennyson has expended his powers in portraying any love that incapacitates for the common duties of life, unless the two 'Marianas' be regarded in this light, which would be a perverse misconception of their main purpose. In 'Locksley Hall' the ghost of a murdered love is fairly laid, and the man comes out of his conflict the stronger and the clearer for his experience. Nothing that can with any propriety be called morbid or unhealthy belongs to any of the great love poems in the collection; and surely the view of the relation of the sexes in the *Princess* is as sound a basis for a noble life as was ever propounded. It would be singular if, with such antecedents, Mr. Tennyson should, in the maturity of his intellect and experience, have descended to exhibit the influence of love upon a weak and worthless character, and have chosen for that purpose a melodramatic story of suicide, murder, and madness, dished up for popular applause with vehement invective on the vices of the English nation, and claptrap appeals to the war-feeling of the day. This, however, is what we are asked to believe of Mr. Tennyson's latest production, *Maud*, by the loudest professional critics of the journals and magazines. The critics give us some gauge of their opinion by tracing Mr. Tennyson's gradual degradation through the *Princess*, lower still in *In Memoriam*, to its climax of weakness and absurdity in *Maud*; and it is but justice to say that these opinions are not now for the first time put forth on the provocation of the last-named poem, but appear to be the deliberate convictions of the writers. We believe that both the *Princess* and *In Memoriam* are in their sixth edition, which, apart from private experience, necessarily limited, of the impression the works have produced, leads to the conclusion that these writers do not in this case fairly represent the opinion of the English public. Whether they represent it any better in respect to *Maud* remains to be seen. Meanwhile it is well not to be frightened out of the enjoyment of fine poetry, and out of the instruction to be gained from a great poet's views of life, as exhibited dramatically in the destiny of a particular sort of character subjected to a particular set of influences, by such epithets as 'morbid,' 'hysterical,' 'spasmodic,' which may mean one thing or another, according to the sense, discrimination, and sympathy of the man who applies them.

There is little question as to the artistic merits of *Maud*. It is only the aim of the poet that has been assailed; his execution is generally admitted to be successful. It may be at once conceded that the writer of the fragments of a life which tell the story of *Maud*, is not in a comfortable state of mind when he begins his record; and that if a gentleman were to utter such sentiments at a board of railway directors, or at a marriage breakfast, he might not improperly be called hysterical. Like the hero of 'Locksley Hall,' his view of the life around him, of the world in which his lot is cast, has been coloured by a grievous personal calamity; and the character of the man is originally one in which the sensibilities are keen and delicate, the speculative element strong, the practical judgment unsteady, the will and active energies comparatively feeble. A Shelley or a Keats may stand for example of his type; not perfect men, certainly, but scarcely so contemptible as not to possess both dramatic interest and some claim to human sympathy. Chatterton, a much lower type than either, has been thought a subject of psychological and moral interest, in spite or in consequence of the vulgar, petulant, weak melodrama of his life and death. You see, God makes these morbid, hysterical, spasmodic individuals occasionally, and they have various fates; some die without a sign; others try the world, and dash themselves dead against its bars; some few utter their passionate desires, their weak complaints, their ecstastic raptures in snatches of song that make the world delirious with delight,—and somehow, for their sake the class becomes interesting, and we are at times inclined to measure the spiritual capacity of an age by its treatment of these weak souls,—by the fact, whether the general constitution of society cherishes such souls into divine lovers and singers of the beautiful, or lashes and starves and changes them into moping idiots and howling madmen. The autobiographer of *Maud* belongs to this class by temperament, as anyone may understand from the turn of his angry thoughts to those social evils which must and ought to excite indignation and scorn in gentle and loving natures that are at the same time inspired with generous and lofty ideas; from the speculative enigmas he torments himself with at the prevalence of rapine and pain in creation, at the insignificance of man in a boundless universe, subject to iron laws; from the penetrating tenderness, the rich fancy, the childlike *naivete* of his love for the young girl who saves him from himself and his dark dreams. There lies in such a character, from the beginning, the capacity for weakness and misery, for crime and madness. That capacity is inseparable from keen sensibility, powerful emotions, and active imagination; and if events happen which paralyze the will already feeble, turn the flow of feeling into a stream of bitterness, and present to the imagination a world of wrong and suffering, the capacity fulfils itself according to the force and direction of the events. In *Maud* the tendency meets with events that carry it on through these stages; and the question is whether any one of these events is impossible or improbable, whether English society is misrepresented when it is made capable of furnishing the unwholesome nutriment for such a character. . . .

The fact is, that Mr. Tennyson, without abandoning his lyric forms, has in *Maud* written a tragedy—a work, that is, which demands to be judged, not by the intrinsic goodness and beauty of the actions and emotions depicted, but by their relation to character; that character, again, being not only an interesting study in itself and moving our sympathy, but being related dynamically to the society of the time which serves as the background of the picture, and thus displaying the characteristics of the society by showing its influence, under particular circumstances, upon the character selected. Mr. Tennyson's critics have for the most part read the poem as if its purpose were to hold up an example for our imitation, and have condemned it because, viewed in this light, it offers nothing but a nature of over-excitable sensibilities, first rendered moody by misfortune, then driven mad by its own crime, and finally recovered to a weak exultation in a noble enterprise it has not the manliness to share. But no one feels that Shakspeare is immoral in making Othello kill himself; no one attributes the cynicism of Mephistopheles to Goethe.

—George Brimley, "Tennyson's Poems," 1855,
Essays, ed. George William Clark, 1868, pp. 75–84

EDMUND CLARENCE STEDMAN "ALFRED TENNYSON" (1875)

Edmund Clarence Stedman was an American literary critic, poet, and essayist. In the following extract, Stedman remarks on the variance in public opinion that Tennyson's *Maud* elicited and sides with those who find the poem weak in construction, thought, treatment, and theme. Stedman agrees that there are parts of the work where Tennyson's lyric musicality affords those moments of beauty with which his earlier poems had made readers familiar, but he says these are few and far between. The great shame, to Stedman, was that just before the publication of *Maud*, Tennyson had recently gained a number of new readers on each side of the Atlantic, having been made the new poet laureate of Great Britain. As a consequence, this new audience was not granted the "real" Tennyson, the poet whose previous verse had been of much higher quality. Stedman claims that these readers will unfairly, but unsurprisingly, continue to think of the poet as being affected and shallow as this was their first impression of the new laureate.

Maud . . . with its strength and weakness, has divided public opinion more than any other of the author's works. I think that his judicious students will not demur to my opinion that it is quite below his other sustained productions; rather, that it is not sustained at all, but, while replete with beauties, weak and uneven as a whole,—and that this is due to the poet's having gone outside his own nature, and to his surrender of the joy of art, in an effort to produce something that should at once catch the favor of the multitude. *Maud* is scanty in theme, thin in treatment, poor in thought; but has musical episodes, with much fine scenery and diction. It is a greater medley than *The Princess*, shifting from vague speculations to passionate outbreaks, and glorying in one famous and beautiful nocturne,—but all intermixed with cheap satire, and conspicuous for affectations unworthy of the poet. The pity of it was that this production appeared when Tennyson suddenly had become fashionable, in England and America, through his accession to the laureate's honors, and for this reason, as well as for its theme and eccentric qualities, had a wider reading than his previous works: not only among the masses, to whom the other volumes had been sealed books, but among thoughtful people, who now first made the poet's acquaintance and received *Maud* as the foremost example of his style. First impressions are lasting, and to this day Tennyson is deemed, by many of the latter class, an apostle of tinsel and affectation. In our own country especially, his popular reputation began with *Maud*,—a work which, for lack of constructive beauty, is the opposite of his other narrative poems.

—Edmund Clarence Stedman, "Alfred Tennyson,"
Victorian Poets, 1875, pp. 173–74

IDYLLS OF THE KING

WALTER BAGEHOT "TENNYSON'S *IDYLLS*" (1859)

Walter Bagehot was an English essayist and journalist who wrote articles on literary, political, and cultural affairs. In the following extract, Bagehot begins by considering the influence that a small but devoted group of poetic devotees can have on the object of their admiration. Bagehot suggests that Tennyson has had such a following until recent years and that these sectarian disciples of the poet had been primarily young men "of rather heated imaginations." It was to these young men of unhealthy mind-set that poems such as *Maud* appealed and for whom several critics charged Tennyson with encouraging immorality with that poem (see the extract by George Brimley contained in this section). In later years, however, Tennyson had drawn a wider popular audience, with the consequence that he could publish his *Idylls of the King* without regard to the unhappiness of those young, and now perhaps previous, devotees. Bagehot says that *Idylls of the King* is the opposite to *Maud*, to such an extent that critics might claim that Tennyson had been toying with his previous adherents in publishing the latter. Every line of his new poem, Bagehot claims, proclaims a delicate taste, refined grace, and maturity. After examining these qualities in a number of the work's episodes, Bagehot states that he is glad that Tennyson decided to divide his retelling of the Arthurian legend into a series of long poems, for the painful nature of the story requires various subplots to relieve the readers' minds. The poet has shown good sense in structuring his tale in such a manner and displayed the talent to prevent any one of these episodes from gaining a prevalence that might threaten the balance and harmony of the poem as a whole.

The only fault that Bagehot finds in the poem, and it is one echoed by several other critics (not only of *Idylls of the King* but Tennyson's work in general), is that the characters in the poem all speak with the poet's full range of gifts; there are simply no individuated conversational styles. Bagehot contrasts this element with the work of Robert Browning, who was praised by most critics for his gift for portraying true, real, believable characters in his dramatic monologues. Tennyson's inability to do so is a failure of "dramatic expression" for Bagehot. Still, relative to the skill displayed in the architecture of the larger cycle of the poem, the critic can comfortably find more to praise than to frown upon.

Bagehot begins to consider Tennyson's place within the pantheon of poetic worthies. He finds both Percy Bysshe Shelley and John Keats to have greater lyric gifts than Tennyson, whose ability does not extend beyond individual lines and images. Tennyson is considered by the critic to have greater intellectual gifts on display in his verse than the young Keats does (although Bagehot recognizes that Keats's early death makes this victory somewhat hollow). Shelley, however, is once again deemed greater than Tennyson insofar as his intellectual gifts are more apparent. However, relative to the romantic elder William Wordsworth, Tennyson is both more humorous (Bagehot claims that there might never have been born a less humorous soul than Wordsworth) and also portrays in his verse a greater and more general picture of human life than the older poet did. Bagehot places Samuel Taylor Coleridge beneath Tennyson as well and concludes that only Shelley might claim to be a greater poet than the author of *Idylls of the King*.

It is a hardship on quarterly reviewers that good books should be published at the beginning of a quarter. Before the next number of the Review appears, they are scarely new books at all. Everything which need be, or ought to be, perhaps everything which can be said, has been said. Doubtless the best remarks are forestalled. Yet what is to be done? A critical journal, which hopes to influence the taste of its time, must not omit to notice any remarkable books. When they are so attractive as the *Idylls of the King*, what critic can neglect a chance of reviewing them? Although, therefore, the last poem of Mr. Tennyson has already been some time before the public, and much has already been written about it, we must devote a few words to the delineation of its peculiarities.

The *Idylls of the King* is, we think, more popular with the general public than with Mr. Tennyson's straiter disciples. It is the characteristic—in some cases it is the calamity—of every great and peculiar poet, to create for himself a school of readers. Wordsworth did so during the first twenty years of the century. For the whole of that time, and perhaps for some years longer, his works could scarcely be said to belong to general English literature: the multitude did not read them. Some of the acutest of those who gave away reputation in those days laughed at them. But a secret worship was all the while forming itself; a sect accumulated. If you read the reviews of that time, you will find that the Wordsworthians were considered a kind of Quakers in literature, that rejected finery, disliked ornate art, and preferred a 'thee and thou' simplicity in poetry. Some of the defects of Wordsworth's poems may be in part traced to the narrowing influence of this species of readers. Even the greatest artist thinks sometimes of his peculiar public. The more solitary his life is, the more he broods on it. The more rejected he is by the multitude, the more he thinks of his few disciples. It is scarcely conceivable that such a habit should not narrow the mind and straiten the sympathies. The class of persons who are the first to take up a very peculiar writer, are themselves commonly somewhat peculiar. 'I am not sure of missionaries,' said some one; 'but I detest converts.' The first believers in anything are rarely good critics of it. The first enthusiasts for a great poet are heedless in their faith; a fault in their idol is like a fault in themselves: they have to defend him in discussion, and in consequence they come to admire the most those parts of his poems which are attacked most frequently: they have a logical theory in defence of them, and are attached to the instances that show its ingenuity and that exemplify its nature: in short, they admire, not what is best in the great writer, but what is most characteristic of him; they incite him to display his eccentricities and to develop his peculiarities. 'Beware of thy friends,' says the oriental proverb; 'for affection is but the flattery of the soul.' Many of Wordsworth's best poems would have been better if he had been more on his guard against the misleading influence of a sectarian sympathy. A few years ago Mr. Tennyson was in a rather similar position. We should not like to specify the date of his ratified acceptance by the public at large; but it is indisputable that at one time he was not so accepted. Everybody admires Tennyson now; but to admire him fifteen years or so ago, was to be a 'Tennysonian.' We know what the *Quarterly* said of his first volume, and the feeling there indicated lingered a long time in many quarters. He has now vanquished it; but an observant eye may still detect in literary, and still more in semi-literary society, several differences in taste and in feeling between the few disciples of the early school and the numerous race of new admirers.

Perhaps the first Tennysonians were not among the wisest of men,—at least they were not taken from the class which is apt to be the wisest. The

early poetry of Mr. Tennyson—and the same may be said of nearly all the
poetry of Shelley and Keats—labours under the defect that it is written,
almost professedly, for young people—especially young men—of rather
heated imaginations. All poetry, or almost all poetry, finds its way more
easily to the brains of young men, who are at once intellectual and excitable,
than to those of men of any other kind. Persons engaged in life have rarely
leisure for imaginative enjoyment: the briefs, the sums, the politics intervene.
Slowly, even in the case of young men, does the influence of a new poet enter
into the mind; you hear the snatch of a stanza here; you see an extract in a
periodical; you get the book and read it; you are pleased with it, but you do
not know whether the feeling will last. It is the habitual pleasure that such
works give which alone is the exact criterion of their excellence. But what
number of occupied men read new poetry habitually? What number of them
really surrender their minds to the long task of gradually conceiving new
forms of imagery, to the even more delicate task of detecting the healthiness
or unhealthiness of unfamiliar states of feeling? Almost all poetry, in
consequence, is addressed more to young men than to others. But the early
poetry of Tennyson, and of the other poets we have named, is addressed to
that class even more peculiarly. In the greatest poets, in Shakespeare and in
Homer, there is a great deal besides poetry. There are broad descriptions of
character, dramatic scenes, eloquence, argument, a deep knowledge of manly
and busy life. These interest readers who are no longer young; they refer to
the world in which almost all of us have to act; they reflect with the strong
light of genius the scenes of life in which the mass of men live and move.
By the aid of these extraneous elements, the poetry of these great writers
reaches and impresses those who would never be attracted by it in itself, or
take the pains to understand it if it had been presented to them alone. Shelley
and Keats, on the other hand, have presented their poetry to the world in its
pure essence; they have not added—we scarcely know whether they would
have been able to add—the more worldly and terrestrial elements; probably
their range in the use of these would have been but limited; at any rate, they
have not tried—parts of Shelley's *Cenci* perhaps excepted—to use them;
they have been content to rely on imaginatively expressed sentiment, and
sentiment-exciting imagery; in short, on that which in its more subtle sense
we call poetry, exclusively and wholly. In consequence, their works have had
a great influence on young men; they retain a hold on many mature men only
because they are associated with their youth; they delineate

Such sights as youthful poets dream
On summer eves by haunted stream:

and young men, who were not poets, have eagerly read them, have fondly learned them, and have long remembered them.—A good deal of this description applies to the writings of Tennyson,—some years ago we should have said that almost the whole of it was applicable to him. His audience formerly consisted entirely of young men of cultivated tastes and susceptible imaginations; and it was so because his poetry contained most of the elements which are suitable to such persons in a country like England, and an age such as this is. But whatever be the cause,—whether or not our analysis of the ingredients in Mr. Tennyson's poetry which attracted young men of this kind be correct or otherwise,—the fact that it did so attract them, and that it attracted but few others with great force, is very certain. His public was limited and peculiar; it was almost as much so as Wordsworth's was at an earlier time.

When Mr. Tennyson published *Maud,* we feared that the influence of this class of admirers was deteriorating his powers. The subject was calculated to call out the unhealthier sort of youthful imaginations; and his treatment of it, so far from lessening the danger, seemed studiously selected to increase it. The hero of *Maud* is a young man who lives very much out of the world, who has no definite duties or intelligible occupations, who hates society because he is bound by no social ties and is conscious of no social courage. This young gentleman sees a young lady who is rich, and whose father has an unpleasant association with his own father, who was a bankrupt. He has all manner of feelings about the young lady, and she is partial to him; but there is a difficulty about their interviews. As he is poor and she is wealthy, they do not meet in common society; and a stolen visit in her garden ends, if we understand the matter, in his killing her brother. After this he leads a wandering life, and expresses his sentiments. Such a story is evidently very likely to bring into prominence the exaggerated feelings and distorted notions which we call unhealthy. The feelings of a young man who has nothing to do, and tries to do nothing; who is very poor, and regrets that he is not very rich; who is in love, and cannot speak to the lady he loves; who knows he cannot marry her, but notwithstanding wanders vaguely about her,—are sure to be unhealthy. Solitude, social mortification, wounded feeling, are the strongest sources of mental malaria; and all of these are here crowded together, and are conceived to act at once. Such a representation, therefore, if it was to be true, must be partially tinctured with unhealthiness. This was inevitable; and it was inevitable, too, that this taint should be rather agreeable than otherwise to many of the poet's warmest admirers. The Tennysonians, as we have said, were young men; and youth is the season of semi-diseased feeling. Keats, who knew much about such matters, remarked this. 'The imagination,' he said, 'of a man is healthy, and the imagination of a boy is healthy; but between' there is an uncertain time, when the fancy is restless, the principles are unfixed, the sentiments waver, and the highest feelings have not acquired consistency. Upon young men in such a frame of mind a delineation like that of the hero of Maud, adorned, as it was, with rare fragments of beautiful imagery, and abiding snatches of the sweetest music, could not but be attractive, and could not but be dangerous. It seemed to be the realised ideal of their hopes, of their hearts, of themselves; it half consecrated their characteristic defects, it confirmed their hope that their eccentricities were excellencies. Such a danger could not be avoided; but Mr. Tennyson, so far from trying to shun it, seemed intentionally to choose to aggravate it. He seemed to sympathise with the feverish railings, the moody nonsense, the very entangled philosophy, which he put into the mouth of his hero. There were some odd invectives against peace, against industry, against making your livelihood, which seemed by no means to be dramatic exhibitions of represented character, but, on the contrary, confidential expositions of the poet's own belief. He not only depicted the natural sentiments of an inactive, inexperienced, and neglected young man, but seemed to agree with them. He sympathised with moody longings; he was not severe on melancholy vanity; he rather encouraged a general disaffection to the universe. He appeared not only to have written, but to have accepted the 'Gospel according to the Unappreciated.' The most charitable reader could scarcely help fancying, that in describing an irritable confusion of fancy and a diseased moodiness of feeling, the poet for the time imbibed a certain taint of those defects.

The *Idylls of the King* suggest to us a peculiar doubt. Was not Mr. Tennyson, after all, laughing at his admirers? *Did* he believe in *Maud*, though he seemed to say he did? We do not know; but at all events we have now a poem not only of a different, but of the very opposite kind. Every line of it is defined with the delicate grace of a very composed genius; shows the trace of a very mature judgment; will bear the scrutiny of the most choice and detective taste. The feelings are natural, the thoughts such as people in life have or might have. The situations, though in a certain sense unnatural, have, we believe, a peculiar artistic propriety. There is a completeness in the whole.

> For when the Roman left us, and their law
> Relax'd its hold upon us, and the ways
> Were fill'd with rapine, here and there a deed
> Of prowess done redress'd a random wrong.
> But I was first of all the kings who drew
> The knighthood-errant of this realm and all

The realms together under me, their Head,
In that fair Order of my Table Round,
A glorious company, the flower of men,
To serve as model for the mighty world,
And be the fair beginning of a time.

The general public will like this, but scarcely the youthful admirers of broken art and incomplete beauties who accepted *Maud* with great delight. The world we know is opposed to earnest enthusiasts and fond disciples, and Mr. Tennyson has sided with the world. . . .

Mr. Tennyson has in the *Idylls* used these elements of the chivalric legend with instinctive felicity and dexterity. The tale of Prince Geraint, as the first Idyll might be called, is, in its main incidents, as pure a tale of chivalry as could be conceived. His love of Enid at first sight; his single combat with her cousin, who keeps her out of her inheritance; the general plentifulness of banditti, and his conquests over them,—are all features belonging essentially to that kind of story. It would be needless criticism to show that the poet has made a great deal of them, that the narrative is very clear and very flowing, that the choice of the events is very skilful; every reader must have perceived these excellencies.

It is more necessary to point out what the careful art of the poet disguises—that he has avoided the greatest danger of such a theme. The danger of a topic abounding in romantic and extraordinary events is, that its treatment may have a sort of glare. The first miracle we meet petrifies us, the next only astonishes, the third tires, and a fourth bores. The perpetual stimulus of such events as those which we have shown to be particularly characteristic of the chivalric legend would become wearisomely tedious, if a relieving element were not introduced in order to prevent it. Mr. Tennyson has found us such an element. He has managed to introduce to us, incidentally and without effort, many pictures of the quieter parts of human nature. He has fully availed himself of the license which his subject gives him. He never goes into any detail of life, which cannot be made attractive, which may have disenchanting associations, which may touch with a prosaic breath the accomplished exquisiteness of his art. But no mistaken hesitation, none of the over-caution which a less practised artist would have felt, has restrained him from using to the utmost the entire range of that part of life which he can make attractive. We have spoken of the first Idyll, as in its story one of the most purely chivalric of the four. Yet even in this there are several relieving elements. There is scarcely anything to be imagined of higher excellence in this kind than the character of Yniol and his wife. Yniol is an old lord who has lost his property, whose followers have deserted him, and who lives in poverty at an old castle upon sufference. He thus describes how his nephew ejected him, and what are the feelings with which he contemplates his life:

'And since the proud man often is the mean,
He sow'd a slander in the common ear,
Affirming that his father left him gold,
And in my charge, which was not render'd to him;
Bribed with large promises the men who served
About my person, the more easily
Because my means were somewhat broken into
Thro' open doors and hospitality;
Raised my own town against me in the night
Before my Enid's birthday, sack'd my house;
From mine own earldom foully ousted me;
Built that new fort to overawe my friends,
For truly there are those who love me yet;
And keeps me in this ruinous castle here,
Where doubtless he would put me soon to death,
But that his pride too much despises me:
And I myself sometimes despise myself;
For I have let men be, and have their way;
Am much too gentle, have not used my power:
Nor know I whether I be very base
Or very manful, whether very wise
Or very foolish; only this I know,
That whatsoever evil happen to me,
I seem to suffer nothing heart or limb,
But can endure it all most patiently.'

The quiet contemplative character, which suffers so many calamities in rude times, and which is often so puzzled to find out why it has experienced them, is a most suitable shading element to relieve the mind from always admiring great knights who strike hard, who throw immense lances, and who can kill anyone they wish. The feminine reflections—if such they can be called—of Yniol's wife, on the changes of her fortune, are equally appropriate, and quite as true to nature:

'For I myself unwillingly have worn
My faded suit, as you, my child, have yours,

And howsoever patient, Yniol his.
Ah, dear, he took me from a goodly house,
With store of rich apparel, sumptuous fare,
And page, and maid, and squire, and seneschal,
And pastime both of hawk and hound, and all
That appertains to noble maintenance.
Yea, and he brought me to a goodly house;
But since our fortune swerved from sun to shade,
And all thro' that young traitor, cruel need
Constrain'd us, but a better time has come;
So clothe yourself in this, that better fits
Our mended fortunes and a Prince's bride:
For tho' ye won the prize of fairest fair,
And tho' I heard him call you fairest fair,
Let never maiden think, however fair,
She is not fairer in new clothes than old.'

The whole story of the dress, of which this is a part, is a very delicate instance of relieving and softening skill; but we have no room to make any more remarks upon it.

Mr. Tennyson has, however, introduced another element into the description of the chivalric state of society, which, though in some sense it relieves it, does not so well harmonise with it. As we have observed, he avails himself of the peculiar manner—the sudden manner—of falling in love, characteristic of that society. In the first Idyll, Geraint falls in love with Enid on the first evening of their acquaintance; he proposes for her at once, fights a tournament, and is accepted the next morning. In the third Idyll we have the reverse history: a young lady named Elaine falls in love at once with the great Sir Lancelot; but as he does not like her as well as the Queen, she is not accepted. These are love affairs very characteristic of a state of society when women were seen but rarely, and even when seen were but little spoken to; but side by side with them in the Idyll there are other scenes indicative of a great familiarity between them and men, full of intellectual friction between the two, showing on both sides the nice and critical knowledge of our civilised world. It seems hardly fair that a writer should insist on the good side of both species of life; upon being permitted to use the sudden love which arises from not knowing women, and the love-tinged intercourse of thought and fancy which is the result of knowing them, together and at once. The nature of the story seems to have led Mr. Tennyson into this complication. The reign of Arthur, as is well known, was believed to have been for many years clouded, and at length terminated, by the unlawful affection of his Queen Guinevere for Sir Lancelot, the greatest and most renowned of his courtiers. This is evidently a very delicate topic for art to handle. King Arthur and Sir Lancelot are both to be made interesting: the Queen, of

> imperial-moulded form,
> And beauty such as never woman wore,

is to be made interesting likewise. A great deal of intellectual detail is necessary for this end; many slight touches of delicate insight must conduce to it; a hundred pencillings of nice art must be accumulated to effect it. If the subject was to be treated for modern readers, some additions to the bareness of old romance and legend were indispensable; and even a critic could hardly object to them. But Mr. Tennyson has gone further. There being a Queen at court who was not immaculate, he has thought it proper that there should be ladies about her who are no better. 'Vivien,' the young lady who gives her name to the second Idyll, is more fitted for the court of Louis Quinze than for that of the saintly king of chivalry. . . .

There is undoubtedly much that is not modern in Merlin's character, or rather in his occupation, for he is a faint kind of being; but the enchanter who has a charm of 'woven paces and of waving hands,' and who has read lines of lore which no other person can read, does not belong to the drawing-room. His pursuits, at any rate, do not. . . .

But however removed from us Merlin's character may be, that of Vivien in its essence rather belongs to an over-civilised and satirical, than to an uncultivated and romantic time. It rather mars our enjoyment of the new book of chivalry, to have a character so discordant with its idea placed in such prominence, and drawn out in such development.

A similar charge cannot, however, be justly brought against the main story of the poem. The contrast of character between King Arthur and Sir Lancelot is one of those which exists in some degree in all ages, but which the exciting circumstances of an unsettled time necessarily tend to bring out and exaggerate. In our last Number we had occasion, in writing on another subject, to draw out at some length the delineation of the two kinds of goodness which have long been contrasted, and always seem likely to be contrasted, in the world,—the ascetic and the sensuous. The characteristic of the latter is to be sensitive to everything in this world, tempted by every stimulus, exposed to every passion; the characteristic of the former is to be repelled from the ordinary pleasures of the world, to be above them, to feel a warning instinct against them. In the course of life the fate of the ascetic character is to be absorbed in a somewhat chill ideal; that of the sensuous character is to purchase a fascinating richness of earthly experience by a serious number of grave errors. We had some difficulty formerly in illustrating the distinction between the two characters at once clearly and expressively, but we should have had no such difficulty if Mr. Tennyson had published his new poem a little earlier. The character of Arthur, absorbed in the ideal conception of a chivalrous monarchy, is the very type of the highest abstract or ascetic character; that of Lancelot, the great knight of many exploits and full-lipped enjoyment, whom Guinevere prefers, is the type of the sensuous and sensitive. . . .

There can be no doubt that Mr. Tennyson has judged wisely in telling the story of Arthur and Guinevere in a series of tales rather than in a single connected epic. The peculiar and painful nature of that story requires, in a singular degree, the continual use of relieving elements; and yet it is of the first importance that no one of these elements should assume an undue prominence, or be more interesting than the story itself. If other interesting characters had been introduced into the main plot of a continuous poem, the latter effect would have been nearly inevitable. The imagination cannot rest with satisfaction either on Guinevere's relation to Arthur or on her relation to Lancelot. In each there is a disagreeable and disenchanting something. If a competing interest had been introduced into the central plot, it could hardly fail to be intrinsically pleasanter, and might have distracted the attention intended from the chosen theme. The form which the poet has adopted—that of a set of stories, with continual allusion to a latent thread—prevents this result, and also gives the requisite shading to the painful subject. There is a continued succession of relieving interests; but there is none which can compete with the central one, or be compared with it.

We have said enough of the merits of this poem to entitle us to say what ought to be said against it. We have not, indeed, a long list of defects to set forth. On the contrary, we think we perceive only one of real importance; and it is very probable that many critics will think us quite wrong as to that one. It appears to us that the *Idylls* are defective in dramatic power. Madame de Stael said that Coleridge was admirable in monologue, but quite incapable of dialogue. Something analogous may perhaps be said of Mr. Tennyson. His imagination seems to fix itself on a particular person in a particular situation; and he pours out, with ease and abundance, with delicacy and exactness, all which is suitable to that person in that situation. This was so with 'Ulysses' in former years; it is so in his 'Grandmother's Apology', published the other day. Unnumbered instances of it may be found in the *Idylls*. But the power of writing a soliloquy is very different from that of writing a conversation; so different, indeed, that the person who is most likely to wish to write one, is most likely not to wish to write the other. Dialogue requires a very changing imagination, ready to move with ease from the mental position of one mind to the mental position of another, quick with the various language suited to either. Soliloquy—prolonged solioquy, at any rate—requires a very steady imagination, steadily accumulating, slowly realising the exact position of a single person. The glancing mind will tend to one sort of composition; the meditative, solitary, and heavy mind to the other. All Mr. Tennyson's poems show more of the latter tendency than of the first. His genius gives the notion of a slow depositing instinct; day by day, as the hours pass, the delicate sand falls into beautiful forms—in stillness, in peace, in brooding. You fancy Shakespeare writing quick, the hasty dialogue of the parties passing quickly through his brain: we have no such idea of our great contemporary poet. He keeps his verses in his head: a meditative and scrupulous Muse is prayed to

> Let him write his random lines
> Ere they be half forgotten,
> Nor add or alter many times
> Till all be ripe and rotten.

The lightly-flowing dialogue is not so written. The lightly-moving imagination which is necessary to its composition gallops quicker, has a more varied tread, alters its point of view more frequently. If we look into the various dialogues of these *Idylls,* we shall not only observe that the tendency to monologue is great, and is greatest at the most striking points and telling situations, but also be struck with what is nearly the same phenomenon in another form—the remarkable similarity of the conversational powers of all the various personages. It is not only that a peculiar kind of language, a sort of a dialect of sentimental chivalry, pervades the whole,—this is quite in keeping with the design, and is perhaps essential to the perfect effect of such a book; but the similarity seems to go deeper: each dramatic personage is fully endowed with the expressive capacities of Mr. Tennyson's imagination; each one has them all, and consequently they are all on a level; no one has a superiority. No fact can more exactly and instructively define the precise difference between a genuine dramatic expression and the superficially analogous, but really different, art of delineative soliloquy. In the latter, it is right that the state of feeling to be expressed should be expressed with all the poet's power: we are representing the man's notion of himself; we take the liberty to say for him what he could never say; we translate into similes and phrases the half thoughts and floating feelings which he never could for a moment have expressed in that way, or probably in any other way. But in the genuine drama we are delineating a scene with more than one actor, and we are to state an imaginary dialogue. The mode in which people express themselves is an essential fact of that dialogue. The degree in which people can express themselves is one of the most dramatic parts of their characters; it is therefore contrary to all the principles of art to give to each character the same command, especially if it be a singular command over very imaginative language. The state of the supposed speaker's mind is no doubt brought out by that mode more effectually than by any other; but the effect of the scene—of the speaking mind which can delineate itself, and of the dumb mind which cannot—is altogether impaired, for the striking contrast is destroyed.

The only other defect with which the *Idylls* are, we think, to be charged, is not so much a positive defect in the poetry itself, as rather a negative deficiency in it when compared with other poems of Mr. Tennyson's that we have known for many years. A certain subtlety seems to pervade some of the latter; and it is in part ascribable to the subtlety of thought, and is greatly heightened by a peculiar subtlety of expression. There are lines in some of the older poems for which perhaps every one has

A pleasurable feeling of blind love.

We know what they express: they *do* express it to us: they dwell in our memories; they haunt us with their echo. Yet, if we try to analyse them, their charm is gone. Is the meaning expressed? Did Mr. Tennyson really mean this?—is there not this ambiguity? Might he not have intended something else? We can conceive a foreign critic, thoroughly acquainted with our language for almost all other purposes, to be quite incapable of seeing the merit of some of the more characteristic of these poems, from a want of those early floating and mysterious associations with language, in the instinctive and delicate use of which that charm consists. We have known literal-minded English persons, who preferred the plainer phraseology—the 'commin print,' as Lisbeth would have called it—of every-day rhymers. And, in some sense, their preference was correct. All that they could perceive was more perfect in the entirely valueless rhyme than in the entirely invaluable. The logical structure is better; it would construe better into other words, or into a foreign language: and this the literal critics perceive. The hovering air of power and beauty which the words really have, they do not perceive. If you were to suggest the existence they would smile. We believe that of this subtle sort of beauty, there is less in the *Idylls* than in Mr. Tennyson's earlier poetry. Perhaps they have not been in our hands long enough for us to judge.

These super-logical beauties, if we may so say, are those which require the longest time to perceive, and the most perfect familiarity to appreciate. Still we do think so. We think there are few passages, considering the length of the poems, which will have years hence that inexplicable and magical power over our minds which some of Mr. Tennyson's old lines have. Perhaps the subject may have something to do with it. The sentiments in these poems are simpler than his sentiments used to be; they are not 'clothed in white samite, mystic, wonderful.' The thoughts are broader and plainer. The old mystic grace of language may, therefore, not have been so much used, only because it was no longer so much needed.

Every poem of Mr. Tennyson's must suggest the inquiry, what is the place which he occupies in the series of our poets? This poem must do so most of all; because, as we have explained, it removes some of the doubts which his warmest admirers formerly felt as to the limits of the range of his genius. It shows that he has the skill to adapt, the instinctive taste and self-restraint to preserve a continued interest of considerable length. Architectonic power the long-worded critics used to say he had not; but we have now discovered that he has it. The puzzling question returns, Where is Mr. Tennyson to be placed in the rank of our poets? We know that he has genius; but is that genius great or small, when compared with others like it?

It is most natural to compare him with Keats and Shelley. The kind of readers he addresses is, as we observed, the same: a sort of intellectual sentiment pervades his works as well as theirs: the superficial resemblances of the works of all the three are many. But, on the other hand, Mr. Tennyson is deficient in the most marked peculiarity which Shelley and Keats have in common. Both of these poets are singularly gifted with a sustained faculty of lyrical expression. They seem hurried into song; and, what is more, kept there when they have been hurried there. Shelley's *Skylark* is the most familiar example of this. A rather young musician was once asked, what was Jenny Lind's charm in singing. 'Oh,' he replied, 'she went up so high, and staid up high so long.' There is something of this sustainment at a great height in all Shelley's lyrics. His strains are profuse. He is ever soaring; and whilst soaring, ever singing. Keats, it is true, did not ascend to so extreme an elevation. He did not belong to the upper air. He had no abstract labour, no haunting speculations, no attenuated thoughts. He was the poet of the obvious beauty of the world. His genius was of the earth—of the autumn earth—rich and mellow; and it was lavish. He did not carry his art high or deep; he neither enlightens our eyes much, nor expands our ears much; but pleases our fancies with a prolonged strain of simple rich melody. He does not pause, or stay, or hesitate. His genius is continuous; the flow of it is as obvious at the best moments as the excellence, and at inferior moments is more so. Mr. Tennyson, on the other hand, has no tendencies of this kind. He broods, as we have said. There are undoubtedly several beautiful songs in his writings,—several in which the sentiment cleaves to the words, and cannot even in our memories be divorced from them. But their beauty is not continuous. A few lines fasten upon us with an imperious and evermastering charm; but the whole composition, as a whole, has not much value. The run of it, as far as it has a run, expresses nothing. The genius of Mr. Tennyson is delineative; it muses and meditates; it describes moods, feelings, and objects of imagination; but it does not rush on to pour out passion, or express overwhelming emotion.

In the special lyrical impulse, therefore, we think it indisputable that Mr. Tennyson is inferior both to Keats and to Shelley. To Shelley he is moreover evidently inferior in general intensity of mind. This intense power of conception is, indeed, the most striking of all Shelley's peculiarities. There is something nervously exciting about his way of writing, even on simple subjects. He takes them up so vividly into his brain that they seem to make it quiver, and that of a sensitive reader at times quivers in sympathy. The subjects are no doubt often abstract; too abstract, perhaps, occasionally for art. But that only makes the result more singular. That an excitable mind should be stimulated by the strong interest of the facts of the world, by the phenomena of life, by the expectation of death, is what we should expect. It is intelligible to our understanding, and in obvious accordance with our experience. But that this extreme excitement should be caused in the poet's mind very often, and in the reader's mind sometimes, by the abstractions of singular tenuity, is what few would expect. So, however, it is. The mind of Shelley seems always to work in a kind of pure rare ether, clearer, sharper, more eager than the ordinary air. The reader feels that he is on a kind of mountainous elevation, and perhaps he feels vivified by it: at times almost all persons do so, but at times also they are chilled at its cold, and half-frightened at the lifelessness and singularity. It is characteristic of Shelley that he was obliged to abandon one of his favourite speculations, 'dizzy from thrilling horror.' Of all this abstract intensity Mr. Tennyson has not a particle. He is never very eager about anything, and he is certainly not over-anxious about phantoms and abstractions. In some respects this deficiency may not have injured his writings: it has rather contributed to his popularity. The English mind, which, like its great philosophers, likes to work upon 'stuff,' is more pleased with genial chivalric pictures than with chiselled phantoms and intense lyrics. Still, a critic who appreciates Shelley at all, will probably feel that he has a degree of inner power, of telling mental efficiency, which Mr. Tennyson does not equal. Horrible as the *Cenci* must ever be, it shows an eager and firmer grasp of mind—a greater tension of the imagination—than the *Idylls.*

Over Keats, however, Mr. Tennyson may perhaps claim a general superiority. We are, indeed, making a comparison which is scarcely fair; Keats died when he was still very young. His genius was immature; and his education, except the superficial musing education he gave himself, was very imperfect. Mr. Tennyson has lived till his genius is fully ripe, and he has gathered in the fruits of his century. No one can read his poems without feeling this: some of his readers have probably felt it painfully. Twenty years ago, when there was an idea in the high places of criticism that he was a silly and affected writer, many ignorant persons thought they were showing their knowledge in laughing at a language which nevertheless was both most emphatic and most accurate. The amount of thought which is held in solution,—if we may be pardoned so scientific a metaphor,—in Mr. Tennyson's poetry, is very great. If you come to his poems a hundred times, it is very probable that you will even to the end find there some new allusion, some recondite trace of high-bred thought, which you had not seen before. His reflections are often not new; he would not advance for himself perhaps, his just admirers, we are sure, would not claim for him, the fame of an absolutely original thinker. But he indicates the possession of a kind of faculty which in an age of intellect and cultivation is just as important, possibly is even more important, than the power of first-hand discovery. He is a first-rate *realiser;* and realisation is a test of truth. Out of the infinite thoughts, discoveries, and speculations which are scattered, more or less perfectly, through society, certain minds have a knack of taking up and making their own that which is true, and healthy, and valuable; and they reject the rest. It is often not by a very strict analysis or explicit logical statement that such minds arrive at their conclusions. They are continually thinking the subjects in question over: they have the details of them in their minds: they have a floating picture of endless particulars about them in their imaginations. In consequence, by musing over a true doctrine, they see that it is true: it fits their picture, adapts itself to it, forms at once a framework for it. On the contrary, they find that a false tenet does not suit the facts which they have in their minds: they muse over it, find out its unsuitability, and think no more of it. The belief of these remarkably sane and remarkably meditative persons about the facts to which they devote their own understandings is one of the best criteria of truth in this world. It is the discriminating winnow of civilisation, which receives the real corn of the true discoverer, and leaves the vexing chaff of the more pompous science to be forgotten and pass away. This kind of meditative tact and slow selective judgment Mr. Tennyson possesses in a very great measure; and there is nothing of which Keats was so entirely destitute. It does not, perhaps, occur to you while reading him that he is deficient in it. It belongs to an order of merit completely out of his way. It is the reflective gift of a mature man: Keats's best gifts are those of an impulsive, original, and refined boy. But if we compare—as in some degree we cannot help doing—the indications of general mind which are scattered through the three writers, we shall think, perhaps, that in these Mr. Tennyson excels Keats, even remembering the latter's early death, and, in consequence, giving him all fair credit for the possibilities of subsequent development; just as we found before that the intellectual balance seemed, when similarly adjusted, to incline against Mr. Tennyson, and in favour of Shelley.

Some one has said that Tennyson was a drawing-room Wordsworth. There is no deep felicity or instruction in the phrase, but it has some superficial appropriateness. Wordsworth's works have no claim to be in the drawing-room: they have the hill-side and the library, and those places are enough for them. Wordsworth, as we know, dealt with two subjects, and with two subjects only,—the simple elemental passions, 'the pangs by which the generations are prepared,' and in which they live and breathe and move; and secondly, the spiritual conception of nature, which implies that the universe is, in its beauties and its changes, but the expression of an inherent and animating spirit. Neither of these subjects suits the drawing-room. The simple passions are there carefully covered over; nature is out-of-doors. Mr. Tennyson, however, has given some accounts of the more refined and secondary passions in Wordsworth's intense manner; and if he does not give the exact sketches of external nature, or preach any gospel concerning it, he gives us a mental reflex of it, and a Lotus-eater's view of what it ought to be, and what it is rather a shame on the whole that it is not, which are not inadmissible in a luxurious drawing-room. A little of the spirit of Wordsworth, thus modified, may be traced in Mr. Tennyson; and perhaps this is the only marked trace of a recent writer that can be found in his writings. If we were to be asked as before, whether Mr. Wordsworth or Mr. Tennyson were the superior in general imaginative power, we think we should say that the latter was the superior, but that Wordsworth had achieved a greater task than he has as yet achieved, with inferior powers. The mind of Wordsworth was singularly narrow; his range peculiarly limited; the object he proposed to himself unusually distinct. He has given to us a complete embodiment of the two classes of subjects which he has treated of: perhaps it would be impossible to imagine one of them—the peculiar aspect of outward nature which we mentioned—to be better delineated; certainly as yet, we apprehend, it is not delineated nearly so well any where else. Although we should be inclined to believe that Mr. Tennyson's works indicate greater powers, we do not think that they evince so much concentrated efficiency, that they leave any single result upon the mind which is at once so high and so definite.

If we were asked, as we shall be asked, why we think Mr. Tennyson to have greater powers than Wordsworth, we would venture to allege two reasons. In the first place, Mr. Tennyson has a power of making fun. No one can claim that, of all powers, for Wordsworth, it is certain: no human being more entirely destitute of humour is perhaps discoverable anywhere in literature, or possibly even in society. Not a tinge of it seems ever to have influenced him. He had, through life, the narrow sincerity of the special missionary; but he had not, what is all but incompatible with it, the restraining tact of the man of the world, which teaches that all things and all gospels are only now and then in season; that it is absurd always to be teaching a single doctrine; that it is not wise to fatigue oneself by trying to interest others in that which it is perfectly certain they will not be interested in. The world of 'cakes and ale,' indisputably, is not that of Wordsworth. There are quite sufficient indications that Mr. Tennyson appreciates it. Secondly, it may be said that, far more completely than Wordsworth, and far more completely than any other recent poet, Mr. Tennyson has conceived in his mind, and has delineated in his works, a general picture of human life. He certainly does not give us the whole of it, there is a considerable portion which he scarcely touches; but an acute eye can observe that he sees more than he says; and even judging exclusively and rigidly from what is said, the amount of life which Mr. Tennyson has delineated, even in these *Idylls* only, far surpasses in extent and range that which Wordsworth has described. Wordsworth's range is so narrow, and the extent of life and thought which these *Idylls* go over, slight as is their seeming structure, is so great, that perhaps no one will question this conclusion. Some may, however, deny its sufficiency; they may suggest that it does not prove our conclusion. In Shelley's case, it may be said that we allowed a certain defined intensity to have a higher imaginative value than a more diffused fertility and a less concentrated art; why is not Wordsworth entitled to share the benefit of this doctrine also? The plea is very specious, but we are not inclined to think that it is sound. Shelley has shown in a single direction, or in a few directions, an immense general power of imagination and mind. We may not pause to prove this: it is in the nature of allusive criticism to be dogmatic; we must appeal to the memory of our readers. On the other hand, we think, by a certain doggedness of nature, by high resolution, and even, in a certain sense, by an extreme limitation of mind, Wordsworth, with far less of imagination, was able in special directions to execute most admirable works. But the power displayed is, in a great degree, that of character rather than of imagination. He put all his mind into a single task, and he did it. Wordsworth's best works are the saved-up excellencies of a rather barren nature; those of Shelley are the rapid productions of a very fertile one. When we are speaking of mere intellectual and imaginative power, we run, therefore, no risk of contradiction in ranking Mr. Tennyson at a higher place than Wordsworth, notwithstanding that we have adjudged him to be inferior in the same quality to Shelley.

Perhaps we can, after this discussion, fix, at least approximately and incompletely, Mr. Tennyson's position in the hierarchy of our poets. We think that the poets of this century of whom we have been speaking,—and Coleridge may be added to the number,—may be, in a certain sense, classed together as the intellectualised poets. We do not, of course, mean that there ever was a great poet who was destitute of great intellect, or who did not show that intellect distinctly in his poems. But the poets of whom we speak show that intellect in a further and special sense. We are all conscious of the difference between talking to an educated man and to an uneducated. The difference by no means is, that the educated man talks better; that he either says better things, or says them in a more vigorous way. Possibly uneducated persons, as a rule, talk more expressively, and send whatever meaning they have farther into the hearer's mind; perhaps their meaning on the subjects which they have in common with educated men, is not very much inferior. Still there is a subtle charm about the conversation of the educated which that of other persons has not. That charm consists in the constant presence and constant trace of a cultivated intellect. The words are used with a certain distinct precision; a distinguishing tact of intellect is indicated by that which is said; a discriminating felicity is shown in the mode in which it is said. The charm of cultivated expression is like the charm of a cultivated manner; it is easy and yet cautious, natural and yet improved, ready and yet restrained. The fascination of a cultivated intellect in literature is the same. It is more easy to describe its absence, perhaps, than its presence. The style of Shakespeare, for example, wants entirely this peculiar charm. He had the manifold experience, the cheerful practicality, the easy felicity of the uneducated man; but he had not the measured abundance, the self-restraining fertility, which the very highest writer may be conceived to have. There is no subtle discretion in his words: there is the nice tact of native instinct; there is not the less necessary, but yet attractive, precision of an earnest and anxious education. Perhaps it will be admitted that the writers we have mentioned— Shelley, Coleridge, Keats, Wordsworth, and Tennyson—may all be called, as far as our own literature is concerned, in a peculiar sense the intellectualised poets. Milton indeed would, in positive knowledge, be superior to any of them, and to many of them put together, but he is an exceptional poet in English literature, to be classed apart, and seldom to be spoken of in contrast or comparison with any other; and even he, from a want of natural subtlety of mind, does not perhaps show us, in the midst of his amazing knowledge, the most acute and discriminating intellectuality. But if we except Milton, these poets may almost certainly be classed apart: and if they are to be so, we have indicated the place which Mr. Tennyson holds in this class in relation to all of them save Coleridge. A real estimate of the latter is not to be expected of us at the end of an article, and as a parenthesis in the estimate of another poet. He will long be a problem to the critics, and a puzzle to the psychologists. But, so far as the general powers of mind shown in his poems are concerned,—and this is the only aspect of his genius which we are at present considering,—we need have no hesitation in saying that they are much inferior to those shown in the poems of our greatest contemporary poet. Their great excellence is, in truth, almost confined to their singular power in the expression of one single idea. Both *Christabel* and the *Ancient Mariner* are substantially developments of the same conception; they delineate almost exclusively the power which the supernatural has, when it is thrust among the detail of the natural. This idea is worked out with astonishing completeness; but it is left to stand alone. There are no characters, no picture of life at large, no extraordinary thoughts, to be found in these poems; their metre and their strangeness are their charm. After what has been said, we need not prove at large that such an exclusive concentration upon such an idea proves that these poems are inferior, or rather indicate inferior imaginative genius to that of Tennyson. The range of the art is infinitely less; and the peculiar idea, which is naturally impressive, and in comparison with others easy to develop, hardly affords scope for the clear exhibition of a very creative genius, even if there were not other circumstances which would lead us to doubt whether Coleridge, rich and various as were his mental gifts, was possessed of that one. On the whole, we may pause in the tedium of our comparative dissertation. We may conclude, that in the series of our intellectualised poets Mr. Tennyson is to be ranked as inferior in the general power of the poetic imagination to Shelley, and to Shelley only;—and if this be true, the establishment of it is a contribution to criticism quite sufficient for a single article.

—Walter Bagehot, from "Tennyson's *Idylls*," 1859,
Collected Works, ed. Norman St. John-Stevas,
1965, vol. 2, pp. 179–207

THOMAS BABINGTON MACAULAY (1859)

Thomas Babington Macaulay was an English poet, author, historian, and a Whig politician. In the following extract from his journal, Macaulay states his great admiration for Tennyson's *Idylls of the King* and that certain passages moved him to tears. He does remark that he found some faults with the poem but not to the extent that they detracted from the pleasure he received from it.

The Duke of Argyll called, and left me the sheets of a forthcoming poem of Tennyson. I like it extremely—notwithstanding some faults, extremely. The parting of Lancelot and Guinivere, her penitence, and Arthur's farewell, are all very affecting. I cried over some passages; but I am now ἀρτίβακρυς, as Medea says.

> —Thomas Babington Macaulay, *Journal*, July 11,
> 1859, cited in G. Otto Trevelyan, *The Life and
> Letters of Lord Macaulay*, 1876, vol. 2, p. 398

W. E. GLADSTONE "TENNYSON'S POEMS— *IDYLLS OF THE KING*" (1859)

William Ewart Gladstone was a liberal politician and statesman and four times prime minister of the United Kingdom. In the following extract, Gladstone presents the possibility of Tennyson's cycle of poems as being part of the epic genre. He finds in the first five poems of the cycle those qualities that might allow such a claim to be made: a moral unity, the poet's concentration on the individual rather than his or her actions, and the interrelatedness of the separate poems. Gladstone holds out hope that the future sections of the whole cycle will continue to produce those epic qualities he believes the initial poems display.

We have no doubt that Mr. Tennyson has carefully considered how far his subject is capable of fulfilling the conditions of an epic structure. The history of Arthur is not an epic as it stands, but neither was the Cyclic song, of which the greatest of all epics, the *Iliad,* handles a part. The poem of Ariosto is scarcely an epic, nor is that of Bojardo; but is not this because each is too promiscuous and crowded in its brilliant phantasmagoria to conform to the severe laws of that lofty and inexorable class of poem? Though the Arthurian romance be no epic, it does not follow that no epic can be made from out of it. It is grounded in certain leading characters, men and women, conceived upon models of extraordinary grandeur; and as the Laureate has evidently grasped the genuine law which makes man and not the acts of man the base of epic song, we should not be surprised were he hereafter to realise the great achievement towards which he seems to be feeling his way. There is a moral unity and a living relationship between the four poems before us, and the first effort of 1842 as a fifth, which, though some considerable part of their contents would necessarily rank as episode, establishes the first and most essential condition of their cohesion. The achievement of Vivien bears directly on the state of Arthur by withdrawing his chief councillor—the brain, as Lancelot was the right arm, of his court; the love of Elaine is directly associated with the final catastrophe of the passion of Lancelot for Guinevere. Enid lies somewhat further off the path, nor is it for profane feet to intrude into the sanctuary, for reviewers to advise poets in these high matters; but while we presume nothing, we do not despair of seeing Mr. Tennyson achieve on the basis he has chosen the structure of a full-formed epic.

—W. E. Gladstone, "Tennyson's Poems—*Idylls of the King*," *Quarterly Review*, October 1859, pp. 479–80

PRINCE ALBERT (1860)

Prince Albert of Saxe-Coburg and Gotha was the prince consort and husband of Queen Victoria. In the following extract from a letter written to Tennyson, the prince requests an autograph. As seen in the previous extract written by the queen, she viewed Tennyson with high regard, and it is clear that the same emotions are felt by her husband when he reads the poet's verse. The prince consort remarks quite sensitively on the commingling of chivalric feeling and the formal qualities of the modern in Tennyson's poem.

Will you forgive me if I intrude on your leisure with a request which I have thought some little time of making, viz. that you would be good enough to write your name in the accompanying volume of your *Idylls of the King?* You would thus add a peculiar interest to the book, containing those beautiful songs, from the perusal of which I derived the greatest enjoyment. They quite rekindle the feeling with which the legends of King Arthur must have inspired the chivalry of old, whilst the graceful form in which they are presented blends those feelings with the softer tone of our present age.

—Prince Albert, letter to Alfred, Lord Tennyson, May 17, 1860

Thomas Carlyle (1867)

In the following short extract from one of Thomas Carlyle's letters to Ralph Waldo Emerson, Carlyle makes note of the pleasure he derived from Tennyson's *Idylls of the King*, while also finding the work lacking in any substance whatsoever. Carlyle feels as if he has been treated as a child on being presented with the tale in the poem, despite its formal excellence.

We read, at first, Tennyson's *Idyls*, with profound recognition of the finely elaborated execution, and also of the inward perfection of *vacancy*,—and, to say truth, with considerable impatience at being treated so very like infants, tho the lollipops were so superlative.

> —Thomas Carlyle, letter to Ralph Waldo
> Emerson, January 27, 1867

James Russell Lowell (1872)

James Russell Lowell was an American poet, literary critic, and diplomat. Lowell levels the accusation against Tennyson's *Idylls of the King* that it is full of childish sham, that the characters are unreal, their emotions and actions staged; equally, Lowell feels that Tennyson's language is a prop for the extended similes deployed in the poems and that they, too, are contrived. Nonetheless, Lowell is not immune to the beauty on display in the verse and remarks that he finds those younger poets to be fools who are telling Tennyson to stop writing now that he has produced his greatest works. Lowell asks what these youths have accomplished when compared to Tennyson? He fears that much of the poet's present criticism is a natural outcome of achieving fame rapidly and too early in his literary career. Nevertheless, the extract ends with Lowell's conclusion that Tennyson's verse is passionate and can still burn brightly in the world.

There are very fine childish things in Tennyson's poem and fine manly things, too, as it seems to me, but I conceive the theory to be wrong. I have the same feeling (I am not wholly sure of its justice) that I have when I see these modern-mediaeval pictures. I am defrauded; I do not see reality, but a masquerade. The costumes are all that is genuine, and the people inside them are shams—which, I take it, is just the reverse of what ought to be. One special criticism I should make on Tennyson's new Idyls, and that is that the similes are so often dragged in by the hair. They seem to be taken (a *la*

Tom Moore) from note-books, and not suggested by the quickened sense of association in the glow of composition. Sometimes it almost seems as if the verses were made for the similes, instead of being the cresting of a wave that heightens as it rolls. This is analogous to the costume objection and springs perhaps from the same cause—the making of poetry with malice prepense. However, I am not going to forget the lovely things that Tennyson has written, and I think they give him rather hard measure now. However, it is the natural recoil of a too rapid fame. Wordsworth had the true kind—an unpopularity that roused and stimulated while he was strong enough to despise it, and honor, obedience, troops of friends, when the grasshopper would have been a burthen to the drooping shoulders. Tennyson, to be sure, has been childishly petulant; but what have these whipper-snappers, who cry "Go up, baldhead," done that can be named with some things of his? He has been the greatest artist in words we have had since Gray—and remember how Gray holds his own with little fuel, but real fire. He had the secret of the inconsumable oil, and so, I fancy, has Tennyson.

—James Russell Lowell, letter to Charles Eliot
Norton, December 4, 1872

ALGERNON CHARLES SWINBURNE
"TENNYSON AND MUSSET" (1881)

Algernon Charles Swinburne was a controversial English poet and critic, who, at one time, was considered by some to be the greatest poet of the Victorian era. Swinburne never recanted this title but was surpassed in the popular imagination and taste by both Tennyson and Robert Browning. Swinburne here criticizes the *Idylls of the King* for the incoherence of its characterization. Tennyson, claims the other poet, has taken aspects of different periods' and different authors' portrayals of Arthur and tried to combine them all into a recognizable whole, a task that Swinburne believes to have been impossible from its flawed conception. The attempt is described as being akin to trying to combine the noble Achilles of Homer with the brutish Achilles of Shakespeare: They are simply incompatible figures. Swinburne states that Tennyson has multiplied the incompatible Arthurs by taking depictions from so many differing sources that nothing at all is left in the end that can cohere into a recognizable human character.

The real and radical flaw in the splendid structure of the *Idylls* is not to be found either in the antiquity of the fabulous groundwork or in the modern touches which certainly were not needed, and if needed would not have been adequate, to redeem any worthy recast of so noble an original from the charge of nothingness. The fallacy which obtrudes itself throughout, the false note which incessantly jars on the mind's ear, results from the incongruity of materials which are radically incapable of combination or coherence. Between the various Arthurs of different national legends there is little more in common than the name. It is essentially impossible to construct a human figure by the process of selection from the incompatible types of irreconcilable ideals. All that the utmost ingenuity of eclecticism can do has been demonstrated by Lord Tennyson in his elaborate endeavour after the perfection of this process; and the result is to impress upon us a complete and irreversible conviction of its absolute hopelessness. Had a poet determined to realize the Horatian ideal of artistic monstrosity, he could hardly have set about it more ingeniously than by copying one feature from the Mabinogion and the next from the Morte d'Arthur. So far from giving us 'Geoffrey's' type or 'Mallory's' type, he can hardly be said to have given us a recognizable likeness of Prince Albert; who, if neither a wholly gigantic nor altogether a divine personage, was at least, one would imagine, a human figure. But the spectre of his laureate's own ideal knight, neither Welsh nor French, but a compound of 'Guallia and Gaul, soul-curer and body-curer,' sir priest and sir knight, Mallory and Geoffrey, old style and middle style and new style, makes the reader bethink himself what might or might not be the result if some poet of similar aim and aspiration were to handle the tale of Troy, for instance, as Lord Tennyson has handled the Arthurian romance. The half godlike Achilles of Homer is one in name and nothing else with the all brutish Achilles of Shakespeare; the romantic Arthur of the various volumes condensed by Mallory into his English compilation—incoherent itself and incongruous in its earlier parts, but so nobly consistent, so profoundly harmonious in its close—has hardly more in common with the half impalpable hero of British myth or tradition. And I cannot but think that no very promising task would be undertaken by a poet who should set before himself the design of harmonizing in one fancy portrait, of reconciling in one typic figure, the features of Achilles as they appear in the Iliad with the features of Achilles as they appear in *Troilus and Cressida*.

—Algernon Charles Swinburne, "Tennyson and
Musset" (1881), *Miscellanies*, 1886, pp. 249–51

DRAMATIC WRITINGS

James Anthony Froude (1875)

James Anthony Froude was an English author, historian, the controversial biographer of Thomas and Jane Carlyle, and the editor of the literary journal *Fraser's Magazine*. In the following letter, Froude expresses great admiration for Tennyson's *Queen Mary*, claiming it as the greatest of all the poet's works. Coming from a historian, such warm appreciation of a piece of historical drama is perhaps slightly biased, but Froude's reasoning is clear: He claims that no English dramatist except Tennyson, and since Shakespeare, has claimed a piece of history and unalterably fixed its perception in the popular imagination.

I cannot trust myself to say how greatly I admire the play (*Queen Mary*). Beyond the immediate effect, you'll have hit a more fatal blow than a thousand pamphleteers and controversialists; besides this you have reclaimed one more section of English History from the wilderness and given it a form in which it will be fixed for ever. No one since Shakespeare has done that. When we were beginning to think that we were to have no more from you, you have given us the greatest of all your works. Once more I thank you for having written this book with all my heart.

> —James Anthony Froude, letter to Alfred,
> Lord Tennyson, May 7, 1875, cited in Hallam
> Tennyson, *Alfred Lord Tennyson: A Memoir*, 1897,
> vol. 2, pp. 180–81

William Watson (1892)

William Watson was an English poet and a staunch defender of Tennyson in the elder poet's latter years of declining popularity. Watson was considered a candidate for the post of poet laureate after Tennyson's death, but his political opposition to the first Boer War (1880–81) meant he was passed over in favor of Alfred Austin. In the following extract, Watson suggests that Tennyson has been less acclaimed for his drama because he has accomplished so much in his lifetime and is judged according to whichever aspect of his body of work is preferred by each critic: Some favor his lyric voice, some his elegiac verse, some the *Idylls of the King*. Watson, in a canny turn of phrase, suggests that Tennyson is, in fact, his own greatest rival.

Another element that Watson believes may have worked against Tennyson in his dramatic achievements is the plays' themes. It is impossible to sympathize with the justly named "Bloody" Queen Mary; of *Harold*, Watson says all Englishmen are as much Norman as Saxon, so the viewer's loyalties are torn; with *Becket*, the several story lines engaged in were too great for the structure of drama, and the audience once more felt its sympathies divided between multiple characters. Despite great poetry in all three plays, the dramas did not allow the necessary sympathies required for an audience's enjoyment to develop.

Readers might contrast Watson's view, remembering that the man was a great admirer and defender of Tennyson, with the volume's final extract, written by Hugh Walker only a few years later. Watson values the lyrical aspects of Tennyson's dramas most highly, seemingly succumbing to the same critical fault that he outlines at the beginning of his own extract. Walker's view of the relationship between Tennyson's drama and his lyric accomplishments might offer readers an alternative perspective on Watson's comments.

Tennyson, the dramatist, labours under the serious disadvantage that he has always to enter the lists against Tennyson the lyrist, Tennyson the elegist, Tennyson the idyllist. He is his own most formidable rival, and perhaps in this fact lies the explanation of that respectful coldness which on the whole has marked the reception of his dramas by both the critics and the public. Then, too—though no one could think of saying that Lord Tennyson had been positively infelicitous in his selection of dramatic subjects—there has yet always been some barrier to complete surrender of one's sympathies to his theme. In *Queen Mary* one could hardly help feeling that the poet, obeying a noble impulse of justice towards the wearer of that ensanguined name, had unduly gone outside himself, by imaginative abnegation of his own prepossessions, to invest her with a pathos too tender for her deserts. In *Harold,* again, the conflicting issues provided a great theme for a poetic-historic study, but impaired the simplicity and singleness of interest which are desirable in a dramatic poem. We have the Norman in us as well as the Saxon. "Saxon and Norman and Dane are we," and more besides; and it is impossible for us to swear undivided spiritual allegiance to the Saxon protagonist. *Becket,* the most ambitious of the plays, and in parts the most splendid and powerful, was embarrassed by too great opulence of material. The struggle of crown and crosier was itself a subject quite large enough for a single play. An enamoured king, an embowered mistress, and a jealous queen, were also in themselves a large subject. And the two interests stood rather apart, over against each other; the effect being variety at the cost of continuity. In all these cases, however, great poetry was achieved in the face of all opposition on the part of refractory history; but the makers of history seem to have been culpably indifferent to form, and negligent as to grouping, and even a master like the Laureate is to some extent their slave. Is it because Lord Tennyson has at times been disposed to chafe against the inflexibility of events, that he has now chosen a theme in which he can evade the dull despotism of the annalist, and reign as supreme in Sherwood as Shakspere in the forest of Arden?

A spiritual or material conflict has in every case formed the basis for the subject-matter of Lord Tennyson's dramas. The struggle (as fought out in England) between Rome and Geneva; between invading Norman and invaded Saxon; between the Church and the English monarchy—these have in turn engaged his dramatic imagination. In his latest production the theme is the contest between arbitrary and misused power, as embodied in the person of Prince John, and the spirit of justice and freedom, as represented by the people and their champion the outlawed Earl of Huntingdon. If Lord Tennyson should see fit to make yet another incursion upon the domain of drama, it is conceivable, and perhaps probable, that he will again look for his material in the incidents of some great conflict or controversy in which opposing principles have incarnated themselves in human agents. Mere dynastic feuds, like those of York and Lancaster, involving no strife of ideas, no oppugnancy of principles, do not seem to attract the author of *Becket* and *Queen Mary*. And, besides, Shakspere has left little to be gleaned in that field. But the great strife of King and Parliament still awaits its great dramatist; and one can scarcely help believing that if the Laureate were to found a play upon the more essentially human as distinguished from the purely political aspects of that struggle, the result might be the most memorable English drama of modern times. Possibly the subject would afford scant opportunity for those lyrical features which are so delightful a characteristic of his plays. But the same defect might have been supposed inherent in the subject-matter of the Laureate's first drama; yet *Queen Mary* contains some of the loveliest of his incidental snatches of song. His sympathy with the aristocratic idea is deep, but his sympathy with popular causes, when such causes are identical with the spirit of justice and the legitimate aspirations of a free-born people, is no less deep; and I can think of no other English poet who has had anything like his natural qualifications and equipment for such a work. To say that Tennyson's genius is worthy of such a subject would be almost an impertinence; but it is, perhaps, permissible to observe that the subject is worthy of Tennyson's genius. On the one hand, there is the immense impersonal pathos of dissolving forces, the tragedy of fading sentiments and perishing ideas; on the other hand, the stirring spectacle of a people for the first time fully confident in itself and the validity of its cause; added to which, the innumerable picturesque personalities of the scene offer an extraordinary range of dramatic material.

—William Watson, *Academy*, April 9, 1892, p. 341

HUGH WALKER (1897)

Hugh Walker was a Scottish academic, lecturer in English and philosophy at Saint David's College, Lampeter, Wales, and a prolific literary critic. In the following extract, Walker recognizes the major aesthetic change and expansion in Tennyson's latter years as being the addition of drama to his output. These plays have been the most critically neglected of all Tennyson's art, but Walker views them as the natural end of the "dramatic element" the poet increasingly sought after producing his earliest poems. Tennyson, Walker claims, went through the same learning process as other artists before him: In seeking to portray reality more ably, the dramatic mode had to rise, of necessity, to the surface of his art. Where Tennyson's earliest verses lack any dramatic sense, by the middle of the century there are, evident in that period's work, more dramatically drawn character sketches. Tennyson has now begun to speak from the point of view of the characters in his art, and it is this trend that he continues for the last 20 years of his life. It is also the cause for the decline in the lyric musicality of his poetry, the quality that so many admirers of his early work had praised highly. There is no surprise then, to Walker's mind, that Tennyson's popularity declined with the removal over time of that aspect of his earliest verse most cherished by the majority of his readers.

Walker believes that an appreciation for the later work of Tennyson will grow in both the critical and popular consciousness. The elderly poet had persevered in writing plays despite lukewarm to hostile responses from critics and public alike. To Walker's mind, the fact that Tennyson's early and rapid rise to fame as a lyricist has blighted attitudes to his later dramatic works will not ultimately hinder an objective appreciation of the plays. While *Queen Mary* is considered to be a failure by the critic, *Harold* is a clear advance away from that early failure; but it is Tennyson's *Becket* that Walker claims to be drama of the highest quality, and he believes it will, in the end, be appreciated as one of the poet's greatest creations. The extract is a sensitive, articulate, and insightful contemplation of not only

Tennyson's drama but also of the movement of the poet's interests over his long lifetime as an artist.

When we come down to later years the principal change visible in Tennyson's work is the development of the dramatic element. The dramas proper have been the most neglected of all sections of his work; but 'the dramatic element' is by no means confined to them. They are rather just the final result of a process which had been long going on. Tennyson, as we have already seen, gradually put more and more thought into his verse. In doing so he felt the need of a closer grip of reality, and he found, as other poets have found too, that the dramatic mode of conception brought him closest to the real. This is all the more remarkable because nothing could well be more foreign to the dramatic spirit than his early work. His youthful character sketches are not in the least dramatic. Neither is there much trace of humour, a quality without which true dramatic conception is impossible. The change begins to show itself about the middle of the century. In 'The Grandmother' and 'The Northern Farmer' we have genuine dramatic sketches of character. The poet does not regard them from his own point of view, he speaks from theirs. 'The Northern Farmer' is moreover rich in humour. Tennyson never surpassed this creation, but he multiplied similar sketches. All his poems in dialect are of a like kind. They are in dialect not from mere caprice, but because the characters could only be painted to the life by using their own speech. Other pieces, not in dialect, like 'Sir John Oldcastle' and 'Columbus,' are likewise dramatic in their nature. Less prominent, but not less genuine, is the dramatic element in the patriotic ballads, such as 'The Revenge.' The greater part of the work of Tennyson's last twenty years is, in fact, of this nature, and herein we detect the principal cause of the change of which all must be sensible in that work as compared with the work of his youth. The old smoothness and melody are in great part gone, but a number of pieces prove that Tennyson retained the skill though he did not always choose to exercise it. It is the early style with which his name is still associated, and probably the majority of his readers have never been quite reconciled to the change. But while we may legitimately mourn for what time took away, we ought to rejoice over what it added, rather than left. If there is less melody there is more strength; if the delightful dreamy languor of 'The Lotos-Eaters' is gone, we have the vivid truth of 'The Northern Farmer' and 'The Northern Cobbler,' and the tragic pathos of 'Rizpah'; if the romantic sentiment of 'Locksley Hall' is lost, something more valuable has taken its place in the criticism of life in 'Locksley Hall Sixty Years After.'

Tennyson's dramas then, surprising as they were when they first appeared, are merely the legitimate and almost the inevitable outcome of his course of development. Inevitable he seems to have felt them, for he persevered in the face of censure or half-hearted approval, perhaps it should be said, in the face of failure. A deep-rooted scepticism of his dramatic powers has stood in the way of a fair appreciation. The fame of his earlier poetry has cast a shadow over these later fruits of his genius; and the question, 'Is Saul also among the prophets?' was hardly asked with greater surprise than the question whether Tennyson could possibly be a dramatist. And, in truth, at sixty-six he had still to learn the rudiments of his business. *Queen Mary* (1875) is a failure. It is not a great poem, and still less is it a great drama. The stage is overcrowded with *dramatis personal* who jostle each other and hide one another's features. *Harold* (1877) showed a marked advance; but *Becket* (1885) was the triumph which justified all the other experiments. It is a truly great drama, and, though not yet recognised as such, will probably rank finally among the greatest of Tennyson's works. The characters are firmly and clearly delineated. Becket and Henry, closely akin in some of their natural gifts, are different in circumstances and develop into very different men. Rosamond and Eleanor are widely contrasted types of female character, the former a little commonplace, the latter a subtle conception excellently worked out. All the materials out of which the play is built are great. No finer theme could be found than the mediaeval conflict between Church and State; and Tennyson has seized it in the true dramatic way, as concentrated in the single soul of Becket, torn between his duty to the Church and his duty to the King, whose Chancellor and trusted friend he had been and to whom he owed his promotion.

—Hugh Walker, *The Age of Tennyson,*
1897, pp. 224–27

Chronology

1809	Born, the fourth of twelve children, at Somersby, Lincolnshire, England.
1815	Attends Louth Grammar School.
1820–27	Withdraws from Louth to be home-schooled by his father.
1821	He composes a 6,000-line epic poetic work.
1823–24	Writes "The Devil and the Lady."
1827	Enrolls at Cambridge University. He publishes *Poems by Two Brothers* with his brother Charles.
1829	Meets Arthur Henry Hallam; awarded a Chancellor's Gold Medal for the poem "Timbuctoo."
1830	*Poems, Chiefly Lyrical* is published. With Hallam, he joins the insurgent army in Spain.
1831	Father dies, and Tennyson withdraws from Cambridge University.
1833	Publishes *Poems.* Arthur Henry Hallam dies.
1836	Meets future wife, Emily Sellwood.
1837	He moves with his family to High Beech in Epping.
1840	The family relocate to Tunbridge Wells.
1842	An expanded edition of *Poems* is published, establishing his fame and reputation.
1847	*The Princess* is published.
1850	Publishes *In Memoriam A.H.H.*; marries Emily Sellwood; is appointed, by Queen Victoria, poet laureate.
1852	Birth of eldest son, Hallam, the future second Lord Tennyson.
1853	The Tennysons move to Farringford on the Isle of Wight.
1854	Son Lionel is born.
1855	*Maud and Other Poems* is published.

1859	Publishes the initial poems of *Idylls of the King,* which sells 10,000 copies in one month.
1864	*Enoch Arden* is published.
1865	Mother dies.
1869	Publishes *The Holy Grail and Other Poems.*
1871	"The Last Tournament" is published.
1872	The verse novellas *Gareth* and *Lynette* are published.
1872–74	Except for the poem "Balin and Balan," he completes *Idylls of the King.*
1875	The play *Queen Mary* is published.
1880	*Ballads and Other Poems* is released.
1883	Tennyson is given the title of baron.
1885	Publishes *Tiresias and Other Poems.*
1886	*Locksley Hall Sixty Years After* is published. His son Lionel dies at sea.
1889	*Demeter and Other Poems* is published.
1892	Tennyson dies after a long illness.

Index